# From the Flood

# ALSO BY SUZANNE JONES

*There Is Nothing to Fix: Becoming Whole
Through Radical Self-Acceptance*

# From the Flood

A MEMOIR

## SUZANNE JONES

LAKE PUBLICATIONS

Published by LAKE Publications, Somerville, Massachusetts
suejonesempowerment.com

Edited and designed by Girl Friday Productions
www.girlfridayproductions.com

Cover design: Emily Weigel
Project management: Reshma Kooner
Production editorial: Katherine Richards
Image credits: cover © Shutterstock/David Whitemyer, Shutterstock/ Ultrashock, Shutterstock/basel101658, Shutterstock/dip

ISBN (paperback): 978-1-7340835-2-1
ISBN (e-book): 978-1-7340835-3-8
Library of Congress Control Number: 2022907999

*To Mom and Dad*
*for making the worst years of your lives the best years of ours.*

# PROLOGUE

The residents of the Susquehanna River Valley of Northeastern Pennsylvania were accustomed to flood advisories. The last significant flood took place in 1936. After the waters receded and the damage was repaired, a new levee system was built to protect the valley. The new levee was five feet above the level of the river when it crested in 1936, and everyone continued on with their lives, feeling free from the danger of any future flooding.

In the northeastern corner of Pennsylvania, situated in the Susquehanna River Valley, sits a small town called Wilkes-Barre—a community that was especially hard hit by the great flood. As the years passed, the town's survivors of the 1936 flood died, taking their stories of devastation and disaster with them to the graves of the local cemeteries. The flood became historic lore, and the next generation of residents paid little mind to the flood advisories that periodically punctuated local weather reports.

Then in mid-June of 1972, a tropical storm began building in the Caribbean region of the Yucatan Peninsula. Reports of the storm barely made the news, even after it strengthened to a category one hurricane before making landfall in the Florida Panhandle on June 19. They named her Agnes.

Agnes quickly downgraded to a tropical depression, with two thousand miles of storm clouds extending from the storm's epicenter and dumping significant rainfall on the states of Georgia, South

Carolina, Virginia, Maryland, and Pennsylvania. It spawned several twisters and significant flooding, impacting thousands of residents before heading east over the Atlantic Ocean.

While Agnes was hovering over the Atlantic, the residents of Wilkes-Barre breathed a sigh of relief, not knowing the storm was gaining strength. Without warning, Agnes whirled sharply west and made a second landfall as an extratropical cyclone. She hovered over the Wyoming Valley, as if to take care of some unfinished business, and unleashed a deluge of torrential rain that lasted twenty-four hours and overwhelmed the region with nineteen inches of rain.

The people's relaxed attitude around any flood advisories shifted. Vigilance kept their eyes locked on the TV and their ears tuned to radio weather reports as they stared in disbelief at the unstopping torrential downpour. They heard the reports of the river level quickly rising, yet assured themselves that the levees were high enough at thirty-eight feet. The river would hold. But as each hour passed, this assurance became a question. Would the levees hold?

Fourteen hundred National Guardsmen along with ten thousand volunteers arrived to pile sandbags along the dikes of the river as the rain continued to pound down upon them. Evacuation seemed imminent. Residents began piling valuables and memorabilia onto second floors or higher surfaces, a precautionary measure against the unlikely event that a couple of feet would fill their basements or ground floors.

In the early-morning hours of June 23, 1972, over two hundred thousand residents of the river valley were evacuated from their homes, including seventy-two thousand residents of Wilkes-Barre. They left their belongings and took a few days' worth of clothing, feeling irritated and inconvenienced.

The river crested at almost forty-one feet, eight feet above the crest level of the flood of 1936. The river water made its way over or through the resistance of the thousands upon thousands of sandbags. In some areas, the river slowly seeped over the dikes and steadily filled the streets and homes, transforming the June landscape filled with the green of new spring growth into a dead-land swamp of stench-filled brown liquid.

In other areas, the river burst through the dikes with a force unequaled before or since. Fourteen trillion gallons of water rushed through the valley, taking down homes as if they were made of cardboard and sweeping away cars like dust bunnies. The water uprooted trees that had been standing strong for a hundred years. Cars, homes, concrete, and steel debris rushed down the now one-mile-wide Susquehanna River, crashing into bridges and testing their engineering. The massive pile of debris crushed and swallowed the steel-and-cement-constructed Pierce Street Bridge, taking the whole thing downriver with it.

The devastation was unlike anything anyone could have imagined. The region was submerged under sixteen feet of river water for days. Houses, torn from their foundations, were found deposited blocks away, some impaled on telephone poles. The water burrowed its way under the earth of a local cemetery and built up enough force to rifle coffins ten feet into the air, spilling out the remains of twenty-seven hundred town ancestors, including those who had lived through the great flood of 1936. Their remains floated down the muddy waters with the fish and the trees and the crumbled houses and the cars and the concrete and the steel and anything else that the angry, brown, swirling, stench-filled water wanted to take. Eventually, the remains that had spilled from their coffins were deposited on front porches, in backyards, and on roofs. Residents came home to find a skull here, a femur there, or a tibia over there.

Local college and town libraries lost every book in their collections, gone with them historical records of the once-thriving coal-mining region. The colossal steel bleachers that surrounded the college football field were swept away and found seventy yards downriver in a twisted, crumpled heap. Every commercial building of the historic town square was devastated after the river rushed in. It smashed every counter, cash register, and fixture through the walls and ceilings of the stores, leaving every inch of the place covered in the gray-brown silt and slime of the flood mud. Fires raged days after the river crested, unreachable by local fire departments and left to burn until the flames met the river water to which they were no match.

The damage was unthinkable and measurable only later in a dollar value of $2 billion—$13 billion by 2022 standards.

When the water receded, home and business owners got to work collecting tools to help them salvage what they could or demolish what they couldn't. Those who were lucky enough to procure a working hose or a squeegee tried their hardest to clean the mess, but nothing touched by the river water was salvageable. Every inch, crack, and crevice was covered, smeared, or filled with flood mud. The slimy, oily mud was nearly impossible to wash off furniture or out of clothing, cushions, and cupboards.

As clean as something might get, nothing could ever get rid of the caustic smell of the flood mud. It was a fetid smell of rotting fish, raw sewage, toxic chemicals, and sulfur that assaulted nostrils like the nauseating smell of carrion. It made the returning residents recoil with dread as they arrived, despondent, to assess the damage to their town and their homes.

The smell would never be forgotten; it remained in the sensory memory of anyone who was unlucky enough to experience it. Decades later, when the smell was detected on books, clothes, furniture, and even inside the ducts of homes that had survived Agnes, it could instantly be proclaimed *from the flood.*

In the years after Agnes devastated the towns of the Susquehanna River Valley, personal memories and historical events came to be marked in history as *before the flood* or *after the flood. From the flood* became part of the local vernacular, with houses, people, and belongings regularly identified as *from the flood.* This proclamation was a way for those who survived the flood to keep it in their memories, lest they forget and lower their guard the way they had prior to June of 1972.

The flood changed the town in ways that held fast. Banks, churches, libraries, courthouses, and other government buildings still all display permanent lines painted on their walls to mark and remember the level of the river water that filled their buildings. A mass grave was dug for the remains of the twenty-seven hundred unidentifiable ancestors, and marked with one large monument. The historic buildings of the town square were demolished and replaced by modest office buildings. Modern red lampposts were erected around the perimeter of the central grassy park in the middle of the square, replacing the historic charm with a space-age look akin to Tomorrowland in Florida's Disney World. Those who remembered the bustling town center grieved the loss.

The unprecedented meteorological event that was Agnes caused such destruction that this was the first of only three hurricane names ever retired from use.

Hurricane Agnes and the flood of 1972 changed communities, people, and families in ways that they could never have imagined.

This is the story of one such family.

# PART I

## *Agnes*

# 1

# *August 1970*

I was five years old and in kindergarten when our family moved to our new house on Birch Street in Wilkes-Barre, Pennsylvania. Dad said our old neighborhood wasn't a place to raise kids, but I liked it well enough, especially at Halloween when my friend Dolores dressed up as a bride and got to wear makeup. I thought Dolores was the most beautiful girl in the world that Halloween, and I begged my mom to put makeup on me, which she did but *just this once*, but she wouldn't let me wear red lipstick like Dolores the bride wore.

My sister Pam was one year and five days older than me and in the first grade, and she didn't need to beg Mom to let her wear makeup to look beautiful because all of the grown-ups around talked all the time about how Pam was a *gorgeous child*, which made me feel ugly.

Pam and I did everything together.

We had our tonsils out together, spent the night in the hospital together, and when we came home, we ate potato chips together even though we weren't supposed to. The potato chips ripped Pam's stitches open, and she had to go back to the hospital, which meant that she got extra toys and made me mad and jealous—until now, I had forgotten that feeling.

Pam was my favorite person. We slept in the same room, and when I woke up crying from nightmares about the Wicked Witch of the West from *The Wizard of Oz*, Pam lay in my bed with me until I fell back to sleep.

We ate alike, dressed alike, and thought alike. When I was three years old and Pam was four, Mom and Dad told us we were going to have a baby sister or brother. Pam and I insisted we pick the name, convinced we would come up with something fabulous!

When Mom and Dad brought our new baby brother home from the hospital, he had a round, bald head and eyebrows that scrunched down, the way mine did when I felt like something was unfair.

Pam and I triumphantly proclaimed that our new baby brother's name was Jonny Quest. But Mom and Dad told us *no*, and that his name was Paul, which—when you said it out loud—sounded like the sound you make at the back of your throat just before you throw up all over the floor.

We liked the new Birch Street house because it was in a neighborhood with lots of other kids we could play with. Sometimes we played *bank* because we had a set of little windows on our back screened-in porch that opened with a crank handle and looked like the drive-up bank window that our mom passed things through. We thought up exciting adventures like digging a hole to China, and all the kids pitched in to dig deep enough that we felt sure we would make it all the way to China—until we got spankings for digging up our backyard and had to fill the hole back in and find another exciting adventure to embark on.

Our new school was called Lafayette Elementary School. I was in kindergarten and only went for the morning, coming home to eat lunch and watch *Sesame Street* and wait for Pam to get home. But after a few weeks, Pam started coming home with her new friend, Amy, and for the first time there was something about Birch Street that I really didn't like.

One day I was in the backyard on our swing set.

"We wanna swing," Pam said, walking through the side path to the backyard with Amy in tow.

"Wait your turn," I said. But what I really wanted to say was *If you didn't bring your stupid friend Amy home, you could swing right here next to me.*

"Fine," said Pam, in a huff. "C'mon, Amy," Pam instructed. Amy dutifully followed Pam to the opposite corner of the yard.

I felt momentarily triumphant, but Pam and Amy huddled together, whispering some secret to one another, then started singing at the top of their lungs.

> My coun-try 'tiiiis of thee,
> Sweet land of liiiiiber-ty,
> Of. Thee. I. Siiiing.

They kept on singing this mysterious song louder and louder. It was like they had a secret that only *they* knew, just because they were in the first grade together and I was still in kindergarten. My chest got hot.

"Hey!" I shouted to them.

> Land where my faaaaa-ther died,
> Land of the pil-grims' pride,
> From e-ev-ree-hee moooun-tain side . . .

They kept loudly singing.

*"Hey!"* I shouted again.

"What?" Pam shouted back, irritated.

I paused. I wanted to tell them how I really felt. That I felt left out and mad and sad, and I wanted stupid Amy to go home and give my sister back to me.

"You can have the swing now," I said instead.

I slid off the swing, spun myself toward the back door, and huffed back into the house. Mom saw that I was sad and made me my favorite snack of saltines and grape jelly, which always made me feel better. But the kind of sad that I felt on the day I realized that even though Pam was my best friend, I might not be her best friend, was not the kind of sad my favorite snack could make feel better.

2

# September 1971

I didn't feel better until the next fall, when I started first grade at Lafayette Elementary School and met my best friend in the whole world, Lowri Jones.

Lowri lived one block away from me. I knew the way to Lowri's house because Lowri's house was also my piano teacher's house, and my piano teacher was Lowri's mother.

Every morning I walked to Lowri's house; then together we walked another two blocks to Lafayette Elementary School, where we met the crossing guard lady, who wore a bright orange sash and carried a stop sign in one hand and looked like a nice old grandma. When she saw us coming, she'd smile and say, *Here come the early birds!* This confused me because when we went back to Lowri's house at the end of the day to eat the bologna and mayonnaise sandwiches and tuna salad sandwiches, Lowri's mom told us that she found out we had been late to school again and could we please stop looking at every leaf and every tree and splashing in every puddle and just get to school on time.

But every day, Lowri and I found things to discover and explore on the walk to school, and we just couldn't understand why we needed to ignore an amazing flower or a struggling worm on the middle of the sidewalk or hurry up past an irresistible puddle that we knew might not be there the next day just to get to dumb old school, which I hated ever since I pooped my pants by accident in kindergarten and cried all the way home, sure that every kid in the class knew what I had done.

Lowri was my first best friend besides Pam, and she felt almost like my twin sister because she had the same last name as me and she loved to suck her thumb as much as I did, so sometimes we sat in front of the TV with a blankie (for her) or a pillow (for me) and silently sucked our thumbs, feeling safe and content without having to talk to each other.

Sometimes Pam and Lowri's little sister, Meghan, played with us, but mostly Lowri and I would really rather be alone, laughing and eating our sandwiches together or watching TV and sucking our thumbs. It helped to have a new best friend, and I started not caring about Pam and Amy singing "My Country 'Tis of Thee" and making me feel left out.

# 3

# *April 1972*

Paul, who was three by the time the spring of my first-grade year came around, had a best friend named Patrick Koons. Patrick was the same age as Paul and had a mom who was named Peggy, just like my mom, but his dad was named Pat, and not Bob like my dad. Patrick came to play at our house every day until he stepped in front of the teeter-totter that Paul was riding and got himself clocked smack in the fore-head and had to be rushed to the hospital to get the cut all sewn up. Patrick's mother screamed like a *banshee* when it happened, which Dad called *a little dramatic*. After that, Patrick Koons didn't come over without his mother.

Sometimes when Peggy Koons came over with Patrick, she'd sit around the kitchen table with Mom, talking about the things moms talk about like what to make for dinner and new stores that opened up and how to get a stain off a new couch that was there because someone ate chocolate pudding on the couch when they were *specifically told not to*. That someone was me, but I never told anyone because I didn't want to get a spanking.

I spent every day with Lowri, my best friend, and sometimes Pam, but Pam also played with Michelle Bedwick, the oldest in a Lebanese family that lived down the street, next to a house that Mom called a *modern monstrosity*. Pam and Michelle ran through the middle of Birch Street, playing *The Partridge Family*, a game that mainly consisted of Pam and Michelle waving their hands and running from the screaming throngs of fans while yelling, "No autographs, no autographs!" Pam, of course, was Laurie Partridge, and Michelle Bedwick was Keith Partridge, and I had to be Danny Partridge because Pam was the oldest and always got what she wanted and Michelle was the oldest and probably also got what she wanted. As usual, I didn't get what I wanted, unless you count playing with Pam, which was what I *always* wanted, especially when I wasn't playing with Lowri, so I pretended to be whatever Pam told me to be, even though Danny Partridge was weird and ugly and didn't really have any fans wanting autographs.

Dad worked at his printing business, which was called Bedwick and Jones because our last name was Jones and our uncle Ray was his business partner and his last name was Bedwick. Even though Uncle Ray wasn't our real uncle, he felt like our real uncle. He was actually Michelle Bedwick's real uncle. On Sunday afternoons, we'd pile into our sedan and go to the house of Uncle Ray's sister, Aunt Sadie—because that was where all the big Bedwick dinners and family action took place. Sometimes the Bedwick kids, who lived next to the *modern monstrosity* house, were there too, and we felt like cousins even though they had dark skin and we had light skin.

When we asked Dad what his job was, he told us it was "making the money that pays for this beautiful house and all of the things in it, in this lovely neighborhood that is safe and clean so you kids can have a better life than Mom and I had."

But that was *before*. Before June 23, 1972, the Birch Street neighborhood *was* quiet, and the streets and sidewalks were wide and clean, and there were hardly any cars because it ended right about where our ranch-style house sat. If you drove down our street past the *modern monstrosity*, past our house, and then past Patrick Koons's house, then tried to keep driving without looking where you were going, you would drive right up that dike and over the hump and land your car right in the Susquehanna River, and unless you had a car like in *Chitty Chitty Bang Bang*, you would be in big, big trouble.

We weren't allowed to climb on the dike because there was a train track there, and Mom told us we could get hit by a train and have our leg cut off or an arm cut off, and that was if we were lucky. A big iron bridge that crossed the river was also only for trains, and we weren't allowed to climb on that either, which was fine by me because I hated bridges and felt sure that if I thought about them collapsing when I was on one and me falling in the water and drowning, I could make that happen just with my thoughts. And sometimes I couldn't stop myself from thinking of scary things that could happen, even if I never ever wanted them to happen.

# 4

# *Wednesday, June 21, 1972*

It started raining in the third week of June, which meant that we couldn't play on our swing set or in our yard or even play bank. Dad said we were getting a *real dumping*, and he seemed very interested in that because when the weatherman came on the television set, Dad told us to be quiet because he wanted to listen *for Christ's sake!*

We hated the news because it was boring and the man on the television, who looked like a grandpa, never smiled and looked like he wasn't any fun at all. But we all liked piling on top of Dad because he was gone every day and when he came home, he let us climb all over him, pretending he was a ferocious T-Rex and we were little dinosaurs attacking him.

But when the rain started, Dad and Mom watched the news, and we had to wait to play our game with Dad, which made us feel grumpy.

Dad said, "Enough of that pouting." Dad sometimes said that, and other times he just said, "Don't give me that look," which meant that I was in trouble unless I changed my face, but I was never sure what to do with it, so I looked up, down, left, right, and all around, hoping that if I just didn't settle on *a look*, it would be OK.

The weatherman came on the screen of our giant wooden console television, and Pam tucked herself under Dad's arm.

"Is everything OK?" Pam asked after the weatherman said *flood advisory* more than once.

"Don't worry, Pamela. The levees are very high, and the river would never get high enough to go over them."

"What's a levee?" I asked, thinking it was a very strange word.

"You know that train track right out there?" Dad said.

"The one that will cut off our leg?" I asked.

Dad chuckled.

"It's not the track that could cut off your leg, Suzanne; it's the train that travels down the track," said Mom.

I still didn't understand how just getting near that track could cut off my leg.

"Well," Dad said, "that's a dike, and it's sometimes called a levee. It is built to keep the river water on the other side, even if it rains a lot and gets really high."

"How do they know how high to build it?" I pressed.

"Well, a long time ago, the river got high and flooded this town, so after that, they built them up as high as they possibly could, and there's never been a flood since!"

The weatherman was saying, "Up to three inches of rain before morning . . ."

We were silent as Dad glued his eyes to the television and Mom watched us carefully.

"Every year they give a flood advisory; it's really nothing to be worried about," Mom assured us.

"I'm bored," I said. Staying inside all day wasn't any fun as far as I was concerned.

"It'll stop by tomorrow," Dad said. Then he said, "Who wants pancakes for dinner?"

"*Yeeeeaaaahhh!*" Pam and I yelled in unison. Paul looked at us and joined in the jubilation even though he probably didn't know what we were cheering about.

Mom made all of the dinners and lunches and most of the breakfasts too, but Dad was the best pancake cook in the world. When Dad made pancakes, it felt like an extra-special morning, but when we had pancakes for dinner, we didn't even know *what* to do with ourselves because it felt so special and wonderful.

Dad got out the Aunt Jemima pancake mix and the Log Cabin syrup. Mom put the syrup on the table along with a tub of Parkay margarine. We sat at the table expectantly.

"Will you make our initials?" I asked Dad.

"You bet!" said Dad.

Dad made pancakes in the shape of our initials, SJ for me, PJ for Pam, and a Z for Paul because of his nickname, which was Za Za Zu. I hated my initials because they sounded stupid. I wanted initials like PJ or even DJ because they sounded happy and made a great nickname. No one would ever use SJ as a nickname because it sounded sad and clumsy, so everyone just called me Suzie, except for sometimes Mom called me Suzanne, especially when I was in trouble.

We ate our pancakes, had our baths, and climbed into bed.

"Pam," I whispered.

"What?" She sounded irritated.

"Are you awake?" I asked, just to be sure.

"Yeah," she said.

I paused.

"What do you want?" Pam asked.

"Are you scared?"

"No." She paused. "Are you?" she asked.

"Kinda," I admitted.

There was a long silence, but my eyes were wide open. I stared through the dark to the ceiling of our bedroom, watching shapes of light move around slowly like a lava lamp.

"Pam?"

"What?" she shot back.

"Can I sleep with you?" I asked.

I was glad that I had a big sister in my bedroom with me, even if she was only one year and five days older than me. Paul was the only boy and slept in a room by himself, and I definitely would not want that. I wondered if he was scared.

"OK," she said.

I climbed into bed with Pam, sleeping with my feet by her head and her feet by my head, like the way sardines fit into their tin.

"Go to sleep, Suzie," Pam instructed. "We can play in the morning."

I slipped my thumb into my mouth, pressed the thumb pad to the roof of my mouth, and made my tongue vibrate. I ran my fingers over the cool wrinkles of my pillowcase and immediately felt like I was wrapped in a warm hug. I fell asleep, thinking of all the games we would play outside once the rain stopped.

# 5

# *Thursday, June 22, 1972*

Pam and I sprang from our beds and ran to the kitchen. I thought we had the greatest house in the world because it had a pink kitchen. Even though I didn't like pink for toys or pink for dresses, I liked having a pink kitchen because we were the only kids with a kitchen like that, and it made me feel special.

Mom and Dad were sitting at the pink linoleum table. Paul was in a high chair making a mess of his cinnamon-sugar toast.

"How come you're not at work?" Pam asked Dad. It was unusual for him to be at home when we woke up in the morning unless it was a weekend.

"Well, girls," he said after taking a deep breath, "it looks like more rain is on the way, and I'm going to go help pile up some sandbags just in case."

Mom looked at him, then back at us.

"It's nothing to be worried about," she said, wiping Paul's face with a wet cloth.

"Nooooo!" Paul shouted as he shook his head back and forth. "I don't wike it!"

Paul couldn't say all his words right yet, so he called a log a *wog* and said *kepitch* instead of ketchup and called my sister *Pam-Pam*.

Mom lifted him out of the high chair, and he ran to the living room, picked up the cylindrical cardboard container of Lincoln Logs, and spilled them all over the floor.

"It's just a precaution," Mom continued.

"That means just in case," Pam said looking at me, as if I were a dummy. I was glad she told me anyway.

"Can we go out and play before breakfast?" we asked with our hands folded the way Pam learned in Sunday school so she could have First Holy Communion. I couldn't wait until I had First Holy Communion and could wear a beautiful white dress like the one Mom bought for Pam and get treated extra special for one day in my life even though Pam would be the first to do it. Pam was the first to do everything, so nothing was as special for me because I was always second.

"Pleeeeaaassseee!" we begged.

Mom looked at Dad, then looked back at us. "OK," she said, then added, "Don't leave the yard, and come in if it starts raining."

Pam and I ran out the side door to the backyard before Paul could see us and tag along.

The rain did not start gradually. We had just begun playing on the swing set, singing "Miss Mary Mack," when the rain suddenly started, like a faucet turned all the way on high, soaking Pam, me, the swing set, and the whole yard with water. The metal sliding board on our swing set became a downhill stream. The yard was all at once covered in puddles so deep that we couldn't walk from the swings to the house without avoiding them. Our feet sunk into several inches of water, soaking our shoes. It didn't matter because the rest of us was so thoroughly soaked that by the time we walked through the side door, we were dripping from our shirts and our pant cuffs. The water made squishing sounds in our shoes. We had to wring out our long hair.

"Take your clothes off," Mom instructed as we stood there, drip, drip, dripping.

I looked at Pam. Water dripped off the tip of her nose, her earlobes, and her eyelashes.

We peeled off our clothes like they were banana skins, leaving them inside out in a wet, heavy heap on the floor.

I was so irritated that it was raining again that I wanted to stomp my feet in protest. Instead, I said, "Mom?"

"Yes?" Mom said as she began wrapping us each in a bath towel before scooping up our sopping wet clothes.

"How long is it gonna rain this time?" I asked.

She let out a big sigh, as if she were tired of us asking the question. "I don't know, Suzanne." Then she added, "Soon."

"Will it stop today?" I asked.

"Maybe," she said as she stared out the window at the torrent of rain. It didn't let up. The puddles in our yard turned to streams, running down our driveway and overwhelming the storm drains on the street. The pounding rain on the metal roof of our screened-in back porch sounded like the freight trains that ran over the forbidden tracks. I was glad we had a house to keep us warm and dry.

"Can we play in the basement?" Pam asked.

"Yes," Mom said, still staring out the window. "Let's get you dry and dressed first," she added. Then, "And take your brother with you."

*"But Mooom!"* I moaned in protest.

"No buts," she said. "I need to clean."

After Pam and I dried off and got dressed, we found Paul in the living room still. He was lying on his belly with one of the Lincoln Logs in his hand. He moved it forward and back on the floor, pretending that it was a truck. *Vroom! Vroom!* he said as he moved it forward. *Eeep! Eeep! Eeep!* he chirped as he moved it backward, the way trucks beep when they are backing up.

"Come on, Paul. We're going to play in the basement," we instructed.

The basement was where all of our toys were kept. There was also a bar down there that we only used to store things. It came in handy when we played hide-and-seek.

"I don't wanna!" Paul protested. He wore a look that said, *Come near me and I'll rip your face off.*

"Mom said," Pam told him.

He began to scream, "No!" and wrapped his arms around his Lincoln Logs.

"You know what? You know what?" I said excitedly. I didn't really know what to say, but Paul was like our old dog Sophie that Dad gave away to a farm. You just had to pretend that something was really exciting, and he would forget all about being mad and follow you.

Paul's face brightened. "What?" he said.

I had to think quick. "I think Mom got you a new truck, and it's in the basement!"

It was a lie, but Paul loved trucks. He especially liked garbage trucks. He loved them so much that when we lived in our old, bad neighborhood, he ran outside and down the street after the garbage truck he had missed because Mom was changing his diaper when the truck stopped at our house. Mom ran after Paul, who was naked as anything, waving his clean diaper in one hand and scooping him up under her other arm, carrying him like a football back to the house while he was kicking and flailing and screaming and crying.

Pam looked at me. She knew I told a lie, and lying was bad. But the situation called for it, so I looked back at her sternly, trying to word-lessly communicate, *Don't you dare tell on me,* which was something that she sometimes did.

Paul jumped up and followed us to the basement with a bounce in his step. I grabbed one of his trucks and gave it to him.

"Here," I said.

"I don't want that!" he grumbled, swatting the truck away.

"This is a new one! It just looks like the old one." It was worth a shot.

Paul examined the truck.

"Come on. Let's play," I said as I started to move the truck back and forth, imitating the *vrooming* and *eeeping* noises Paul had been making. He joined in and seemed to forget about being mad. Paul was really dumb sometimes.

We could hear the rain, even though we were all the way in the base-ment. Mom was vacuuming above us. We could hear the furniture being moved aside and the vacuum banging into the baseboards.

Pam and I sorted through our toy box and pulled out a Sunset Malibu Barbie and a Skipper doll. We played in the basement with our Barbies. Pam had the Malibu Barbie and pretended she was the mom. I had Skipper, and I had to be the kid.

"You've been a bad kid," Malibu Barbie said to Skipper.

"Hey!" I protested.

"It's just pretend," Pam reminded me.

"Why do I always have to be in trouble?" I meant it, and I wasn't just talking about Skipper.

"Because you do dumb stuff," Pam said. Then she added, "And now your father is going to give you a spanking when he gets home."

This made me furious. A red-hot wave filled my face, moved down into my chest, then down through the arm holding Skipper, and it made me whip the Skipper doll at Pam, hitting her in the head.

*"I'm telling!"* Pam screamed, and she ran upstairs.

I sat in the basement, listening to Paul blather on with his trucks, waiting for what was always coming.

"Suzaaaaanneee!" Mom yelled.

"I didn't mean it!" I yelled back. I mostly loved Pam more than anyone, but I hated her right now. I waited for what was next, but nothing came.

Just then, I heard Dad come through the door.

"Look at you!" Mom exclaimed. "Don't come in—I just cleaned! Let me get towels."

Paul's ears perked up, and he yelled, "Daddy!" then ran up the stairs.

I wasn't going to go upstairs unless I had to, afraid that if I did, I would get a spanking for throwing Skipper at Pam's head. I crept up the stairs to listen. Paul left the door to the basement open, and the low voices of Mom and Dad carried the smell of lemon pledge down to me.

"How is it?" Mom asked as she switched on the television.

"Not good," Dad said. He told her he'd never seen anything like it. He described standing in an assembly line. The guys at the end filled pillowcases, garbage bags, or any sack they could find with dirt and sand. They passed them down the line to the end, where they were piled a dozen high, stretching for miles along the dikes.

"I've never seen rain like this," he told her.

"Are we gonna be OK?" Pam asked with a lilt of worry in her voice. Retired General Sergeant Frank Townsend, who Dad told us was a very important man who was the chief of something called the Civil Defense Department, soberly updated us over the television on the status of the river.

"May begin evacuating hospitals and nursing homes as a precautionary measure . . . ," he was saying.

Dad peeled off his soaked clothes and dried his head and face with a towel. "It's a lot of rain, that's for sure," he said. "But those dikes are higher than this river has ever gotten. Five feet higher than the worst flood ever. Everything's going to be fine."

Everyone was so interested in the rain and the old man on the television and hearing Dad talk about what it was like outside that they didn't talk at all about Skipper hitting Pam on the head. I quietly moved up the stairs and peeked my head through the doorway.

"It must be coming down over an inch an hour out there," Dad told Mom. "One fella had a can of spray paint. He was marking the water level on the river side of the dike, but as soon as he sprayed a line, it was covered up again! He just kept spraying and spraying."

"What do you think?" Mom asked, looking at Dad with an expression that looked less like worry and more like she was trying to make some sort of decision.

If she had asked me that question, I would have told her I thought Pam was a snot and a tattletale and that *she* should be the one to get in trouble for making me be naughty Skipper and making her Malibu Barbie act like a mean grown-up.

Dad pulled on a clean dry, shirt, took in a deep breath, and said, "I think we should put some things up. We might get some water in the basement."

Then he scooped Paul up off the floor, pretend threw him on the couch, and growled, "Rooowwwwweeer! T-Rex is *huuuuunnngggrrryy!*"

Paul giggled, and Pam and I jumped on Dad and laughed and laughed. Pam and I forgot all about our fight, and I felt like this was a very special day because Dad was playing and laughing with us instead of being at work. If a whole lot of rain was what it took for that to happen, then it was fine by me.

When the five-o'clock news came on the television, Dad told us all to *shhhhhh* so he could hear about the weather.

A man stood under an umbrella in the torrential rain. He had a yellow rain slicker on with the hood pulled up. He held a large umbrella over his head, and we could barely hear him above the noise of the rain.

"Tropical cyclone Agnes isn't letting up, with river levels topping out at thirty-five feet so far . . . ," he was saying. It was raining so hard, the rain looked like it was coming through his umbrella. Water dripped off the front edge of his hood. He didn't bother to wipe any of it off.

"Expect it to continue for several hours . . . expect some flooding in basements of low-lying homes and businesses."

"What a pain in the ass," Dad said when he heard *expect some flooding.*

"What about the shop?" Mom asked.

We called Dad's printing business *the shop.* The shop was in a town called Kingston, which was across the river from Wilkes-Barre, where our house on Birch Street was. The shop wasn't as close to the river as our house was, and Dad didn't seem too worried.

"I'm not worried," he assured, then added, "Let's put some things up on the bar just in case we get a little water."

"Can I help?" I asked.

"Me too!" Pam echoed.

"C'mon, girls," Dad answered as he waved for us to follow him down to the basement. Paul toddled after us, holding on to the banister and carefully making his way down by stepping his left foot, then his right foot, on each stair.

"I'm going to start dinner," Mom said as she disappeared into the pink kitchen.

Dad began piling a few things on top of the bar in the basement. His golf clubs, some photo albums, and some tools balanced atop one another precariously. Pam and I had immediately gotten distracted with a game of jacks.

"If you don't want your toys to get wet, you better bring them over here," Dad warned.

We rifled through our toy box and grabbed as much as we could. Paul brought Dad a toy truck. Dad found a place for everything on top of the bar and proudly proclaimed, "That should do it!"

He paused and looked at all the stuff on the bar, seeming lost in thought.

"C'mon, girls!" he yelled excitedly. "Let's go for a ride!"

"Me too!" Paul chimed in.

"OK, buster, you too," Dad agreed.

"But it's raining," Pam reminded Dad. She was always very practical.

"Don't worry. I have a gigantic umbrella that will keep us all dry," Dad assured. He fetched the umbrella from the corner of the basement where his golf clubs were usually kept. Gripping the umbrella in his hand, he thrust his arm straight forward to show us the umbrella, which he used when he played golf on rainy days.

"The rain never stops a game of golf!" he always told us, but Mom usually rolled her eyes when he said it, so we weren't sure if it was really true.

We ran excitedly up the stairs from the basement, using both our hands and our feet, which made it feel like we were going twice as fast up those stairs. We waited in the kitchen for Dad to catch up to us, but when he did, Mom put her hand on his shoulder to stop him from walking to the door that led outside.

"Are you sure this is a good idea?" she asked Dad in an almost whisper.

"What are we gonna do, hang around here all day, sitting on our hands?"

Mom just looked at him, silently.

"It'll be fine. They'll be fine," he assured.

Mom still didn't speak. We all held our breath.

Finally, Dad said, "I'll have them back within the hour."

Mom took her hand off Dad's shoulder and let him pass.

Dad led us out to the driveway under the pounding rain, which made the driveway look like a stream and the streets look like rivers.

We climbed into the Chevy, and Dad drove us through the streets of town. They were empty until we arrived at the Market Street Bridge, a formidable beige stone bridge with four stone arches. Two arches framed the road on one side of the river, the other two on the other side of the river. Each stone arch had a gigantic eagle on the very top, with its wings outstretched, as if about to take flight. The Market Street Bridge was the only bridge that I wasn't too afraid to drive over, on account of the fact that it was so solid looking and it didn't have metal grates with holes that you could look down through to see the distance you would fall into the water if the bridge collapsed, which I was almost always sure would happen if I thought about it too much.

Dad pulled the car over to the side of the road and tucked it into a space that had been recently vacated in the middle of a line of parked cars. He opened his door, stuck the umbrella out into the hard rain, opened it, and held it in one hand while he scooped Paul under his other arm, exited the car, and hooked Paul onto one hip. He held the umbrella over our heads as we got out of the car. That umbrella was so big, all four of us could stand under it and stay mostly dry, even though we could see some water seeping through the umbrella because it was raining so hard. It sounded like popcorn that never stopped popping.

The air felt cool like a damp washcloth on your face, and it smelled tinny. The entire sky was like one big blanket of low and dark clouds, casting gray over everything. *What's the big deal?* I thought. *I hate this stupid rain.*

Dad led us to the chunky cement railing of the bridge. The thick, curvy cement spindles were completely obscured by hundreds and hundreds of sandbags piled one on top of the other, spanning the entire length of the bridge. We could see hundreds of men piling more sandbags on top of the dikes that ran on either side of the river. They didn't have raincoats or umbrellas or anything to keep them dry. They were soaked through, their shirts and pants sticking to their bodies and dripping with so much water, it looked like they might have had a hose under there somewhere. *Why do they get to be outside in the rain when I can't?* I felt irritated. I wondered if this was the place where Dad was piling sandbags earlier in the morning.

"Did you put these here, Daddy?" Pam asked before I could.

"Not these," he said. Then he pointed to the dikes along the river that bordered Kirby Park, which was where Dad took us to sled and ice-skate in the winter. "I helped pile those over there," he added.

I was glad that Dad made sure to keep Kirby Park safe from the brown river water that, when he lifted me up to see over the sandbags, I could see was so high that if the bridge did collapse, which I tried my hardest not to think about, you wouldn't fall at all before splashing into the water.

I could tell that Pam was nervous. "Are we gonna be OK?" she asked Dad. She was right on the verge of busting out crying because she was giving Dad *those cow eyes* as he called them.

But this time he didn't say, *Don't give me those cow eyes* to Pam, and instead he said, "Don't worry; we're gonna be fine."

Paul was stretching his arm, trying to reach out from under the umbrella to feel the rain. The umbrella was too big, which made Paul lean his little body away from Dad, making it hard for Dad to hold him.

"Come on back, buddy," Dad said to Paul as he tried to pull him back in with the same arm he was holding him with.

Pam was not so quick to accept Dad's assurances. "Why is the man on the television saying the river will flood?"

She had a point, I thought.

Dad squatted down to face Pam, bringing the umbrella and a wriggling Paul with him.

"You know the story of the boy who cried wolf?" he asked Pam.

"Yes," she said.

Of course we knew it. The adults were always reminding us of that story when we *exaggerated* things.

"Well, every year, the weatherman says the same thing. It rains a lot, and they warn us of a flood advisory. And every year, we're perfectly fine because the levees are so high, the river would never reach the top," he explained.

"Then what are all those sandbags for?" Pam was a lot smarter than me.

"It's just a precaution," he explained.

There was that word again. *Precaution.* If that meant doing things like piling sandbags or not doing things like playing outside in the rain, then why didn't we use *precaution* other times, like when we had to cross bridges and be scared that they would collapse? Why didn't we just not go over the bridge? I made a note to suggest that to Mom and Dad.

Pam seemed to accept Dad's explanation. Paul was getting very *antsy*, as Mom would say, so it was time to get back in the car and return home and sit around inside feeling irritated again because we couldn't play outside.

After we ate the lasagna that Mom made for dinner and Paul was put to bed, Pam and I sat out on our screened-in back porch with Dad, who was teaching us how to play gin rummy. Dad was a great teacher because he explained everything really well and never lost his patience when we didn't understand something. It was usually me that didn't understand, because Pam was seven years old and almost in the second grade, and she already knew a little about playing gin rummy.

It was past our bedtime, and Dad was tired from standing in the pouring rain and piling all those sandbags earlier in the morning, but earlier, when Mom was doing the dinner dishes and Dad was drying them, I heard them talking with bowed heads in hushed tones, catching only pieces of their conversation. *Occupy the girls . . . pack some clothes . . . in case we have to evacuate.*

I didn't know what *evacuate* meant, and I didn't care because when Dad was with us, time felt special, like when he gave us baths and sang the "Do-Re-Mi" song from *The Sound of Music* as he soaped up a washrag and helped us scrub ourselves from top to bottom. Or when he made going to bed a fun game by giving us *a sack of potatoes*, which was really just a way for him to throw us over his shoulder like a sack of potatoes and carry us to bed. And when we came home from a long car ride, I pretended to stay asleep so I could feel the specialness of being lifted out of the car and carried to my bedroom and tucked into my bed, which was great for me because Pam was usually the special one because she was older. I wanted to stay small forever so I would never be too big for my dad to give me a *sack of potatoes*.

But this day, I already felt special even before our sack of potatoes because Dad didn't go to work and was home most of the day, and that made me feel like everything was going to be all right.

Pam was winning because she could do most things better than I could, except when we played *go fish*, which is a game that our great-grandmother Nana taught me before she taught Pam, so I could usually beat her. But this was gin rummy, and I was getting jealous and angry as usual, but I stopped myself from throwing stuff at Pam, remembering that I avoided a spanking for hitting her with Skipper earlier in the day.

"No fair!" I yelled after she won a hand and flashed a glib smirk in my direction. I really wanted to throw my cards in her face.

Dad pulled me onto his lap and said we would be teammates, except he kept turning his head to look into the kitchen to see what Mom was doing, so I felt like I only had half of a teammate. We had to almost shout over the noise of the hard rain pounding on the metal roof of the porch as my mom shuffled around the house organizing this and that, washing and folding laundry, and wrapping up the tray of leftover lasagna. She then carried the tray down to the basement.

After Dad gave us a sack of potatoes, and Pam and I were in our bedroom, I couldn't get myself to go to sleep. The rain was beating hard on the roof above our bedroom. It had been raining this way all day long, and I just wanted it to stop and be quiet.

"Pam?" I asked.

"What?" she said.

"Do you hear the rain?"

"What do you think?" Pam shot back.

I felt dumb. But I really just wanted Pam to tell me that everything was going to be all right. "If the river comes over the dike, are we gonna drown?"

I imagined the river rushing over the dike next to our house and filling it up so fast, we didn't stand a chance. Pam and I were already learning how to swim, but Mom and Paul couldn't swim, so on top of worrying about me and Pam and Dad drowning, I worried even more about Mom and Paul. Sometimes I didn't know why bad and scary thoughts kept coming into my head.

"Suzie, you heard Daddy. The river won't hurt us. This happens all the time," she assured me.

I trusted Pam because she was right about a lot of stuff. I tried not to think about the river or the Wicked Witch of the West and eventually fell asleep.

# 6

## *Friday, June 23, 1972*

It was still dark out when I awoke to the sounds of my brother, Paul, crying, Mom and Dad shuffling about, and a truck with a bullhorn passing in front of our house. There was that word *evacuate* again. I still didn't know what it meant, but it must have been serious because there was a lot of commotion. The lights in my house and in all the neighbors' homes turned on. Like strings of lights that rimmed porches and wrapped around front-lawn shrubs at Christmastime, the homes on our street lit up one after the other after the other.

"Pam! Are you awake?" I asked her. I was confused and frightened.

"Yes," she said.

"What's happening?" I asked.

"I don't know," Pam said. If Pam didn't know something, it made me really worried.

Just then, Dad opened the door to our room. We saw Mom down the hall past our doorway, carrying Paul, who was flailing his arms and legs about, crying as loud as I had ever heard him cry.

"Come on, girls. We're going for a ride," Dad said.

"Where?" we wanted to know. We had never gone for a ride in the morning before the sun came out.

"It's a surprise," Dad said. Then, "You can keep your nightgowns on. And grab a toy if you want."

He swiftly left the room. Pam and I looked at each other, confused.

Pam and I rubbed the sleep from our eyes and walked into the living room. Dad was now holding Paul, telling him the same thing he had just told us. We were *going for a ride*. I didn't understand why Paul was crying when we were *just going for a ride*. I figured it was because he got woken up in the middle of his sleep, because that's what babies do. Paul really wasn't a baby anymore, but he wasn't a kid like Pam and I were kids, so he sometimes acted more like a baby than we did.

Mom was on the phone, which was also strange. Why was everyone so awake this early? The only day we woke up before it was light out was Christmas morning, and Mom and Dad always told us it was *too early for God's sake* and to go back to bed. But it wasn't Christmas. It wasn't anything special that I knew about, yet the man shouting over the bullhorn was waking up the whole neighborhood.

"Who's Mom talking to?" I asked.

Dad said, "Uncle Ray."

*Why is Uncle Ray awake?* I wondered.

"OK, we're coming," Mom said before she hung up the phone.

"We're going for a sleepover at Aunt Sadie's!" Mom said, sounding kind of excited.

"Now?" Pam asked.

"Yes, it's a surprise one-night sleepover. Isn't that fun?"

I don't think Mom really wanted us to answer because as soon as she asked the question, she walked away and went back to her bedroom.

We loved Aunt Sadie. Aunt Sadie's face looked like Uncle Ray's face. It was brown and round with a large nose in the center and large lips with white teeth below that. Whenever Aunt Sadie saw us, her face instantly illuminated, and she smiled with her cheeks as round as apples, cooing *Helloooooo, honey! It's so good to seeeee you!* It always felt great to walk through Aunt Sadie's door and see her happy face, but we usually just went there for spaghetti dinners with all of Aunt Sadie's and Uncle Ray's other brothers and sisters and kids and nieces and nephews, but we never ever had a sleep-over at Aunt Sadie's, which sounded *great*, so I didn't really care what time it was.

Mom walked out of her bedroom with a small bag. "Girls, grab a change of clothes for tomorrow. And bring a toy if you want," Mom instructed. Then she added, "We won't be staying long."

Pam and I rifled through our dresser and found identical brown slacks and long-sleeve T-shirts. Blue for her, and pink for me.

"Can we trade?" I asked Pam. I wanted the blue shirt.

"No way," Pam quickly quipped.

"*Whyyy?*" I begged.

"Because the pink shirt is yours," Pam stated.

"I hate pink!" I grouched.

Pam turned to walk out of the room, taking the stuffed floppy-eared dog she got as a gift when we had our tonsils out. I left the fluffy pink-and-white kitty that I got because I really would have rather gotten that dog and was mad because, once again, Pam got the thing that I wanted, and she never wanted to trade. Instead, I brought the Sunset Malibu Barbie.

We gave our clothes to Mom, who put them in her bag. She grabbed Paul's favorite pillow that smelled like maple syrup and had a dent in it because Nana taught Paul to rock his head back and forth to help put himself to sleep.

Outside it was still raining as hard as I'd ever seen. The storm drains on the street were overwhelmed and backed up so much that the street looked like a big stream. We saw the Koonses, the Bedwicks, and all of our other neighbors sloshing through the ankle-deep water and trying to stay dry under umbrellas as they dashed from their homes to their cars.

Were they having sleepovers too?

"Dad?" I asked as he was opening the trunk of the car.

"Hmm?" he answered, preoccupied.

"What's *evacuate* mean?" I could still hear the man on the bullhorn shouting *evacuate immediately*.

"It means everyone has to leave their homes for the night," Dad said.

"Why?" I asked.

"It's just a precaution."

That word again.

Paul sat on Mom's lap in the front. Pam and I climbed up onto the back dash of the car, where there was enough room for us to lie sardine style, like we did in the twin bed. I looked up through the back windshield and watched the wires on the electric pole move up and down and up and down. I stared at the smooth motion of the wires, wondering if they would hypnotize me.

Pam wriggled and shoved me deeper into the back dash until I was smooshed between the dash and the windshield. My nose fogged the glass when I breathed in and out as I watched the rain hit the glass. The water smoothed the edges and colors of the outside world. I thought about the sandbags on the Market Street Bridge. I wondered if the brown river water was reaching them. Were they piled high enough to keep it in place?

"Daddy, are we gonna be OK?" I asked this time.

"We're gonna be fine," he said.

"Why did we have to leave our house?" Pam asked.

"Just to be on the safe side," Mom quickly piped in. She did this sometimes when she didn't want Dad to say something to us that he shouldn't.

There was a pause. Paul was asleep in the front seat with his head on Mom's lap. She tucked a small blanket that Nana had crocheted for him when he was a baby a little tighter around his toddler body. She turned her head to look at Dad. They shared a silent glance, then both looked forward through the windshield as the wipers moved back and forth, in competition with the driving rain.

"It's just for a day or two," Dad said.

I stuck my thumb in my mouth. It always made me feel safe.

*Just for a day or two,* I thought.

We arrived at Aunt Sadie's house as the obscured sun was just fighting to bring light into the sky. The heavy rain, rain, rain was still pounding down on top of our car, filling the sidewalks, the streets, and the yards with more water than they could handle. They called Aunt Sadie's neighborhood *the hill,* which meant that the rainwater washed away down the hill, which meant that the yards and streets in the valley had water coming from the rain and water coming from Aunt Sadie's hill too.

Uncle Ray, who lived right next door to Aunt Sadie, ran under the cover of a big umbrella to our car and tried to keep us kids dry as he led us through the back door that opened directly into the kitchen. We breathed in the intoxicating fragrances of cardamom, cinnamon, cloves, and honey. These were the smells of Aunt Sadie's house, and in this moment, I didn't care what was happening down in the valley or on Birch Street or with the river because the smell of Aunt Sadie's kitchen felt like pure love.

Aunt Sadie turned from the stove and flashed a wide, happy smile. "*Ya Habibi!* My loves! Come in! Sit down!" she chimed as she turned to face us, but instead of wiping her hands on her apron to clean off pasta dough or ground lamb that she prepared when we visited her for dinner, she wiped off eggs and bacon grease and pastry flour before embracing us with her strong arms. Aunt Sadie's hugs felt like sinking into a giant beanbag chair made of the best stuff in the world, and we felt content and warm and forgot about anything that was happening below *the hill*.

The hill was the neighborhood where all the Lebanese people lived, except Michelle Bedwick and her mom and dad and sisters and brothers. They lived on Birch Street near us. Because the houses on the hill were not down in the valley where the Market Street Bridge was, Uncle Ray invited us for a sleepover; getting water in your basement wasn't fun, but getting to sleep over at Aunt Sadie's felt like a special occasion.

Aunt Sadie and Uncle Ray's family was very big. They had lots of brothers and sisters who all lived on the hill because Uncle Ray and Aunt Sadie's mother had been sent from Lebanon to America on a boat when she was fourteen years old to meet her preselected husband-to-be. Her husband had come over to America some months prior in order to start a wholesale fruit and vegetable business. When Uncle Ray and Aunt Sadie's mom arrived, she started having babies right away when she was fifteen and didn't stop until there were eleven babies, so who had time to be moving around? Everyone just stayed up on the hill, and everyone went to Aunt Sadie's house for dinner and sat around her giant rectangular kitchen table.

Dad met Uncle Ray when Dad got out of the army and Daniel, Dad's grandfather and his Nana's husband, who had raised Dad from age three, called Dad a bum and told him to *get a job* and tossed a newspaper opened to the classifieds right on Dad's stomach before he could even get out of bed. That is precisely what Dad did that very day, and that job is where he met Uncle Ray.

Dad's job was in the printing department of Planters Peanuts. Every label had a smiling peanut man who wore a top hat, monocle, shoes, white gloves, and carried a cane. Uncle Ray worked at Planters Peanuts too but not in the printing department. Uncle Ray worked in the accounting department and met Dad one day in the lunchroom, where they decided they wanted to *be their own bosses* and made plans to start their own printing business in the basement of Uncle Ray's house, which was right next door to Aunt Sadie's.

After Mom and Dad got married, we referred to the rest of Uncle Ray and Aunt Sadie's gigantic family as aunts and uncles, and every time we went to Aunt Sadie's for dinner, I felt I was a part of the family. I didn't look like anyone else in the family. I was white. They were dark. My nose was small and looked like a ski jump. They had the same big nose, even the kids like Michelle, who had a kid-sized version. I wished I looked Lebanese, but instead, I felt boring and unexciting. And even though I didn't look like anyone else, the members of this giant Lebanese family told me over and over and over they loved me, and it made me feel safe and special and loved and a part of something so big that it would never go away completely.

We were all tired from being woken up by the bullhorn, and we wiped the sleep from our eyes. Aunt Sadie said, "Sit! Sit! Come eat!" after kissing us all on the forehead. We sat down at that giant table in the center of the kitchen while Aunt Sadie began to lay out platters and dishes and bowls of food that I recognized, like scrambled eggs and bacon, and foods that I didn't that had weird round-shaped beige beans that Mom said were called chickpeas. I imagined little baby chicks laying those beans like chickens lay eggs.

There were pastries dripping with honey and layered with walnuts and pistachios and yogurt so thick you could almost cut it with a knife. There was cheese fried in a pan, which you could definitely eat with a fork and a knife, except Aunt Sadie showed us how to pick up all the food with pieces of soft, flat bread that had some funny green stuff on it that Mom called *herbs* and was warm right out of the oven.

I liked the bread OK after I scraped off the green stuff, but Paul took one look at the bread and blurted out, "Yuck!"

"This is Syrian bread," Aunt Sadie proudly stated as she smiled a wide gap-toothed smile. "It's fresh from the oven!"

"I want pancakes!" Paul shouted. Sometimes three-year-olds were so rude.

"I'll make you pancakes tomorrow, deal?" Dad assured him before turning his head back to the television in the kitchen, where a newsman was standing in the rain next to a bridge. The river looked gigantic and angry, and it carried cars, pieces of houses, and large debris down current and smashed them into that bridge.

"Is that near our house?" Pam asked, alarmed.

"No. It's nowhere near us," Dad lied before quickly shutting off the television.

Paul began crying and kept demanding pancakes. Mom picked up Paul and whisked him out of the kitchen. She turned her head on her way out the door and blurted out, "Keep the TV off!"

I picked up and placed on my plate a sweet and gooey pastry that made my mouth water and my fingertips sticky. I popped some bacon in my mouth, biting down with a crunch.

Dad didn't eat a thing. He kept walking out of the kitchen to talk with Uncle Ray and Mom in the other room before returning to the table, where he silently sat and stared blankly into space.

Pam and I kept real quiet and tried to listen in on the grown-ups' hushed tones as they periodically whispered to one another in the corners of the kitchen or over the sink as they washed and dried the dishes. When they talked to us kids directly, they had smiles on their faces and tried to sound happy. But when they looked away or talked to each other, we saw those expressions immediately change from smiling and happy to frowning and worried, which was unusual, especially for Aunt Sadie, who was almost always smiling. I knew that something really serious was going on, and when kids know that something really serious is going on, they also know enough to *keep quiet* and *stay out of it* and let the *adults take care of things*, so after we ate, Pam and I went into the living room. Mom was sitting on a rocking chair, singing "Bingo" to Paul. We sat on the couch, listened to "There was a farmer had a dog and Bingo was his name-o!" and waited to be told what to do.

Not long after we arrived, Momo walked through Aunt Sadie's back door, which was very, very strange because she wasn't usually invited to Aunt Sadie's house. Momo lived in an apartment down in the valley close to the river and had also been woken up by the man with the bullhorn who was telling everyone to evacuate. Because the same man had made us leave our house on Birch Street, Momo didn't have a place to go, so Aunt Sadie told Mom to *bring her on up!* which made Pam very happy because ever since she was a baby, she spent every single Saturday night having a sleepover with Momo. I stuck my thumb in my mouth and vibrated my tongue to make me feel better because having Momo around was just going to remind me of how special Pam was and how *unspecial* I was.

Momo was Mom's mother. Mom said Momo was a strong and independent woman because when Mom was twelve years old, Momo grabbed her and her brother, Uncle Bob, and walked out on our grandfather who we called *Pop-Pop-with-the-Screwdriver* because he was really handy with tools.

Mom said it wasn't like they were leaving much because they were poor and took baths once a week in a tin tub, taking turns using the same water. But after Momo took Mom and Uncle Bob to go live on their own, Uncle Bob joined the marines and Momo got a job at Planters Peanuts, and I wondered if my first job would be at Planters Peanuts too because that seemed to be where everyone had their first job.

Mom said Momo taught her that women needed to be able to take care of themselves and have minds of their own, so when Momo told Mom she should breastfeed her babies that is what Mom did, even though when Pam and I were born, it was considered old-fashioned and an embarrassment.

Mom said Aunt Sadie was very generous because, between the Bedwick family and our family and now Momo, there weren't enough beds, and we had to sleep on the couches and the floor. Mom and Dad slept at Uncle Ray's house.

Pam and I were still in the living room, waiting for something. We didn't really know what. Paul fell asleep, and Mom laid him on the couch and covered him with a blanket before going back into the kitchen to greet Momo, who had joined in with the secret conversations that were happening in there.

Through the doorway, we could see Aunt Sadie leaning her back against the kitchen counter, with her hands deep in the pocket of her apron. She was fiddling around with something in there. Her knuckles poked the fabric of her pocket out and in, out and in. When things got quiet in there, we heard whatever was in her pocket clicking around.

I was just about to go in there and ask Aunt Sadie what she was fiddling with deep in her apron pocket, when I heard a sound I had never heard before. It was a siren, but not like a fire engine or a police car or ambulance siren. This siren was so big, it needed time to wind up in order to get real loud. Once it was as loud as it could be, it stayed there for what seemed like a long time, then wound down. All the adults in the kitchen were silent as the siren repeated its wind-up, wind-down screaming.

"Oh my God," Mom whispered loudly, slicing through the silence. We heard her start crying. It sounded like Dad was crying too, which made us very worried because Mom almost never cried and our dad never cried because dads aren't supposed to.

"Turn on the TV," Momo said. We heard it switch on.

Aunt Sadie pulled a string of pretty beads with a cross dangling from the end out of her pocket. She was gripping the beads between her fingers one by one and whispering something to herself. I wondered why she wasn't wearing them around her neck.

Pam looked at me with worry. "Suzie, I'm scared," she said.

"Maybe it's a *precaution*," I said with my thumb still in my mouth, so it sounded like *precauthion*. It seemed like the right thing to say.

Pam and I left Paul sleeping on the couch. Paul hated loud noises. He always cried when we went to see fireworks, and he even made Mom miss a ferry ride on the *Mini Ha-Ha* because he had a fit when the loud ferry horn blew. But he wasn't waking up from the noise of the siren, and I was relieved because I didn't think I could take Mom *and* Dad crying and Paul screaming his head off at the same time.

We stopped in the doorway. Mom and Dad were hugging each other. Aunt Sadie put her necklace with the cross back into her pocket and rubbed Mom's back. When the commercial ended on the TV, everyone watched and listened in silence.

An old man with hair parted in the middle and greased down to his head was talking. He had a mustache that started out fat in the middle but got really skinny and pointy at the ends. He was talking about helicopters and boats and rescues.

The TV then showed people climbing out of the windows of their homes into boats and being rescued from rooftops in helicopters. No one said anything. The man came back on and said something about the Pocono Downs Racetrack being converted into an evacuation center.

"Who is that man?" Pam asked from the doorway.

"That's Dan Flood. He's a congressman," Momo told us.

"He works with President Nixon and is going to help get everyone to safety," Aunt Sadie added.

Mom turned to look at us. "Girls, go play upstairs."

What was *that* supposed to mean? There was nothing upstairs to play *with*.

"I'm scared," Pam said to the grown-ups this time.

I was too busy wondering why this Dan guy put all that grease in his hair, because it made it look dirty and like he needed a shampoo.

"Nothing to worry about, Pamela. We're safe up here, and everything is going to be fine," Dad said.

When Dad said everything was going to be fine, it usually was.

Later that day, it was still raining hard outside. When Paul woke up from his nap, Mom told us to *play with your brother*, so Pam and I took him upstairs and tried to play with the only two toys we had. Mom and Dad took Momo over to Uncle Ray's house across the driveway after telling Aunt Sadie that she didn't want the news on the television in the kitchen or *anywhere else for that matter*, unless it was over at Uncle Ray's house. Aunt Sadie came upstairs and started folding laundry in the room next to where we were playing.

Pam and I couldn't convince Paul to play upstairs with the toys we brought, and he started screaming again. We asked Mom if we could play hide-and-seek because the suggestion made Paul shut up and it was a good indoor game. Mom said *yes we could* and to *not be too loud*, so we made Paul be *it* because we could boss him around like that. He only knew how to count up to twenty, so we told him to do that three times and then yell *Ready or not, here I come* so we would know when he was starting to look for us. I always liked when Paul was *it* because he wasn't very good at the game, and I got to hide for a lot longer than when Pam was *it*. I was *great* at hiding because I was small and skinny and I could squeeze myself into tight spaces like inside the front-loading dryer and under cabinets.

I ran into the kitchen, which was empty at the moment. This was unusual because there were almost always a few people like Aunt Sadie, her sister Mary, and her brother Johnny in there wearing aprons and preparing food for the big dinner or sitting at the big kitchen table playing a game of cards.

The table was covered in a cloth that wasn't fabric but didn't feel exactly like plastic. It had a floral pattern on it and was a little textured but smooth and shiny enough that you could wipe it with a wet cloth. The underside of the tablecloth was like felt. When I sat at Aunt Sadie's table and ran my fingers across the felt, I determined that I could suck my thumb and use the underside of the tablecloth to run my fingers across in a pinch.

I climbed under the table but quickly determined that it wasn't a good hiding place because the tablecloth didn't go all the way down to the floor. I crawled out from under the table and located a cabinet that had enough room for me to crawl into and close the door. I felt a giddy thrill as I congratulated myself on finding such a fantastic hiding space, thinking, *He'll never find me here!*

I heard Paul's dull footsteps as he ran around upstairs and worked his way from room to room, looking for us. A minute or two later, I heard Mom and Dad and Uncle Ray come into the kitchen and sit down at the table. I breathed a sigh of relief that I hadn't used it as my hiding space!

"I'm going down," Dad said.

"Bobby," Mom replied, as if to warn him that his idea was definitely a bad one.

"Peggy, it's OK. I just want to take a look at the house if I can. I'll walk along the dike."

"What if you can't get through?" Then she added, "I don't like it. Stay here until we know more."

"I can't just sit over there, watching the place get buried under water on the news. I'll go crazy."

It was quiet for a while. I thought maybe they had left the kitchen, but then I heard Mom softly crying. I had never seen or heard her cry, and now she was crying a lot in just this one day.

"Please don't do anything stupid," Mom pleaded.

"I won't. I'm just going to take a look," Dad said. He paused for a moment, then said, "I just have to see for myself what I'm up against."

Mom cried a little harder. Then I figured that Dad gave her a hug, which I almost never saw with my own eyes either. But when she said, "I'm so scared," through her sobs, her voice was muffled as if she were tucking her face into Dad's neck. I couldn't really picture Mom hugging anyone, because she wasn't like Aunt Sadie, who hugged and kissed everyone and called everyone *Ya Habibi*. I wasn't sure what *Ya Habibi* meant exactly, but I knew it meant something good because Aunt Sadie always kissed us on the face after she said it. I thought maybe Mom just had her face in her own hands. I put my thumb in my mouth and regretted my decision to move from under the table. I vibrated my tongue, wondering why Mom was crying about some water in our basement.

After Dad left, Mom went back to join Momo at Uncle Ray's house. Pam, Paul, and I finished our game of hide-and-seek and tried to think of another game to play. Aunt Sadie and lots of other Lebanese grown-ups, who we also called aunt and uncle, all put aprons on and started working in the kitchen. They didn't seem all that worried about the river water. They had turned on the TV in the kitchen, but the volume was turned all the way down. Dan Flood was still talking away on the screen. They also showed more people in boats and streets filled with water and whole neighborhoods that, from above, looked like big lakes with lots of houses that looked more like thousands of little islands.

I thought about how close our Birch Street house was to the dike and the river. I wondered if our house looked like a little island in a big lake too. I wondered the same about Lowri's house and Patrick Koons's house and the Bedwicks' house and the *modern monstrosity* next door.

When we sat down for dinner, there was hardly any room in the kitchen because the big table with the plastic tablecloth was full of so many people from Aunt Sadie and Uncle Ray's family and now Mom and Momo and us kids. For dinner, we had a giant platter of spaghetti and meatballs, and for dessert, Aunt Sadie had made a big sticky sweet tray of baklava that Pam never ate because she didn't like walnuts, so there was more for me. Usually, I ate as many pieces of the sticky sweet baklava as I could until the taste of sweet had coated my mouth and hurt my throat and I felt a little bit sick. I always wished I could restrain myself like Pam did with things like candy and ice cream, but I never could, which made me feel like a greedy little pig.

Dinner at Aunt Sadie's was always so wonderful. I felt happy in my heart, like I was a part of this family, because even though they weren't *real* family, they treated us like they were. We didn't have a lot of *real* aunts and uncles and cousins who lived nearby and came over for dinner every night. We did get to visit Nana and Momo, but they lived alone, and their houses were so quiet, you could hear the clock ticking.

There were never *so many people* that you could barely follow conversations like at Aunt Sadie's house. There weren't lots of grown-ups wearing aprons and always cooking or playing cards or chiming *Ya Habibi* and kissing and hugging us all the time like at Aunt Sadie's.

And we never saw our other grandmother, who was named Gertrude and was Dad's mom, because we never went to visit her at her house. Mom said Grandma Gertrude and Dad had gotten into *a disagreement* and hadn't talked to each other in a couple of years.

But now that we were living at Aunt Sadie's, I felt like a part of this gigantic Lebanese family and community up *on the hill*. I had never felt so safe and loved, and sometimes I forgot about what was happening down the hill until I saw Dan Flood, a.k.a. *Dapper Dan*, as I heard the adults call him, on the TV.

Dad hadn't returned when we sat down for dinner, which seemed to worry Mom because even though she was talking with Aunt Sadie and the rest of the Bedwicks, she wasn't smiling and kept looking toward the door as if expecting Dad to walk in any moment, which he didn't.

Finally, when dessert was served and I started to sink my teeth through a piece of baklava, made thick with dozens and dozens of layers of phyllo dough, honey, and walnuts, Dad walked through the back door. His face looked like it was too heavy for his skull. It sagged down as if it would fall right off if it weren't attached to the rest of his head. The kitchen instantly went quiet. Mom stared at Dad. It was as if no one knew what to say or do.

Finally, Aunt Sadie, still wearing her apron with the necklace in the pocket, quickly got up and fixed Dad a plate. "Sit down, Bobby. Eat. You must be hungry," she encouraged.

Dad sat down and let out a giant sigh. He picked up a fork and began to push some pasta around on his plate. He poked at a meatball.

We always got scolded for playing with our food, but no one seemed to mind when Dad did it.

"Did you see the house?" Mom finally asked.

Dad was quiet as he looked over at me and Pam.

"Did you?" Pam asked.

Dad seemed to think about what to say and how to say it. "I drove down as far as I could, then walked about two miles down the railroad tracks on the dike right to our house, so I got a good look."

I wanted to tell Dad he shouldn't walk on the railroad tracks because he could get his leg or arm cut off. I made a mental note to bring this up later.

"Did we get water in the basement?" I asked.

"A bit," he said. He looked at my mother with a grave expression and held her gaze, which wasn't something we saw him do very often.

"Did you see the shop?" Mom asked.

"I couldn't get there," Dad said.

It was quiet again for what seemed like a long time. Finally, Paul broke the silence by demanding another meatball.

"Say *please*," Pam told him.

"Please!" Paul demanded. His eyebrows furrowed, and his mouth made a grimace.

Mom looked to be lost in thought. She had a blank expression on her face and said, "I put a lasagna in the basement fridge."

For a moment, the room felt like it shrank, and I felt like I was in that kitchen cabinet again. I stared right at Mom, who kept staring off into space. Her trance was broken by a gleeful announcement from Aunt Sadie. "Oh! We make the *best* lasagna!"

She stood up, wiped her hands on her apron, and began clearing plates as she smiled and said, "We'll make it for dinner tomorrow!"

The room opened up again. Mom forced a smile; then everyone started talking about how *much influence* Congressman Dan Flood had in Washington and how President Nixon was going to visit the valley any day now.

*Thank God for Dapper Dan,* they all said.

That night, Mom and Dad went next door to Uncle Ray's to watch the news. Mom and Dad didn't want us to see the news because they didn't want to upset us, so the TV in Aunt Sadie's kitchen was kept mostly off, except when *Marcus Welby* came on because it was Aunt Sadie's favorite show and one of the only times we saw her take her apron off and sit down.

When it was bedtime, the three of us were told we would sleep in Aunt Sadie's son's room, which meant that he had to go stay at a friend's house. Me and Pam slept in the single bed, sardine style as usual, and Paul slept in a foldout cot that creaked with an *eek eek eek* as he rocked his head back and forth on his pillow to get himself to sleep.

Because of that rocking, all the hair on the back of Paul's head was tangled up like a *rat's nest*, which was what Mom called it. But there were more important things on Mom's and Dad's minds, which I knew on account of overhearing them from my hiding place earlier that day, and getting the tangles out of the back of Paul's head was not one of them.

As much as we loved Aunt Sadie, that first night we were nervous without our parents in the house with us.

"I can't sleep," Pam whispered, so as not to wake Paul, who had already rocked his head and put himself to sleep.

"Me neither," I whispered back.

"Let's play bicycle," she suggested.

Pam and I had come up with a strategy that we called *bicycle* for whenever we couldn't sleep. We put the soles of our feet together, the sole of her right foot on the sole of my left foot and vice versa. When our soles were connected, we started pushing and pulling them back and forth in a pumping motion. Her left foot pushed my right as my right knee bent up toward my nose. At the same time, my left foot pushed her right, sending her right knee toward her nose. Back and forth and back and forth we moved until we felt so tired, we fell asleep, but not before I tucked my thumb into my mouth.

# 7

# Saturday, June 24, 1972

We woke up early on the morning after our first night at Aunt Sadie's because it was Saturday and that was the only day that shows for kids were on TV. It had stopped raining, and now the sun was shining and the sky was blue.

We ate our breakfast as fast as we could, then ran next door to Uncle Ray's because he had a big color TV. Mom and Dad were already awake watching the news. Dapper Dan was still yacking away about donations of food and clothes being brought from all the surrounding towns to the local airport. When Mom saw us, she quickly switched off the television.

"Can we watch cartoons?" I asked.

"OK," said Mom, and she turned the TV back on, but there were no cartoons showing! Mom switched back and forth between the three television channels as I kept a watchful eye for *Hong Kong Phooey*, or *Yogi Bear*, or *Josie and the Pussycats*, or my favorite show, *Scooby-Doo*. But all we saw was news and Dan Flood's stupid mustached face and big crowds at the airport standing in line for clothes and food.

"I don't think cartoons are on this morning, kids," Dad said.

"That's not fair!" we all chimed in unison because *now* we were going to have to watch cartoons like *Davey and Goliath* the next morning, which was Sunday. We didn't like those cartoons because they were boring, and Davey and Goliath talked real slow, like there was something a little wrong with them, but cartoons were cartoons, and I would take what we could get.

"Why don't you go outside and play?" Mom said.

We hadn't been outside to play in what felt like a very long time, but Aunt Sadie's house didn't have a big yard with a swing set like our Birch Street yard had. We also didn't know any kids to play with, but we said OK anyway and left Uncle Ray's house.

"Do you want to learn how to play jacks?" Pam asked Paul.

"No!" he said. "I want cartoons!"

"There aren't any cartoons today," I told him. I looked at Pam, who shrugged her shoulders, then said to Paul, "Come on. Let's go play jacks on the front porch. You'll like it!"

Paul grumbled but followed us down the driveway toward Aunt Sadie's front porch.

We found Aunt Sadie's son, whose name was Leo, and a neighborhood boy, who was also Lebanese, sitting on the front porch playing cards.

"Hiya, Spook!" Leo's friend, whose name was George, said to Paul when he saw him. Paul smiled wide, exposing his small square baby teeth.

"His name is Paul," Pam corrected George.

"OK if I call you Spook?" he asked Paul as he held up his hand for a high five.

"Yeah!" Paul replied.

We liked George instantly.

"Wanna learn a card game?" George asked.

We told him, yes we did, and not because we really did but because when you met a teenager who was nice to you and made you laugh and gave you nicknames, you wanted to spend as much time with them as you could.

We walked up the porch stairs. The sun was shining, and it was starting to get hot. Aunt Sadie brought out a large pitcher of ice tea that looked like it had more orange halves in it than tea.

She set down the pitcher and some lidless jars that had different

Looney Tunes cartoon characters on them and once contained grape jelly.

"For you, my loves. It's getting hot!" Aunt Sadie chirped through a wide smile.

Aunt Sadie handed me the glass with the Tasmanian Devil on it because she knew it was my favorite.

"Thank you, Mama," said Leo. Aunt Sadie kissed his forehead before disappearing back inside.

George began to shuffle the cards in a way that I had never seen before. When he noticed my amazed wide eyes, he said, "You wanna learn how to do this? It's easier than it looks!"

I told him *yes, I do!*

"This is called the bridge," he said as he split the deck in two piles, then feathered them together. He then bent the cards up in an arch that looked like a bridge and let them fall down flat, collected them together, then did the whole thing again.

I tried to do it, but it didn't work, and the cards flew everywhere.

"Forget it!" I screamed. My chest got really hot.

"Let me try!" Pam grabbed the cards. She concentrated hard, but the same thing happened to her.

"You stink!" I shouted. Pam usually did *everything* better than me, so I felt that pointing out that there were some things she wasn't good at was appropriate.

"I'm telling," she stated flatly.

"Like fun you are," I challenged. I hoped she was bluffing.

But it wasn't a bluff, and Pam headed down the porch and back up the driveway to tattle to Mom and Dad. Pam sometimes acted more like a grown-up than a kid, and it made me even more mad than I was when I couldn't do the bridge.

"She's a snot," I told George.

"It just takes some practice," he said, and that was the day I vowed that I would practice every day until I could shuffle the cards in the bridge.

I ran after Pam to see where she was going. Paul ran after me, lagging behind. Before Pam reached the back door of Uncle Ray's house, Dad came out.

"Daddy!" Paul yelled. He ran past us and up to Dad, who scooped him up and twirled him around before hooking him onto his hip.

"Za Za Zu!" Dad said.

"I'm Spook!" Paul corrected him.

Dad looked at me and Pam, then said, "Is that so?"

"We played with a neighbor boy who called Paul *Spook*," Pam explained.

"All right, OK," Dad said, then added, "There's no rule that says you can't have two nicknames." He smiled and set Paul on the driveway.

"Suzie laughed at me and said I stink!" Pam reported. She made me so mad, I wanted to explode.

"No I didn't!" I lied.

"Yes she did!" Pam protested.

"Girls, try to get along, OK? We're guests here, and we all need to be polite and well behaved."

I looked down to the ground and felt stupid. But I was also glad that I didn't get a spanking and felt a bit of satisfaction that Dad didn't yell at me but told both of us to behave.

Pam shot me a look that said, *Don't think I'm going to forget this.*

I didn't care. Back on Birch Street, I had panicked when Pam got mad at me because Pam had been my best friend all my life, and before we moved to Birch Street and I met Lowri Jones, Pam was my *only* friend. But now I wasn't afraid if Pam got mad at me because there were so many people around to make me feel better. I was starting to think that maybe I wanted to live at Aunt Sadie's forever.

"Come with me; I want to show you something," Dad said.

He led us behind Aunt Sadie's house where there was a green garden hose that had a sprayer that looked like a gun. Next to the hose was a brown and *stinking to high heaven* piece of wet and crumpled-up clothing.

"When I went to check on the house yesterday, I found this floating in the water next to the dike. So I rescued it!" Dad said, trying to sound excited, but his face didn't look excited at all. And anyway, what was exciting about a gross, stinking heap of fabric?

"It smells like a fart!" Paul said. He wasn't wrong.

"What is it?" Pam asked.

Dad bent over to pick it up. He pinched a tiny section of fabric between his thumb and pointer finger and lifted the thing up. It was so heavy, it dropped right out of his fingers.

"I'm going to find some gloves," he said. "Wait right here."

He disappeared into the house. Pam, Paul, and I sat there, looking at the stinking brown heap and wondered why it wasn't in the garbage.

"Get a stick," I said.

"What for?" Pam quipped.

"I want to pick it up," I responded.

"Suzie, no," Pam said. It sort of sounded like she scolded me.

*There she goes again, acting like a grown-up,* I thought. It always confused me when she did that.

I ignored her and went hunting for a stick under a rhododendron bush next to the fence that enclosed Aunt Sadie's small back area. I found a stick that was thinner than I wanted but grabbed it anyway.

When Paul saw my stick, he got excited. "Poke it!" he squealed.

I slipped the stick under the thing and began to lift it up. It was so heavy that as soon as I started to lift it, the stick broke.

"Get another stick!" Paul squealed again.

*Finally, we are having some real fun!* I thought.

"Suzie, leave it alone!" Pam scolded.

Just then, Dad came back with some gloves. He grabbed the thing more firmly this time and lifted it up.

"This, Pamela, is your First Holy Communion dress. And we're going to clean it up good as new," Dad promised.

Pam wore a grimace. "It's gross," she said.

"Well, the river is full of stinky mud and slime, but we're going to give it our best shot," Dad said.

Just then, Mom came outside.

"They are delivering Sears catalogs to every house in town so we can mail order some clothes," she told Dad.

When we left Birch Street after the man with the bullhorn told us to, Mom and Dad brought one change of clothes for each of us. Why did we need more clothes if we just had some water in the basement?

"When are we going home?" I asked. What I wanted to ask was

*Can I live with Aunt Sadie from now on?* I decided I wanted a big Lebanese family.

Dad said, "We can't even go down into the valley until the water recedes."

"Why?" Pam pressed.

"Well, because there isn't any electricity or running water. And because of the river water, it's too dangerous to try to clean up until the water dries up."

Secretly, I was happy we would be staying at Aunt Sadie's for a little longer. I kept my mouth shut.

Mom walked up to us. She looked at the brown mess and asked, "What are you going to do with that?"

"We're going to clean it," Dad said. Then he added, "At least we'll try."

I looked at the wet, stinky pile. The smell was so bad, I wished Dad would just throw it away. When Mom bought the dress for Pam, I thought it was the very definition of beautiful and feminine and wondrous and magical and it looked like it would be worn by a princess or a bride with its tiara and a chiffon veil edged in lace cascading down your back in case you needed anything else to make you feel like the most beautiful seven-year-old in the world. I had planned on asking Mom if I could wear the dress and be a bride for Halloween, hoping Mom would let me wear red lipstick one day. But that was when the dress was white and lacy and frilly and bright and beautiful and didn't stink like it had been dipped in raw sewage and dragged through a sardine factory before being rolled in an oil slick.

Dad turned on the hose and began spraying the dress with the gun. I prayed and prayed that the hose would somehow get that dress clean as new. Dad sprayed and flipped, then sprayed and flipped the dress some, and I hoped that enough spraying and flipping and spraying and flipping and rubbing and rubbing would make that dress release its stronghold on the mud that had now become part of its very fabric. But the dress held fast to the mud, as if the clothing couldn't imagine an existence without it. Uncle Ray and Aunt Sadie's son, Leo, and his friend George came around back to help, because with such a near-impossible job as getting mud out of a First Holy Communion dress, you needed all the help you could get.

It took hours and hours to get that dress looking almost as white as it once was, but there was just no getting rid of that smell, and I decided that I didn't want to wear that dress anymore because of how it smelled, and I wasn't going to let Mom make me.

After Dad got the dress as clean as he could, he hung it outside to dry. No one wanted to bring the dress inside on account of how bad it stunk, so it stayed outside in the baking summer sun.

Later that day, Momo found us playing hopscotch on the driveway. She told us she was leaving to go stay with her sister because Aunt Sadie had *enough of a houseful* and her sister lived alone and did not get floodwater in her house. Mom told us she was driving Momo to her sister's place, which was close to the airport, and that she would pick up some clothes for us to wear until the clothes she ordered from Sears arrived in the mail.

I walked into the kitchen. Aunt Sadie and one of her brothers, my uncle Johnny, were sitting at the big kitchen table, watching the television. She had the beaded necklace with the cross on the table and was fiddling with the beads one by one as she stared at the black-and-white screen.

Before she could turn it off, I saw Dan Flood again. He was saying, "It's one flood against another!" I was mad that Dan Flood canceled our cartoons, and I was sick of seeing him and his stupid mustache.

*"Ya Habibi!"* Aunt Sadie said with a smile. "Come here, my Suzie," she said as she waved for me to sit down. I took a seat next to her. She was still wearing her apron.

"What's *Ya Habibi* mean?" I asked.

"Oh, that's Arabic. It roughly translates to 'my love,'" Aunt Sadie explained.

"What is that?" I said pointing to the beaded necklace. I had saved up all my questions in my head and was glad I finally had time alone with Aunt Sadie to ask them.

"That's a rosary," Aunt Sadie said. "You pray on it when you want God to hear you."

"Why don't you wear it?"

Aunt Sadie laughed, then wrapped her arm around me, squeezing me tight before kissing me on the head. "Oh, my Suzie, you make me laugh!" she said through a wide smile.

I was so close to her, I could see a few gray wiry hairs sticking out of her chin. I didn't know what was so funny.

"The rosary is for prayers. Every part of the rosary has a specific prayer."

She spread the necklace out so I could see all the beads and the big cross with Jesus at the end.

"This has a special prayer you say as you touch it." She pointed to the cross.

"These big beads have a prayer, and the little beads have a different prayer," she said, pointing to each bead. I could see the remnants of some sort of bread or pasta dough under her fingernails.

"Even the chain has a special prayer," she said.

"It's pretty," I said.

"You try it. Do you know how to say the Hail Mary?" she said as she gathered up the rosary and placed it in my hand. The beads made a satisfying chorus of click clicking as they piled into my hand.

"A little," I said.

I looked at the rosary and ached so badly to put that thing around my neck. It looked like it was made of jewels.

Aunt Sadie said, "Hold this bead between your fingers." Then she started, "Hail Mary, full of grace." She looked at me expectantly. "The Lord is with thee," I continued with her. I didn't know what those weird words meant, but I was happy to be all alone with Aunt Sadie, so I didn't care.

"Aunt Sadie, why do you pray?" I asked. It seemed kind of stupid to be fiddling with a rosary and praying all day when you could be outside having fun or playing dress-up.

"Oh, *Ya Habibi*, there are many reasons that I pray," she said. "Today I'm praying for everyone who had to leave their homes, like your dad and mom and Momo and you kids. Sometimes I pray for the people who I loved but are gone like my mother and father. But most times I pray because I am devoted to God."

"Why?" I wanted to know. This seemed extreme.

"Because God loves and protects all devoted Catholics. He hears our prayers," she explained. I wondered why no one prayed for the river not to flood.

It sounded to me like God was sort of like Santa Claus. Santa Claus could see if you were a good kid or a bad kid, so it was important to be a good kid so we could get the presents we wanted on Christmas. But we didn't get *all* the presents we wanted, just some of them.

Maybe God was the same, except instead of bringing presents, he answered prayers, but not all of them, and maybe people did pray for the river not to flood, but God decided not to answer that one. I decided I would pray for presents on the rosary to God. I hoped God would answer that one.

# 8

# Sunday, June 25, 1972

Sunday morning was bright and sunny. Pam, Paul, and I woke up early to watch stupid *Davey and Goliath* on TV. Aunt Sadie, wearing her apron, was in the kitchen, rolling out dough, chopping nuts, and squeezing oranges. Besides hugging and kissing us, the only other things Aunt Sadie seemed to do were hang clothes on the clothesline out back, watch *Marcus Welby*, and play cards. But on Sundays, the whole family went to church, and Mom said we were going to go too.

Most mornings, we ate cereal, except weekends when Dad made his famous pancakes. But Mom said while we were at Aunt Sadie's, we had to sit down with the rest of the family for Sunday breakfast and be polite and eat what we were given.

The table was full of dishes that I had never seen before. There was yogurt and honey with little nuts sprinkled on top. Pastries with sesame seeds on top and cheese inside. I didn't know why anyone would want to eat a pastry with cheese in it, when you could have one with fruit or custard and frosting.

I grabbed a pastry and scraped all the cheese off the honey-drizzled dough. Mom shot me a sideways glance.

"I don't like the cheese," I said softly.

Mom paused, not saying anything. Then she sat up in her chair and said, "After breakfast, get dressed. We're going to church with Aunt Sadie."

I would have really rather stayed home and watched bad Sunday-morning cartoons, but Mom kept telling us we had to be polite and behave because we were guests in Aunt Sadie's house, so I decided to make a list of all the things I would pray to God for. I added getting to stay at Aunt Sadie's house forever to the top of the list.

The church was called Saint George's. It was located at the top of Aunt Sadie's street, which was called Lloyd's Lane. The street was so skinny that it only took a few steps to get over to the house across the street.

The whole family walked up the steep hill to get to church. Aunt Sadie and all her sisters had something that looked like a doily on their heads. They didn't ask me if I wanted to wear a doily, but if they had, I would have told them I'd much rather wear a veil like the one that came with Pam's First Holy Communion dress.

The church was sandwiched between two aluminum-sided houses. In front of the church were two sets of steep stone staircases, one on either side, that you had to climb just to enter the front door of the church. Saint George's was where all the Lebanese families who lived on the hill went for Sunday mass.

I walked in, holding Aunt Sadie's hand. I hoped that Pam could see me because I wanted her to see that even though she was Momo's special kid, I could be a special kid too, and Aunt Sadie gave a lot more hugs and kisses than Momo anyway.

Aunt Sadie showed me how to dip my fingers in the water bowl and touch my forehead, heart, left shoulder, and right shoulder. When we walked through the doors to where everyone was sitting, there were more heads with doilies on them. We slid into a pew, and I grabbed a book from the holder on the back of the pew in front of me. Its pages were thin as tissues. The front part of the book was written in English, but I didn't know what it said. The back part of the book was written in strange curlicue shapes, and it looked completely foreign to me.

The mass was partially recited in Arabic, which I thought sounded very funny because the priest kept making sounds like he was trying to clear his throat. I didn't understand a thing he said.

The only person who didn't go to church that morning was Dad, which didn't surprise us because Dad never went to church with us but instead went golfing ever since he joined a private golf club that Mom said we couldn't afford.

Mom started taking us to church so that we could receive First Holy Communion and wear that beautiful white dress. Pam was first, as usual, and I didn't think it was fair that I had to start going to church and, after that, to Sunday school exactly when Pam did but I wouldn't get to wear the white dress until a year after her.

We used to think Dad didn't come to church with us because it was always so long and boring and he was allowed to weasel out of it because he was a grown-up, but when we asked Mom why Dad didn't have to come to church, she said, "Because he's Protestant." We didn't know what that had to do with anything, but we shut up about it.

Aunt Sadie and all the women sat in the pews in front of us. And we watched the doilies on their heads go up and down and up again and down again as we all stood up and sat down then stood up again, then kneeled before standing up again. The priest hocked and spewed in that funny language, and even though I didn't understand a word he said, I still said *Peace be with you* and *Glory be to God* and *Amen*, and I threw some prayers in there in between because Aunt Sadie told me God was always listening.

When the mass was over, we all walked out the door and down the steep steps, then down the steep hill of Lloyd's Lane to Aunt Sadie's house while the church bells banged and bonged as if to celebrate the fact that church was over. Which, in my opinion, was definitely worth celebrating.

Aunt Sadie and everyone else took the doilies off their heads, put their aprons on, and got busy preparing a big Sunday meal. Mom and Dad went over to Uncle Ray's to see if there was any news about when people could go down to the valley and start cleaning up their homes and businesses. They were checking the TV and the radio all the time because there wasn't any newspaper delivery on account of the newspaper factory getting flooded and all the paper and machines being full of water. Dad kept saying how much *he hated waiting* and just wanted to *get down there* to see the damage, but Dan Flood told everyone to stay put because it was too dangerous right now. So Dad waited.

Pam and I were in the living room showing off our gymnastic moves to anyone who was around. We both could lie on our stomachs, push our torsos up with our arms, lean our heads back, and bend our knees to touch our toes to the tops of our heads. We felt like we were really something when Aunt Sadie poked her head in and told us we were *amazing*, which made us pop back up to our feet, jump up and down, clap our hands with glee, and ask if she wanted to see *what else we could do.*

Aunt Sadie wiped her hands on her apron and watched as we exhausted our repertoire of gymnastic moves, which really amounted to just a couple of backbends. Aside from the one on our stomachs, we showed off how we could lie on our backs, place our hands on the floor below our shoulders, bend our knees with our feet planted on the floor, and push up to a backbend, allowing our head to dangle down so our long hair could brush the floor. Aunt Sadie acted as thrilled as ever, and I was sure that I was just a little bit better at being flexible than Pam was, which made me feel pretty good.

"I have something for you," Aunt Sadie said, taking a step into the living room.

"For me?" I asked excitedly.

"And Pammy too," Aunt Sadie said.

*Of course,* I grumped to myself.

Aunt Sadie put her hands in her apron pocket, pulled out cards, and sat down on the couch.

She handed us the cards. Each card had a lady on it, and each lady was wearing a long scarf on her head and looking up to the sky.

"These are Saint Mary and Saint Theresa," Aunt Sadie said. "You can pray to them too," she told us.

I was starting to feel like there were too many people to pray to. It didn't feel the same as having lots of Aunt Sadie's family around making me feel so great. I never saw God and Saint Mary and Saint Theresa and never got a hug from them or heard *I love you* from them, so even though Aunt Sadie told us that everything would be all right if we prayed, it felt different than the feeling of everything being all right because we were at Aunt Sadie's house with the big Bedwick family.

"Are they just like God?" I wanted to know.

"They are married to God. All of the saints are married to God," said Aunt Sadie.

This made me really confused because, as far as I knew, only one man and one woman could be married at one time, and I wondered if maybe a lot of very unusual exceptions were made for God.

It was just as confusing when I was told that God was Jesus and Jesus was God and they both were the Holy Ghost. I imagined the Holy Ghost was like the bad guy on *Scooby-Doo* who was always caught in the end by the meddling kids who pulled off the bad guy's mask to reveal his real identity. Except the mask never came off because I never saw a picture of the Holy Ghost, so he was always wearing either the mask of God, who was an old man with a long beard and long white hair, or the mask of Jesus, who was young and looked like one of the hippies that Mom said were protesting the war when I asked her why they looked so mad and were shouting whenever we saw them on the TV news.

And even though Aunt Sadie told us that God and now Saint Mary and Saint Theresa were watching us and would take care of us, I thought it was really Jesus who was watching because whenever I walked by the picture of Jesus that Aunt Sadie had hung on the wall by the staircase leading up to our bedrooms, I noticed that Jesus didn't take his eyes off me no matter where I moved.

# 9

# *Thursday, June 29, 1972*

Aunt Sadie kept the black-and-white TV off when us kids were around, but sometimes we heard it from the living room when she thought we weren't listening. Exactly one week after the man with the bullhorn told us to leave our homes, Dapper Dan Flood said everyone could go down to the valley and start cleaning up.

I peeked around the corner into the kitchen and saw Aunt Sadie standing with her hands in her apron pocket, fiddling with her rosary, and staring at the television. Dad walked through the back door, wearing tall rubber boots and clothes I didn't recognize. He turned to the television then stared at it as well. No one turned the volume down.

"Praise God for Dan Flood," Aunt Sadie said.

No cars were allowed because the mud on the streets was too thick. Everything on the screen looked brown and crumpled. There were houses that had completely collapsed or had been washed from their foundations. Trees were uprooted; streetlights and stop signs were mangled. People trudged through the thick mud, carrying shovels and pickaxes, blank expressions on their faces.

A man in uniform was on the TV, telling people what to do.

> If your house was flooded, look for sinking founda-
> tions, cracks in walls or baseboards, and other signs
> of collapse. You may have to scrape mud off the walls
> with a shovel or wash down the walls with a hose to
> prevent rotting.

The television showed trucks with snowplows scraping thick mud off the streets, carting it off, and dumping it at some unknown location. Fire engines sprayed the sidewalks and pumped out basements. Store owners emptied out every last thing that had been in the store, through broken storefront windows. Massive piles of mud-covered items lined the streets. Scavengers picked through the piles, taking whatever they wanted. The shop owners didn't care; the thought of trying to clean an entire inventory of goods was too overwhelming.

The man on the TV was telling people where to stand in line for volunteers to clean up their homes. Where to stand in line for tools and clothes. Where to stand in line for food.

Earlier that week, Dad had gone to the airport to get clothes and tools for cleaning up. *Because it's gonna be a dirty job,* he told us when we asked why he needed such big boots and gloves and shovels and buckets.

> If your basement is still flooded, do not pump it out
> too fast, as the pressure of the surrounding earth may
> cause the walls to collapse. Do not attempt to turn on
> your own electricity if any water is still in the house,
> even a damp floor. Do not connect any electrical appli-
> ances that have been under water.

Dad switched off the television. He didn't say a word to anyone. He just turned and walked out the door with his shovel.

# 10

# *The Week of July 7, 1972*

It was just over a week after Dad had first walked down to the flood zone and came back telling us it was like *walking on the moon*. Dad told us that some houses were submerged in toxic water all the way up and over the roof and some had four or six or eight feet of water filling the basement and first floor.

He described people looking like a *pack of hyenas* as they sorted through what they could salvage and what they couldn't. Entire pieces of furniture like dining room hutches and upright pianos were smashed to smithereens or caked through with mud, whereas delicate teacups or china sets were found untouched and fully intact. Some came home to rooms covered with flood mud, everything inside destroyed except for a clean white ceiling that was punched through with holes from bobbing furniture.

"It just depends on where your house is," he told us, shaking his head. He told us that the hot summer sun was baking the stinking mud, so now instead of everything being wet and slimy and hard enough to get clean, everything from the streets and sidewalks to cars, street signs, trees, and inside and outside every house was now caked in dried and cracked mud that had turned gray and was as hard as cement. Dust was everywhere. It was hard to breathe.

When we asked him if he went to our house, he told us *not yet* and that he needed to clean the shop so people could *get back to work*. We tried not to ask him too many questions.

After that, every day for a week, Dad walked down the hill, across the town of Wilkes-Barre, and over the bridge to the town of Kingston to the shop. He left in the morning before it got light, and he returned after it was dark. Every night he came home covered in mud and dust. He smelled disgusting, like the First Holy Communion dress. He didn't say anything but went directly to the shower at Uncle Ray's house before walking into Aunt Sadie's kitchen, where she warmed up a plate of leftover dinner for him. He never ate much. He didn't call us by our nicknames or grip our knees with his fingertips or even make pancakes in the shape of our initials. He just left in the morning and came home at night.

The shop had filled up with stinky, slimy muddy water that left mud on every surface and in every nook and cranny of anything that hadn't washed away or been smashed to smithereens. One night, we heard Dad and Uncle Ray arguing in the kitchen about what to do with the printing presses.

"That's crazy," Dad said when Uncle Ray insisted they try to clean and reuse the printing presses. "There are too many moving parts, and they're filled with mud. They'll never work properly."

But Uncle Ray insisted.

"Look, Dan Flood is working on getting low-interest loans available," Dad said. "Why don't you go stand in line and apply? Make yourself useful." That made Uncle Ray mad, and he walked out of the house, slamming the door behind him.

Uncle Ray hadn't walked down to the shop with Dad. Some of the guys who worked at the shop were there every day helping Dad clean, but Uncle Ray stayed home and dressed like a businessman and said he was making phone calls to customers, letting them know the presses would be running soon. It wasn't exactly the truth.

Dad wasn't much fun at the moment; Uncle Ray was always mad; and Mom was sad. But as long as I was at Aunt Sadie's house, I didn't care, because Aunt Sadie was always smiling and always made me feel like I had warm honey inside my body.

We had been to Saint George's at the top of Lloyd's Lane two more times since that first Sunday, and I took every opportunity to pray to God for presents at Christmas and to stay at Aunt Sadie's, and I prayed especially hard at church because Aunt Sadie told me that the priest is God's representative on earth. Now that Mom and Uncle Ray and Dad were spending all their time being sad or mad or quiet, Aunt Sadie and her big Lebanese family felt so wonderful that I sometimes didn't even notice.

After staying with Aunt Sadie for almost three weeks, I was convinced that God had heard my prayer. But one night after dinner, Mom and Aunt Sadie sat talking at the now-empty kitchen table while Pam and I played Barbies in the living room. Mom said that cleaning the shop would take months and that Dad and Uncle Ray had decided to move it to a new building out of the flood zone, which would also take time.

"What about the house?" Aunt Sadie asked.

"He hasn't even been there," Mom said. "It's too overwhelming. He needs to wait until the shop is up and running."

They both were quiet for a long time. Then Mom said, "You've been so kind and generous to us, Sadie."

"You're family," Aunt Sadie said.

Was God answering my prayer? *She said we were family!* I thought excitedly.

"We'll never forget it," Mom said. After a pause she said, "We're waiting for HUD to come through for us."

Who was this HUD guy? Dapper Dan Flood seemed to be a friend of his.

"I pray for your family every day," Aunt Sadie said. She fiddled with those rosaries every spare moment she had. Then she added, "God will guide you."

"We're going stay with my father until we can get a trailer. I put our name on the list for one last week. I hope we get it soon," Mom told her.

If God loved me so much, he wasn't showing it very well. I didn't want to leave Aunt Sadie and her house full of relatives and our big dinners with a kitchen packed full of people around the table, giant sticky trays of baklava, and neighbor boys who called Paul *Spook* and even the church where the priest hocked and spit his way through Mass. Things were happening down in the valley that made Dad quiet and made Mom sad and made everyone on the TV mad because they weren't getting enough help fast enough. But up on *the hill*, I was insulated from all of that by the Bedwick tribe. I could just be a kid and play with Pam when she wasn't acting like a grown-up and Paul when he wasn't acting like a baby.

We left Aunt Sadie's in the morning, exactly three weeks after we had arrived there in the early hours of June 23. Mom and Dad packed up the Chevy sedan with everything we had collected over those weeks. Dad's shovel, buckets, squeegee, and pickax were covered in dried, dusty gray mud. They stunk like the First Holy Communion dress.

"Put them in the trunk," Mom said. "And wrap them in a tarp," she added.

Aunt Sadie gave Mom a few sets of sheets, blankets, and pillowcases. Mom put the clothes she got at the airport and the clothes that arrived from the Sears catalog in the pillowcases and squeezed them into the back seat floor.

Aunt Sadie also brought out a giant pan of lasagna *for your first dinner at your father's*, she told Mom. Mom looked at the lasagna. There was a tray just like it still in the refrigerator at Birch Street. It had been baking in the hot summer sun for three weeks, but Dad was still cleaning the old shop and opening the new shop, so the lasagna would have to stay there a little longer.

George came down the hill, holding a pack of cards in his hands.

"Here," he said. "So you can keep practicing the bridge."

"What do you say, Suzanne?" Mom asked.

I wanted to say, *I can't wait until I can finally do the bridge and show off to Pam because for once I might do something that she can't, and I am still mad at her for telling on me.* But instead, I said, "Thank you."

Mom took the tray of lasagna from Aunt Sadie and put it on the front seat between her and Dad.

"I have one more thing," said Aunt Sadie. I was hoping it was a tray of baklava.

She sunk her hands deep into her apron pocket and pulled out her rosary.

"This is for you, *Ya Habibi*," she said, handing the rosary to me. "Pray with it every day, and God will protect you."

I didn't want God's kind of protection; I wanted Aunt Sadie's. I kept my mouth shut about it and said thank you as she poured the rosary into my hand and I closed my fingers around the beads. The click, click, clicking sound seared into my memory. *This is Aunt Sadie's sound,* I thought.

We all climbed into the car. Every Bedwick who lived on *the hill* had gathered to wave goodbye to us. I waved at everyone through the back windshield as I watched them get smaller and smaller in the distance until we turned the corner and I couldn't see them anymore.

I opened my fist, spread out the rosary, put it around my neck, climbed up onto the back dash so I could look out the rear windshield, and stuck my thumb into my mouth. Being at Aunt Sadie's was the only thing that made me feel like I felt when I sucked my thumb.

# 11

# The Week of July 14, 1972

Pop-Pop-with-the-Screwdriver's house wasn't a kid house—it was an old-person house. Everything in his house smelled like mothballs and coal dust and Vicks VapoRub, and the chairs and couches were covered with woven scratchy material that was worn and sagged and was made scratchier in the spots where they got sat on for as many years as my grandfather and his mother, Mum, who lived in that house with him, were alive.

Everything inside of that house was old and rickety and faded. The outside of his house was gray and peeling and dull and drab and barely visible behind shrubs that were towering and scraggly and wild. Out behind his house, near a back alley was a detached garage where he kept an old car, like the ones I saw in pictures when my mom was little. It had round fenders over the tires and a curvy hood and a round roof and looked like it had been blown up like a balloon. It was just as junky looking as the house and the yard.

The inside of my grandfather's house was quiet. Too quiet. There were no smells of delicious food being prepared all day long or exclamations of *Ya Habibi* whenever one of us kids was spotted. There was no big kitchen table surrounded by a big lively, smiling family. There was only the tick-ticking of the kitchen clock in the summer, accompanied by the dull roar of the coal stove in the living room in the winter. The house, like my grandfather, was peculiar in a quiet, sad, and puzzling way. Both had the mark of a long-forgotten garden, gone wild in some places and withering and dying in others.

My grandfather was also quiet. When he did say anything, it was a barely audible mumble, like he didn't really want us to hear what he had to say anyway. We never saw him without a wad of chewing tobacco stuffed down behind his lower lip, which made his mouth look all funny and bulging, and we thought that maybe it was not that he didn't want us to hear what he was saying but the funny shape of his lips that made him mumble in the way that Popeye from the old cartoons sometimes did.

Glass jars of brown tobacco spit sat on top of wooden tables next to his old chair or worn couch with the wooden legs and scratchy fabric because once you sat on that sagging couch or chair, you didn't want to have to get back up to go find a jar to spit your tobacco into. Next to the jars full of dark amber-colored spit, Pop-Pop-with-the-Screwdriver kept aluminum pie pans where he placed his globs of used chewing tobacco after scooping it out from behind his bottom lip and pressing it together into a ball with the tips of his calloused fingers to save for later. And next to all those things were giant tinfoil balls and lamps that Pop-Pop had made out of Maxwell House coffee cans.

So, besides the smell of old and the smell of rickety and the smell of mothballs and the smell of coal dust, there was also the smell of that chewing tobacco spit in mason jars and those balls of used chewing tobacco in aluminum pie pans.

Pop-Pop's hair had a good deal of black running through it, and he wore it just long enough that he could slick it back off his forehead and curl it up at the back of his neck. He looked like he had a black-and-white-striped ducktail at the base of his skull.

He was small, almost kid sized, but his skin was dark and wrinkled. He dressed like a car mechanic, with navy-blue work pants and a navy-blue work shirt—the kind that would have his name embroidered on the pocket if he worked at a gas station.

He had dark, dark bushy eyebrows that seemed to grow longer at the ends and stuck straight out toward you in all kinds of crazy directions. When Pop-Pop-with-the-Screwdriver talked to us, he lowered his chin and moved those bushy eyebrows up and down and up and down as if he were trying to distract us from looking at the minty glob of tobacco stuck behind his mumbling lower lip.

For as small and quiet as Pop-Pop-with-the-Screwdriver was, his mother, Mum, was even smaller and quieter. She stood less than five feet tall and pinned her gray hair back in a bun, with all of it, from her forehead down to the back of her neck, held in place with a net made of threads that were as thin as hair. She had the same bushy eyebrows and wore a dress that looked like a smock and simple shoes that Mom called *orthopedic*.

Her hands looked more like claws, with misshapen fingers bent all this way and that, and bulbous knuckles that made it difficult for her to do anything with them. She found a way to fit her hands together, one on top of the other, and that was how she kept them on her lap. She didn't say a word but would once in a while say, *Mmmmm*, as if to agree with what you had just said.

When we asked Mom why Pop-Pop-with-the-Screwdriver was so strange, she told us that his mother, Mum, became *in a family way* when she was just a teenager. The family wanted to keep the pregnancy a secret, so when she was shipped to Saint Joe's home for unwed mothers in Scranton, she was only allowed home once she gave birth to my grandfather, where she was told to pretend that she was a big sister and not a mother to that baby. It wasn't until Pop-Pop-with-the-Screwdriver was twelve years old that he was told his sister was really his mother, and that he would be going to live with her and her new husband, who was twice as tall as Mum. I figured that maybe what Mom was trying to tell us was that when you are told to keep a secret as big as that for as long as Mum did, you end up keeping your mouth shut for good and that maybe Pop-Pop-with-the-Screwdriver was so strange because his mother was quiet all the time.

By mid-July, the baking summer sun had dried up all the river water and hardened the flood mud like cement. Every morning when we woke up, Dad was already gone. Every evening he didn't return until after dinner. We barely saw him, and when we did, he was as quiet as Mum.

We could hear Mom and Dad talking in the kitchen when they thought no one was around. They started talking about HUD more than they talked about Dan Flood, and Dad said that it was ridiculous that we had to wait so long just for a *god-damn trailer for Christ's sake*, and everyone seemed to be mad at this guy HUD because they talked about it on the news. Mom said we didn't have a place to put that trailer anyway, so let's not put the *cart before the horse*.

Every time we asked Dad if he'd seen our Birch Street house, he said *not yet*. He said he needed to get the shop up and running while they were waiting for their loan, which Mom told us was money that Dapper Dan Flood got the government to give people so they could fix up their homes and businesses and that was the money that Dad was building the new shop with and the money that Mom said would *make ends meet*.

The first week of our stay at Pop-Pop-with-the-Screwdriver's house was quiet and boring. Mom took us to the grocery store, where Pam and I begged for her to buy us sugar cereal. She told us each to pick one box but to not eat it all at once because it was an *indulgence*. I didn't know what that meant, but as usual, Pam picked boring Franken Berry and I picked Count Chocula. When we got back to the house, Pam wanted to save her cereal because that way it would last a long time, but I wanted to eat a bowl right away because I could never wait and didn't see the sense in saving something delicious when you could eat it right away. Mom was putting the groceries away, and I sat at the kitchen table, which was not like Aunt Sadie's big kitchen table, but small with metal legs and a Formica top.

I missed the big dinners at Aunt Sadie's with huge platters of spaghetti and sauce and meatballs and trays of baklava with diamond-shaped pieces that I couldn't resist but always regretted eating. Now we ate stringy pot roast and sandwiches made with *monkey meat*, as Mom called it. It came in a fat tube and tasted like bologna, except it had chopped-up pickles in it and you squeezed it out of the tube onto spongy white bread, then spread it around before putting the top piece on, and you had yourself a monkey meat sandwich.

Sometimes we ate ketchup sandwiches, also on spongy white bread, and when we hankered for something sweet, we had butter and sugar sandwiches, and on very special mornings, like this one, we got to eat sugar cereal, which not only tasted delicious but came with a hidden prize inside every box!

I poured a bowl of Count Chocula into a ceramic bowl that Mom said Pop-Pop-with-the-Screwdriver got with green stamps. I waited. I sat at the table and listened to the sound of the coal fire burning in the kitchen stove, the loud ticking of the clock, and the opening and closing of cabinets as Mom put away canned string beans and corn, Sunbeam white bread, Peter Pan peanut butter, Welch's grape jelly, and Pam's coveted box of Franken Berry cereal that she was saving for later.

After Mom put all the groceries away, she brought to the table a spoon and a carton of milk and sat down next to me. She gave a weary smile.

"Want to see a trick?" she asked.

I wanted more than anything to shove my arm deep into the dry cereal and rummage around for the hidden prize, but since we left our Birch Street house in the middle of the night, Mom hadn't really paid this kind of attention to *just me*. I didn't want to act like a greedy little pig and make Mom walk away from me, so instead I said, "Sure."

"Well, when I was a kid, I didn't like my cereal to get soggy, so this is what I did," she said as she picked up the milk carton and poured just a small amount of milk into the bowl. "Just put a little milk in the bowl, and push all the cereal to one side," she told me as she demonstrated.

I watched her fingers wrap around the spoon and begin to push all the cereal to one side. Her fingernails were thin and fragile. They curled up a bit, instead of down, and they were long enough that they could easily bend backward if she wasn't careful. I felt worried for her because of those nails.

"There," she said. "Just take a little at a time from here, and leave the rest on the side so it doesn't get soggy. You can always add more milk if you need it."

It felt good to sit with Mom, even if I preferred to eat my cereal the old way, letting the milk soak up the chocolatey flavor from the cereal so I could drink it down at the end. Unless milk was sugary or choco-latey from my cereal, I hated the stuff.

Mom got quiet and watched me eat my Count Chocula, moving a little at a time down into the milk before scooping it into my mouth and biting down with a loud crunch-crunch. Pam came back into the kitchen, probably to gloat that she had more cereal left than me.

"Why does Pop-Pop save all this stuff?" she asked Mom as she pulled a chair out from the table and sat down.

"Because of the Depression," Mom answered.

"What's that?" I asked.

"That was a time that your grandfather lived through when people were very poor and needed to be creative to make ends meet."

"Was it a long time ago?" Pam asked.

"Yes, it was before I was born," Mom said.

We looked at her blankly, wondering what saving tins of chewing tobacco balls and jars of chewing tobacco spit, and making lamps out of Maxwell House coffee cans had to do with something that happened before Mom was born. Mom paused, appearing to be lost in thought. Then she said, "I guess some things just stick."

## 12

# *The Week of July 21, 1972*

After the first week at Pop-Pop's, we got tired of exploring his peculiar house and his wild and overgrown yard. Pop-Pop-with-the-Screwdriver's neighborhood wasn't full of warm and loving Lebanese people who were always hugging us and telling us they loved us and were always around yelling *Suzie!* or *Pammy!* or *Spook!* whenever we walked out the door because the houses were so close to each other on Lloyd's Lane.

Pop-Pop-with-the-Screwdriver's yard was no good for playing tag, and on the other side of the alley behind his house was a giant old, abandoned factory warehouse with huge windows made of little panes that were mostly smashed in by rocks that kids threw. It was as dilapidated as the rest of Pop-Pop-with-the-Screwdriver's house and neighborhood.

We were sick of playing with the couple of toys and stuffed animals that we had brought when we loaded into our car when it was still dark and drove away from Birch Street a month prior. And because it was still summer, we didn't have school to go to, so Pam and I decided to make up a game that we would call *school*.

Mom bought us construction paper and markers and tape and scissors and folders and graph paper. We created student profiles and subjects like math and English, and designed tests that we made twelve copies of and filled out under each student's name and then graded and filed in each student's individual file, along with performance notes.

One day, we were playing school in the front room. Mum was in the sitting room, doing her damnedest to crochet pot holders, though her gnarled and deformed fingers made it slow and tedious work. The big potbelly coal furnace sat in the opposite corner, and a big wooden hutch sat in another. We caught Mum looking up from her rocking and her crocheting every now and again, as if the task were so difficult, she needed to take frequent rests. "Mmmff," she mumbled, and stared off in the distance for a few seconds before returning to her work. She never said anything else. I wished she knew how to at least say *Ya Habibi*.

Paul, who was still only three years old, was our only real live student, and we gave him the name *Mike Smith* because we already had a Paul Jones in our class and he was trouble. We taught Mike Smith how to add and subtract, and he took our tests and did very well, whereas the made-up Paul Jones failed all his tests and had discipline reports written up on him.

"Why does Paul Jones have to be the bad kid?" Paul grumped one day, his brows furrowed down as far as they could go.

"Because he comes from a bad home," Pam said.

"No I don't!" Paul protested.

"You're Mike Smith. Mike Smith is an excellent student," Pam explained.

"I don't want to be Mike Smith! I wanna be Paul Jones!" Paul growled.

"You can't," Pam said flatly. "We're the teachers, and you're Mike Smith, and Paul Jones is a bad kid. It's make-pretend."

Paul began having what Mom called a *conniption*.

*Three-year-olds are unreasonable*, Mom would tell us whenever it happened, while Paul kicked and screamed and wailed and she stayed as calm as could be, which I didn't understand because I would have done anything to make him stop.

Mum put her crocheting in her lap and stared at us but still said nothing. Mom came in from the kitchen, telling us to *put it away* if we couldn't *all get along.*

"I guess we're done playing," Pam said.

"Awww, come on! Let's keep playing," I pleaded. Whenever Pam played with me, I just wanted to make it last as long as I could.

"Nope. Mom said," Pam said.

There she was, acting like a grown-up again. Why couldn't she make up her mind whether to act like a kid or act like an adult? It made me so mad, my blood felt like red-hot lava, and I wanted to throw something at her, but I didn't because I was trying to do what Mom had told me and *control my temper.*

Pam picked up our school papers and put everything in the appropriate folders, stacked them all in a neat pile, and decided she would tuck them into the corner hutch of the living room for safekeeping until the next time we played school. And that was when we discovered that Pop-Pop-with-the-Screwdriver kept bags and bags of Brach's spearmint leaves and mandarin orange slices candy in the drawers of the hutch, and I forgot all about being mad at Pam.

"Can we have one?" I asked.

"We have to ask," said Pam—the rule follower.

Mum silently rose from the rocking chair, grasped a bag of candy between her gnarled fingers and knobby knuckles, and opened it with the few teeth she had in her mouth. She handed each of us a candy, which made us like being at Pop-Pop-with-the-Screwdriver's house a little bit more even though it didn't feel as wonderful as Aunt Sadie's.

And Mum must have said a few words, at least to Pop-Pop-with-the-Screwdriver, because from that day on, he agreed to give us a little bit of candy every day, and after that we decided we liked him all right even though his house smelled peculiar and he mumbled.

Toward the end of the second week at Pop-Pop-with-the-Screwdriver's house, Dad came home earlier than usual one evening, wearing his usual mud-covered clothing that smelled of putrid, sulfuric flood mud. But instead of heading straight to the bathroom where he took off his clothes and washed the mud and stink off him before shaving and splashing on some Aqua Velva, he called us kids and Mom into the kitchen because he said he had an announcement.

"Well, kids, HUD finally came through with the trailer, and the club came through with a place for us to put it," he told us with a weary smile.

The golf club that Dad belonged to and the friends that Dad had met there decided to level a piece of land near the golf course so that members of the club that were homeless because of the flood would have a place to put the trailers they got from HUD.

"It's not much," Dad said, "but it's a place to stay put for a while." I noticed lines on his face that weren't there before. Instead of looking happy that HUD had finally given us the trailer we had been waiting for, Dad just looked tired.

I didn't want to live in a stupid trailer if it didn't make Dad feel happier, so I wished that we could go back to living with Aunt Sadie, where at least some of the adults were smiling and happy.

After staying at Pop-Pop-with-the-Screwdriver's house the past couple of weeks, I decided that the good feeling I had when lots of people were around depended on the *kind* of people that were around. And now we were going to have to go live someplace new, and I wasn't especially happy about it because we had spent every day making a quiet and peculiar house with quiet and peculiar people a fun place to be with our games of school and hide-and-seek. And if Dad wasn't even happy about it, I sure wasn't excited about having to do it all again in another house that was really a trailer that some guy HUD was giving us next to a boring old golf course.

I might have had a worried look on my face, because Mom seemed to know something was on my mind and said, "We'll have a place to live that's all our own. We'll make it nice." She wore a tired smile.

"When can we get our things from Birch Street?" Pam asked, not knowing what Dad knew in his heart even though he hadn't been to the Birch Street house yet—that the house was likely destroyed along with everything in it. And after weeks sitting in the baking hot summer sun while Dad worked on cleaning the shop, it was probably not going to be salvageable at all.

Mom and Dad shared a look. There was a pause. Pam looked at me. I shrugged.

"Tell you what," Dad chirped, trying and failing to look enthusiastic. "Once we get all settled, I'll take you girls to see the house."

Mom shot him a sharp, angry look.

"Once I get it all cleaned up," Dad added.

Mom held his gaze a little longer, then suddenly said, "Come on, girls; it's bath time," before pushing her chair away from the table and summoning us to follow her upstairs to the bathroom.

# PART II

## *The Trailer*

# 13

# *August 1972*

Once again we packed up what few things we had into the Chevy sedan. Pam and I begged to bring our school supplies, and Mom said *OK*. Pop-Pop-with-the-Screwdriver gave us a full bag of Brach's mint leaves and a full bag of Brach's mandarin orange slice candies to take with us.

We said *thank you* after Mom asked us, *What do you say?*

Pop-Pop-with-the-Screwdriver mumbled through his bulging lower lip and moved his long wiry eyebrows up and down and all around. We didn't hug. He didn't say *I love you* or *Ya Habibi*. He just stood there in his work pants and work shirt, next to Mum, who waved at us with her clawlike hand, wearing a solemn look in characteristic silence. As we drove away, I thought I heard her mumble, "Mmmmff."

I watched the telephone wires move up and down and up and down through the back windshield as Dad drove us across the valley and over the bridge to the Sans Souci Parkway, where he eventually pulled into a small parking lot and announced, "Here is where the new shop is going to be."

We looked out toward a boring one-story brick building with large windows in the front. I slid down into the back seat and saw two men hanging a big sign made of letters that lit up from the inside above the windows. It said *Bedwick and Jones Printing*. Dad got out of the car and was met by one of his pressmen, whose name was Junior. I didn't know why they called him Junior because he wasn't a kid and he wasn't even small. He was old and shaped like a pear.

I didn't much care *where* the new shop was. I just wanted to see our new home that we were going to *make nice*. I was glad we weren't living with Pop-Pop-with-the-Screwdriver and Mum anymore because Mom was always telling me to *shhhhhh*, which meant Pam told me to *shhhhhh*, which was her favorite thing to say, and I always got so angry when she *shhhhhed* me.

"How long are we gonna be here?" I asked Mom, feeling irritated.

"Not too long," Mom said.

I hated that answer. *Not too long* never ever meant soon. It meant *It'll take as long as it takes, so just shut up about it.*

I grumbled under my breath and shoved Paul with my elbow.

"Quit it!" he whined.

I shoved him again.

"That *hurts!*" he yelped. Then he screamed, *"Mom!"*

"Suzanne!" Mom scolded.

*"I didn't do anything!"* I protested.

"Yes she did!" Paul whined.

"Suzie's lying. She shoved Paul," Pam reported.

*Why can't Pam ever be on my side!* I thought angrily. *It's not fair!* And with that, I folded my arms across my chest and slumped down into my seat, trying to disappear.

Just then Dad returned to the car. He slid into the driver's seat without a word and began driving up a dirt road that led around the back of the new shop. Everyone was silent, including Paul, who was usually making some nonsense noise or whining or crying about something.

We continued up a steep hill and down another piece of dirt road that ended at a flat piece of land that had eight randomly placed plain trailers. There were no sidewalks or streets. No one had any plants or bushes or driveways or lawns. Each trailer had a set of stairs that looked like they were made of scrap wood that had been nailed together. There were cars in front of one or two of the trailers, but we didn't see any people around.

Dad pointed to an ugly pea-soup-green trailer. "That's ours," he said flatly.

"That's our house?" Pam asked.

Mom said, "It's our *temporary* house."

We sat in the car, staring in silence at the ugly rectangular corrugated metal box. Dapper Dan Flood seemed very excited when we saw him on the news telling us that his friend HUD was giving us trailers. I didn't think Dapper Dan or HUD were so great, now that I was looking at our new ugly home.

"How long are we gonna have to be here?" Pam asked.

"As long as we need to," Dad barked. We shut up.

When we stepped into the pea-soup-green trailer for the first time, the sharp smell of plastic and the dull smell of rubber made our noses crinkle.

"It smells funny," Pam said.

"It's just because it's brand new. Like a new-car smell," explained Mom. "Let's air it out a bit." And she began to open all the windows.

We thought the trailer looked like a train car, long and skinny. When we started looking around, we felt happy because we had our very own bedrooms. The bedroom for Pam and me was at one end of the trailer, Mom and Dad's was at the other end, and Paul had a bedroom in the middle next to the bathroom. Paul never had to share a room because he was the only boy, but I didn't mind because when Pam and I were in bed at night, she usually acted more like a kid and was nice to me, and we laughed and giggled and played Elvis and Pricilla, with me being Elvis, of course. Sometimes we got so *rambunctious* that Dad would come to just outside our door and warn us with a low and stern *Girls!* sometimes followed by *Don't make me come in there!*

Unlike at Aunt Sadie's or Pop-Pop-with-the-Screwdriver's, we had our own beds and drawers for our clothes. In the middle of the trailer, there was a living room with a couch to sit on, and a kitchen was next to that with a table.

After we brought our few belongings from the car into the trailer, Mom said she was going to do some shopping and get supplies.

"Can we come?" Pam asked.

I was hoping we might convince Mom to get us something fun to play with, so I folded my hands together in front of me, jutted them out toward Mom, and said, "Please?"

Mom said, *We'll see,* which almost always meant *No.* We followed Mom all around the kitchen and continued begging until she said, "All right! All right!" and Pam and I looked at each other, each flashing a huge smile. Pam and I wore Mom down, and we did it *together,* which felt just as exciting to me as going to the store with Mom.

We left Dad and Paul in the trailer and drove all the way up the mountain to the Sears department store, because the Boston Store was downtown, so it was all emptied out and still stinking of flood mud, which by now everyone in the town could recognize with just one sniff. If something smelled of flood mud, it immediately meant that it was ruined, just the same as if milk smelled sour. You just threw it out.

We bought sheets and towels. We bought soap and toilet paper and cleaning supplies and a broom and toilet brush. Then we went to the grocery store where we again begged Mom to buy us more sugar cereal.

When we got back to the ugly trailer, we saw Paul standing out front in his favorite pair of green Toughskin jeans, which he never took off, and his favorite Incredible Hulk sweatshirt with the puffy appliqué that made you want to reach out and touch it. A boy stood in the open doorway of our pea-soup-green trailer. He looked to be the same age as Paul. He had a mess of hair the color of butter and was wearing absolutely no pants, which I thought was strange. Except for the time that Paul ran out of our old house to chase after the garbage truck before Mom could put a clean diaper on him, he was usually wearing pants when he was outside.

I grabbed a bag with our new things from Sears from the car and walked up the three steps to the door.

"Hi," I said to the boy.

"He's my new friend," Paul said.

The boy stuck his toddler fingers deep down into a Dixie cup that he was holding, pulled a Froot Loop out with his fingers, and examined it, as if it were a rare diamond. He then popped it into his mouth and bit down with a crunch.

"His name is Christopher," Paul continued. "He lives over there."

Paul pointed to a trailer on the other side of the patch of dirt that was our new neighborhood.

Just then, a tall, thin woman emerged from Christopher's trailer. Her slim legs were like stilts, and she had fabulous hair the color of driftwood that bounced with large looping curls like Farrah Fawcett.

She began walking toward us, each step was twice as long as Mom's would have been. She looked a little bit like a flamingo with those legs. She had on a pair of jeans that hugged her hips and a worn red T-shirt that said Coca-Cola on the front. She made the outfit look glamorous.

She arrived at our green trailer, took a cigarette out of a red-and-white box that she had been holding in her hand, put it in her mouth, and struck a match to light it. She sucked in a sharp breath of air and breathed out a plume of smoke while saying, "There you are," matter-of-factly.

Her voice was low and gravelly like Lauren Bacall. She glanced over at Mom and said, "If he's too much, just send him *hayome*," adding a couple of extra syllables to the word *home*.

I had never heard anyone talk like that before and didn't know until later that it was a sophisticated way to speak.

She turned and looked at me and Pam, taking another suck of that cigarette. "I'm Rosalie," she said. "But you can call me Ms. Patton." Pam and I looked at each other. We had never heard the word *Ms.* And we definitely had never met someone like Rosalie. We were both instantly enthralled with her.

Mom told us she had met Rosalie once or twice at a golf club event. Christopher's father was Ted. Ted and Dad had become close friends because they both belonged to the golf club, but Mom and Rosalie didn't know each other all that well.

"When did you get here?" Mom asked Rosalie as she walked toward her with a bag of groceries in her hand.

"About a week ago," Rosalie answered. "We were trying to stay on the second floor of our *hayome* while we cleaned it out, but we just couldn't do it."

"Come on in," Mom said. It felt comforting that there was another mom nearby that Mom could sit and talk about mom stuff with, just like she always did with Patrick Koons's mother when we lived on Birch Street. *Maybe things will start to feel a little back to normal,* I thought.

Rosalie walked right up the scrappy stairs and past Christopher with her lit cigarette in her hand. Christopher was silent; the crunch-crunch of that Froot Loop was the only sound I heard Christopher make.

After Mom and Rosalie went inside the trailer to talk, we heard a shout from across the dirt patch.

"Hey!"

It was Patrick Koons, whose father belonged to the same golf club as Dad. That meant that they were our neighbors here in the group of trailers, just like they were our across-the-street neighbors on Birch Street. I was happy that Mom would have a friend so nearby. Paul's face brightened; he was clearly happy to see someone he knew from before the flood.

"Guys!" he yelled as he ran with his little legs across the dirt. "Wanna catch frogs?"

Christopher silently put his Dixie cup carefully down on the railing of the scrappy stairs, wiped his sugar-coated fingers on his T-shirt, spun around, and cautiously climbed backward and pants-less down the stairs before running off with Paul to catch up with Patrick, who hadn't waited for Paul and Chris to answer before turning to run down a dirt trail toward the woods to catch frogs.

"Wait up!" Paul shouted.

Christopher silently ran behind Paul, his messy butter-blond hair bouncing up and down with each step.

Mom poked her head out of the trailer and saw Paul and Chris run after Patrick. She didn't call after them but looked at me and Pam and told us to come help her put some things away.

When we walked inside the trailer, Rosalie was still smoking. Mom disappeared into the bedrooms and the bathroom to make up the beds and put the bath and cleaning supplies away before rejoining Rosalie at the kitchen table.

Pam and I dug through the bags that remained on the counter and pulled out the boxes of sugar cereal we had convinced Mom to buy. We tore open the inner wax bag and stuck our arms as deep as they could go down into the dry cereal until we could feel the plastic wrap of the toy with our fingers. We grabbed it and pulled it out while trying not to spill the dry, uneaten Cap'n Crunch and Honeycomb all over the place.

Besides the things we took with us from our Birch Street house on the night of the bullhorn and the school files that Pam and I so painstakingly made and organized while we were at Pop-Pop-with-the-Screwdriver's strange and quiet house, the cheap toys found at the bottom of these sugar-cereal boxes were the only things we had to play with.

Rosalie talked to Mom about her job as a nurse and her fancy nursing school in the Philadelphia Main Line, which was where she picked up her accent and *it just stuck*. We heard her talking about someone named Marty, who lived in the trailer next to Ted and Rosalie and Christopher's.

Mom told Rosalie about our time at Aunt Sadie's and Pop-Pop-with-the-Screwdriver's and how Dad had been spending the last few weeks cleaning and moving the shop so hadn't had a chance to even look at how damaged our Birch Street house was.

I couldn't stop staring at Rosalie. I was trying to work out how she made a faded T-shirt and jeans look so sophisticated. I was pretty sure Mom didn't even *own* a pair of jeans, even before the flood and even after Mom bought all new clothes at Sears on account of leaving the Birch Street house with just an outfit or two.

"Three hundred patients were moved to other hospitals!" Rosalie was telling Mom. "Do you know what a logistical nightmare that was?"

Mom had a glazed look, not able to comprehend the *logistical nightmare* Rosalie was complaining about.

"No rest for the wicked, you know? I didn't miss a day of work—they just moved me to the General Hospital. Who knows how *long* it will take before the Mercy is up and running!" Rosalie continued.

Mom said, "Thank God for people like you. I can't imagine having to go to a job when everything you own is being destroyed by that river!" She shook her head.

"It was such chaos. But it took my mind off things while I was there. I mean, it was better than sitting around, watching the news, and worrying."

Mom looked off into space for a second. "Yeah," she said in sort of a dreamy, far-off voice.

"At that point, whatever was gonna happen was gonna happen, you know?" Rosalie said before taking a last drag of her cigarette and asking Mom if she had an ashtray.

Pam and I felt bored. We were tired of hearing about the flood and all the things the grown-ups around us had to do and think about and worry about, and all the complaining about the government and how slow they were and when the loans were going to be handed out and how Rosalie had to *go to work, of all things!* So we slipped out the door to try to find where the boys were catching frogs.

We walked down the dirt path and arrived at the edge of the woods. We could hear the boys yelping with excitement, but we didn't see them until we walked deeper into the woods. The woods were thick and moist, with moss and ferns and trees with branches that twisted and turned this way and that. It felt magical, like we could spend hours in the woods discovering a secret world of frogs and caterpillars and salamanders and ferns and sticks and moss-covered logs.

We followed the boys' voices and found them crouched over a hole that they had dug. Their hands were brown with mud, and they were poking at a dozen frogs ranging in size from as small as a fingernail to as big as a piece of Aunt Sadie's baklava.

Paul heard us approach and turned his head. "Look at our frogs!" he said proudly.

"Those aren't frogs—they're toads," Pam said in her know-it-all voice.

"No they're not!" Paul protested.

"They're frogs!" Patrick chimed in.

Christopher stayed quiet. He didn't even say *crunch-crunch*, which I was glad about because the only things around for him to crunch on were those tiny frogs.

"Frogs live in water," Pam said. "Toads live in the woods. These are toads."

Paul frowned and drew his eyebrows down over the top of his eyes. "Too much sisters," he said grumpily. "Go away," he added.

I was interested in the hole full of frogs or toads or whatever they were, but I wanted to be with Pam more. "Let's go look for salamanders," I suggested.

Pam and I found a spot near the boys and began turning over rocks. We found pill bugs and spiders and some tiny toads that we didn't tell the boys about. Finally, we found an orange salamander with purple spots. It felt like the greatest discovery in the world. We yelled with excitement and ran to show the boys, because when you found something as cool as an orange salamander with purple spots, it was easy to forget all about being mad.

We played in the woods together, finding more treasures and feeling so happy that we had this magical treasure trove that we could play in every day because it was just down a dirt path and right next to the patch of land where our trailer sat.

"I like it here," I said to Pam.

"Me too," she said as she turned up both corners of her mouth, making dimples appear on both cheeks.

It gave me a good feeling inside. For as much as I missed living at Aunt Sadie's, I liked having Pam a little more to myself. And it felt good not to have to share her with Momo.

The next morning, I was awake before the sun came up. I was excited to go back to the woods to discover what other treasures were in there.

"Pam!" I whispered loud enough so that if she was still asleep, she would hear me.

"What?" she answered. She didn't sound sleepy, which made me think that maybe she had been awake for a while and was as excited as I was about the woods.

"Let's play in the woods today," I said.

"OK," Pam said. She wasn't very talkative.

I began to plan out the day in my head. Pam and I would spend the day in the woods, just me and her. We would discover more salamanders and find precious rocks and climb trees and maybe even play hide-and-seek, and I would hide behind anything in those woods that was big enough to block me, because even though I had turned seven that month, I was still skinny and good at hiding.

"Let's not bring Paul," I said.

"OK," Pam agreed. She paused, then added, "As long as Mom doesn't make us."

I felt irritated. I didn't understand why Pam was always thinking of what Mom or Dad might want, and what we might have to do. It was times like these that I just wanted Pam to think more like me. I only wanted to think about all the fun things I wanted to do, and not what Mom and Dad might ask me to do.

"Let's go early," I suggested, thinking that we might be able to sneak into the woods before anyone noticed.

When the sun started to come up, Pam and I ate our cereal. On most mornings, we ate our cereal still wearing our nightgowns, but on this morning, we got dressed first. Mom was already in the kitchen cutting up pieces of peanut butter and jelly toast for Paul to eat.

"You're dressed early!" Mom exclaimed when she saw us.

Pam started to say, "We're gonna go pl—" but I interrupted her. Pam always told the truth, which wasn't always the best thing to do as far as I was concerned.

I cut in, "Can you wash our nightgowns? They smell bad." It was a lie, *and a pretty good one*, I thought to myself.

Mom gave us a puzzled look. "Okaaaayyy?" she said, making it sound more like a question than an answer.

After we ate, Pam and I went back to our bedroom to wait until Mom took Paul into the bathroom to sit on his potty, like she did every morning after breakfast.

"Suzie, you shouldn't lie!" Pam said, using a scolding tone that made her sound like a grown-up.

"Mom would make us take Paul!" I protested.

"It's a sin," she told me, which I already knew from my catechism class that Mom made me start attending every Sunday after church.

I thought about God and Jesus and Santa and considered my chances at getting my prayers answered and getting what I wanted for Christmas. I had a long, long list because after we left Birch Street in the middle of the night, I didn't have any toys to play with anymore. I considered that Pam might get more than me because she didn't do things like throw Skipper dolls at my head or lie, and I got mad at myself for not being able to be more like Pam.

"Okaaaaa*yaa*!" I said, with the emphasis on the *yaa*. "I won't do it anymore!" I said, but I felt irritated and stupid because I might have blown my chances with God and Santa.

"Good," Pam stated, apparently satisfied.

We heard Mom take Paul into the bathroom and close the door.

"Tell me a story," he demanded. Paul wouldn't poop on the potty unless Mom, or sometimes Dad when he was home, told him the story of "The Boy Who Cried Wolf," except every time he wanted it to be some kind of animal instead of a boy. Every day it was "The T-Rex Who Cried Wolf," or "The Rhinoceros Who Cried Wolf," or "The Giraffe Who Cried Wolf." If anyone tried to tell the story of "The Boy Who Cried Wolf," Paul would scream, "No not that!" and he would start making a big fuss, so everyone did what they were told so that he would use the potty.

"Let's *go*," I urgently instructed Pam.

We quietly slipped out of the trailer, then ran down the dirt path and into the woods.

Everything was wet with dew. Ferns, moss, leaves, sticks, and rocks all glistened with tiny drops of moisture that reflected any light that was able to penetrate the thick forest through the tree canopy.

We got to work turning over rocks and logs, looking for anything amazing that lived under there. We found worms, more bugs, more tiny frogs, and one more salamander. Pam squealed with excitement, and I was so relieved she was acting like a kid again and not scolding me for lying.

"Hey!" we heard from a short distance. It was Paul. He must have heard our squeals and decided to come find us.

I looked at Pam with disappointment. "Darn it!"

Before Pam could say anything, Paul was approaching us, breathless from running. Behind him was Christopher, with the same mess of blond hair but with pants on this time. Paul was grinning from ear to ear, even though he was running and breathing heavily. I realized that I hadn't heard Paul cry or *act unreasonable* since we left Pop-Pop's. I silently asked God to keep it that way because when Paul was screaming and crying, it was a real pain.

Patrick Koons was behind Christopher, and behind Patrick was a boy I had never seen before. This new kid was wearing a pressed pair of khaki pants and a pink T-shirt with Josie and the Pussycats on the front. His hair was sandy brown, parted cleanly on the side and neatly brushed. He was wearing what looked like a broach on his chest.

All four boys stood there panting for a second or two; then finally Paul said, "We wanna play."

Pam and I decided it would be OK.

"This is Jamie," Paul said. "He lives next to Christopher."

"Hi," I said. "I'm Suzie, and this is my sister, Pam. I'm seven and she's eight." Then I added, "We're one year and five days apart." I had gotten so used to saying this because every time Mom took us somewhere, people asked if we were twins.

"They're one year and five days apart," Mom would say. But Mom wasn't in the woods with us, so I said it instead.

"Oh, *helloooo!*" Jamie sang, with a smile on his face as wide as I had ever seen. He stood with one hand on his hip, which was cocked to one side, and the other hand on his heart, as if to say, *Well bless my Lord, aren't you two as cute as the dickens!*

"He's five," Christopher said. It was the first thing I had heard him say since meeting him yesterday. I was beginning to think he didn't know how to talk.

"Kids," Jamie said, still a bit breathless from running into the woods behind the other three boys. "I know a *great* place where we can play house!"

"Yeah! Let's play house!" Patrick shouted with enthusiasm.

"Follow me!" Jamie commanded, and he turned on his heels and began leading us out of the forest, still holding one hand to his heart and raising his other arm straight into the air with his pointer finger extended. He didn't lower his arm until we emerged from the forest. He then pointed to each one of us, counting silently to himself, finally pointing to himself and saying out loud, "Six! OK, let's go!"

Jamie led us to a patch of green in the middle of the dirt and rubble of the trailer park. It was a small circular stand of trees—a little oasis that we hadn't noticed before, but it seemed to be there just for us.

Jamie seemed very comfortable taking charge of our game of house. He told us we would be two families with babies. Paul and Christopher were the babies, he was the mother, and Patrick was his husband, which left me and Pam.

"I'm older, so I'm the mom," Pam said, which meant that I was the husband, just like I had to be Elvis and Danny Partridge.

"Fine," I said. *If I'm the dad, then all I have to do is act grumpy and quiet,* I thought, because most of the dads acted like that lately. And so that's what I did.

Jamie told us that we needed to collect food and look for shelter high up in the trees because the flood was coming and *Lord knows we need to get ready and make sure we could feed our families and make it to higher ground.*

Jamie had an endless list of things that needed to be taken care of, thought about, and attended to, and he knew the things that had to be done just so, because you never could be too careful when the weatherman on the TV was warning that a flood might be coming.

Pam already acted like a grown-up sometimes, so I decided it made sense that she was the mother. I didn't complain about having to be the dad because I wasn't really given a choice, so I told the kids to *sit down* and *keep quiet* and *help your mother* and I told them not to cry or I would give them something to cry about, which never made much sense when Dad said it because we were *already* crying, so we didn't need anything more to cry about. I said it anyway because I knew I couldn't get in trouble for being mean because it was a part of our game, and when dads had to take care of things that got ruined in the flood, they got a lot less fun and spent less time playing and making special pancakes and more time telling the kids to behave and to *keep it down to a dull roar.*

Every day I thought about Aunt Sadie's house, the sad I had when we left wasn't there as much anymore. I wasn't sad at all about not living at Pop-Pop-with-the-Screwdriver's weird and quiet house. There wasn't room for any of that because every time I stepped out of the trailer, there were kids to play with and adults to ask for things if you needed them, and so for the rest of the summer, Pam, Paul, Christopher, Jamie, Patrick, and I played in the woods, digging for treasures or catching frogs and salamanders, or we played house in the stand of trees in the middle of the dirt patch. We always pretended that the flood was coming because it felt like an adventure. For variety, we sometimes made it a tornado. It didn't matter what kind of disaster was coming to destroy your house because we all knew what needed to be done to get out of our homes and make sure there was enough food and clothing and that everyone was safe.

One day we were playing house in the stand of trees, collecting food for our impending evacuation. Jamie ran around frantically, trying to get the kids hidden and safe, just in case we were caught in the tornado. "You kids go hide in the house with the chickens!" Jamie commanded in his motherly tone, while he whisked them off with his pretend dish towel, saying, "Go, go, go!"

"I don't wanna hide with the chickens!" Paul protested. "I wanna go catch frogs!" Catching frogs had become Paul and Christopher's favorite activity, which Pam and I stayed away from because we felt sorry for the frogs.

"No," Jamie said. "It's my job to keep you safe, and there is a disaster coming, and you need to go hide with the chickens while I make some food to bring with us so we don't all starve to death!" Then he looked up to the sky, put his hand to his heart, and said, "Lord God, help me, this kid will be the death of me!" which was something his mother, Marty, said.

Mom said Marty looked like Ali MacGraw, and Mom was very impressed that Marty's wedding dress was made of macramé. I didn't think a dress made of macramé sounded very nice, and I definitely did not want a First Holy Communion dress made of macramé. We had a hanging plant holder made of macramé, and it looked ugly and full of holes to me.

Marty sometimes came to our trailer with Rosalie to smoke cigarettes and drink Tab and talk about all the things we were tired of hearing about like the cleanup and HUD, but sometimes we heard her asking Mom and Rosalie what she should do about Jamie and how Jamie's father, Al, was fed up with Jamie playing with dolls and wanting to play dress-up in Marty's dresses. I thought about Jamie in Marty's macramé wedding dress, and the thought made me laugh.

After Jamie shooed the *children* away with his dish towel, he said, "Let's make some pies," and began to dig a hole. He threw dirt and leaves and a little water into the hole and began mixing them into a paste. Pam, Patrick, and I all watched, mesmerized by Jamie's hands as he patted and shaped each mud ball into a patty. His hands were covered in mud, but his nails were very tidy and cut and filed perfectly. Mine were ugly and bitten, and I knew that even if I tried to get my fingernails to look nice like that, I couldn't. They just grew ugly.

I could smell the mud that Jamie was making. It smelled musky but not bad like the mud on the First Holy Communion dress. It looked smooth and shiny, and I wished that we really could eat what Jamie was making with the mud. I was just about to reach down and plunge my own hands into that mud when Jamie looked up at our gawking faces and stopped patting his mud pie.

"A little help please?" he said, sounding irritated.

"I'll get some sugar," Pam said. She turned and pretended to open a cupboard, which was really the trunk of a tall tree. She opened the cupboard and loudly exclaimed, "Oh fart! We're out of sugar!"

Jamie's irritation immediately disappeared, and he busted out laughing with a force that seemed like it had been bottled up and pressurized and was just waiting for something to allow it to unleash. He rolled onto his back, looking like a beetle that couldn't right itself as he wriggled his arms and legs and giggled with a nonstop rat-a-tat-tat sound that reminded me of a machine gun.

Pam began laughing, then me and Patrick and Paul and Christopher, and pretty soon we were all laughing so hard, we couldn't stop, and we forgot all about preparing for the disaster that was coming to wash our homes away. *I could live here forever,* I thought to myself.

The best thing about Jamie was he laughed all of the time and his laugh was contagious, like a yawn was. He made me feel like Aunt Sadie did, even though he was a kid. Jamie was like a mom, and we all loved being around him because he never seemed to hesitate when it came to deciding what to do or how to do it. He just somehow knew.

One Saturday morning near the end of August, Pam and Paul and I were watching *Hong Kong Phooey* on TV when we heard shouts coming from outside. I shot up to look out of the window and saw Jamie running toward our trailer, flailing his arms all about and yelling, "Kids! Kids!"

All three of us ran out the door to see what Jamie was so excited about. When Jamie was this excited, it was always something good.

He stopped in front of our trailer, half bent over with his hand on his heart. Through his panting breath, he said, "I found something *amazing*! Follow me!"

Christopher and Patrick had also heard Jamie's shouts and came running out of their trailers. Christopher had grape jelly smeared all over his mouth.

"Wait for me!" he shouted to all of us. We just kept running, and Christopher ran behind us, following us following Jamie down the dirt path and into the woods.

Jamie stopped at a tree that had a large thick branch that was close to the ground and ran horizontally. Patrick and Christopher caught up to us, and we all looked at the branch, then back at Jamie.

"Climb on!" he ordered.

We all climbed on, straddling the branch horseback-riding style, one behind the other.

"Now bounce!" Jamie shouted, and we all started bouncing up and down and up and down, and Jamie started laughing his rat-a-tat-tat laugh, so the rest of us started laughing and whooping and shouting, and we could not believe how much fun we were having. The branch was the most ridiculous carnival ride ever in the world, and even when we got thrown off, we climbed back up and bounced and bounced some more and felt sorry for anyone who wasn't us because the world outside our trailers was so truly, truly amazing.

I had seen a branch like that one time when Dad and Mom took us for a ride into the country and then for a walk in the woods to look for bright red or yellow or orange leaves to bring back home to press in the back of the *Encyclopedia Britannica*.

"Why is that branch so funny looking?" I asked Dad.

"Trees are pretty incredible," Dad said.

"But why does it look like that?"

"Trees get their nutrients from their roots and branches. The roots drink up water, and the branches reach for the sun, which is like food for the tree. This branch has had to grow in whatever way it needed to so it could get to the sun."

I stared at the branch and tried to imagine drinking water with my feet and eating food with my arms.

Then Dad said, "Trees don't always decide where to grow, but wherever they find themselves, they figure out a way to survive."

One night Dad came home early and sat down at the table with us for dinner, which was unusual because ever since we left the Birch Street house, Dad was almost never home for dinner, and when he was, he usually sat silently in front of the television while we sat at the table.

"Come join us for dinner," Mom would tell Dad.

*I had something at the club* was all he would say, and that would be the end of it.

But on this night, Dad left his boots and his dirty clothes on the steps outside, showered the stink and the mud off him, and sat down at the dinner table. He smelled like Irish Spring soap and Vitalis aftershave.

"I have an announcement," Dad said as he removed a slice of pizza from the cardboard box and put it on a paper plate.

Mom was busy cutting Paul's pizza into little squares.

"*We* are going to be building a brand-new house for us to live in up in Mountain Top." Dad emphasized the word *we*.

"But we like it here," Pam said.

"Yeah, can't we stay here?" I added.

"It will take some time to build our new house, so we're not leaving the trailer anytime soon," Mom chimed in.

We were quiet for a few minutes. Then Pam asked, "Why can't we go back to our old house?"

*Why can't we just stay here?* I thought. *Or go back to Aunt Sadie's?*

"Because it's too close to the river," Mom offered. If either one of them said it was a *precaution*, I thought I might scream so hard I would turn inside out.

Dad told us that he hadn't seen our house until that day because he was too busy cleaning the shop. He said that even though we couldn't go back and live there, he needed to clean the place all out anyway so someone would want to buy it.

"Can we help?" Pam asked.

"It's too dangerous," Dad said. "There is a group of hippies that have volunteered to help me clean."

I imagined hippies with bell-bottoms and Afros and headbands and suede-fringed jackets holding up peace signs with their fingers. I couldn't picture them helping Dad clean up a house filled with mud and stinking of flood mud, but after that, Dad continued to come home day after day, leaving his high rubber boots outside before walking into the trailer and heading straight to the bathroom to wash the stink off himself, but not before saying, "Thank God for those hippies!"

One day Dad came home with a black vinyl La-Z-Boy recliner hanging out of the car's trunk, tied down with some rope.

"What's this?" Mom asked, wearing a grimace.

"Some guy was selling them off the back of a truck," he said, then added, "Ted bought one too."

We could all tell that Mom didn't like it. Mom was never good at faking how she really felt about things. Just the look on her face, a look that made it seem like she was smelling something bad, was enough for Dad to protest.

"Jesus Christ, Peggy, I'll take it back!"

"No, no. It's fine, it's fine. If Rosalie is OK with Ted's chair, then I'm OK with it. Bring it in," she said, trying to reverse the message that her face had sent.

Dad sat in the black recliner every night after that, and Mom told us he needed to *unwind*. Mom had bought a *state-of-the-art* stereo with an eight-track player. She got Dad a big pair of puffy headphones to wear on his ears so he could listen to Neil Diamond and not get irritated by all the *Goddamn noise*.

One Sunday night, after dinner and after we took our baths and Mom helped us wash and rinse our hair, we sat in front of the TV, watching *Mutual of Omaha's Wild Kingdom* and then *The Wonderful World of Disney* while Dad sat in his La-Z-Boy, listening to music with his puffy headphones on. Mom brushed and sprayed our long, long hair with *No More Tangles* by Johnson & Johnson, which was not the same as *No More Tears* by Johnson & Johnson, because our hair was so long and there were so many tangles that the brush snagged and pulled over and over until our skulls felt sore and there were most certainly a few tears every time.

Mom was just finishing up with our hair, and I was imagining what my hair would feel like when it got as long as Cher's from the

*Sonny and Cher Comedy Hour,* or at least as long as Susan Dey's from *The Partridge Family,* which I was sure it would be someday.

There was a knock at the door, and we all looked at each other, silently thinking, *That's strange,* because by now no one knocked on our trailer door and instead everyone just walked right in.

Mom walked over to the door and opened it. It was Uncle Mark, Dad's stepbrother. Uncle Mark had never come to the door of our trailer before, and besides, he was a *teenager* and hung out with his friends all the time getting into trouble when really what he needed was a *Goddamn job.*

Mom didn't invite Uncle Mark to come inside, and instead we heard him whispering to Mom in a way that the grown-ups did right after the flood when they didn't want us kids to hear what they were saying. Mom pulled her head back into the trailer and waved Dad over.

"It's Mark," Mom said.

"Mark?" Dad said, surprised.

Dad got up out of his black recliner, went over to the door, and walked outside, closing the door behind him.

"Why is Uncle Mark here?" Pam asked.

We didn't see Uncle Mark very much since Dad and his mother, Grandma Gertrude, got into a fight and stopped talking a couple of years back, but when we did go visit, he sometimes made us laugh. Other times he made us scream because he told us that if you hold a gerbil or a Chihuahua upside down by their tails, their eyeballs would fall out. Then he would pretend to pick up Chi-Chi, Grandma Gert's pet Chihuahua, by the tail, and we would scream, "No! No! No!" because we didn't want Chi-Chi's eyes to fall out and drop on the floor.

"He needs to talk to your father," she said solemnly. We knew by the tone in her voice to keep our mouths shut.

We just waited quietly for Dad to come back into the trailer as we watched Marlin Perkins in his khaki pants and his khaki shirt with an ascot stuffed down into his collar sitting in a Jeep on the safari and talking about the lion and gazelle and the cruel magnificence of nature. I wondered if getting eaten by a lion was anything near as painful as getting your long, long hair full of tangles sprayed and brushed by your mother on Sunday night, and before I could decide which was worse, Dad came back into the trailer.

"Where's Uncle Mark?" I asked Dad. He didn't say a word. He just walked over to his black La-Z-Boy recliner, put on his puffy headphones, reclined his chair, and closed his eyes.

"Come on, girls; it's time for bed," Mom said. It felt like something fishy was going on, but we also knew that when something felt fishy, we should keep our mouths shut.

Once Pam and I were settled in bed, I whispered to Pam, "Why do you think Uncle Mark came here?" Pam usually had answers.

"I don't know," she said.

"Why didn't he come in?" I asked.

"I don't know," she said.

"Why do you think Dad didn't say anything?" I asked.

Pam became irritated. "*Suzie!* I don't *know!*" she barked.

I shut up.

The next morning, when we woke up, Dad wasn't there. Mom was already giving Paul his breakfast. We sat around the table eating our cereal in silence. The only sound was the crunch-crunch of our cereal as we chewed it up. Finally, Mom said, "Girls, I have some news to share."

We stared at her blankly, waiting for whatever it was she had to tell us and feeling pretty sure that it wasn't something fun and exciting.

"Last night, Uncle Mark came to give Dad some bad news," she started. "Grandma Gert had an aneurysm in her brain last night, and she died."

We weren't exactly sure how to feel. We hadn't seen Grandma Gert in a long time, on account of the fight that Dad was having with her. She had asked Dad to give Uncle Mark a job at the shop, which he did. But then he fired Uncle Mark because he was *unreliable,* and Grandma Gert got so mad at Dad that she stopped talking to him, and they hadn't talked at all for at least two years, and now she was dead. She was fifty-two years old.

"What's an aneurysm?" I asked.

"It's when a blood vessel ruptures in your brain," Mom said.

I tried to work out how and why that would kill you. It wasn't a gunshot wound or a stab wound or a heart attack. I didn't quite understand, but I didn't ask any more questions.

After the night that Uncle Mark came to our door, Dad was quieter than ever. And even though I didn't know Grandma Gert all that well, and wasn't all that sad, I couldn't make sense of how someone can be living and doing things like watching TV and making dinners and brushing hair and listening to music on headphones, and then the next day just be gone. From then on, I added some prayers to my conversations with God, asking him to please not let Mom or Dad or Pam or Paul die like Grandma Gert. And I made a vow to be nice to Pam and play with Paul and be a good kid for Mom and Dad so that God would grant me that wish along with all the Christmas presents I had been praying for. Then, I made the same prayer to Jesus *and* the Holy Ghost *and* Saint Mary and Saint Theresa from the cards that Aunt Sadie gave us just to make sure that I had all my bases covered.

Not too long after Uncle Mark came to the trailer, we began to notice little changes in Mom. Before the flood, when we lived in the Birch Street house, and even the house before that, in the bad section of town, Pam and I would lie on our bellies with a box of Crayola crayons and a coloring book while we watched Mom getting ready for the day. Mom listened to Petula Clark sing "Downtown" while she looked in the mirror and combed pieces of her long jet-black hair in a backward fashion, then held it all in place with a couple of short, strategic sprays from an aerosol can with the words *Aqua Net* down the side.

When Mom's hair was perfectly shaped like Marlo Thomas's in *That Girl*, she changed out of her housecoat and into a dress. She collected her stiff white patent leather handbag with the gold clasp at the top and gathered us up to accompany her while she ran errands to the bank or the market.

After we moved into the trailer, we noticed that she stopped spending time on her hair, instead parting it in the middle and letting it hang straight down to her shoulders. She started wearing jeans and polo-style T-shirts that had three or four buttons at the top and were made of soft jersey fabric. She bought a pair of weird-looking sandals that had a wooden sole, and one thick leather strap that ran across the front of the foot. The strap had a brass clasp in the middle that you could move to tighten the strap to fit your foot.

"Those shoes are ugly," we told her when she showed them to us.

"These are Dr. Scholl's," she informed us proudly, as if that were to mean something to us. We stared at her blankly.

"They were designed by a *foot doctor.*"

*A foot doctor with terrible taste,* I thought. We didn't say anything.

"They are good for your feet," she added.

We shrugged and went back to what we were doing. I wouldn't wear anything that ugly no matter *how* good they were for my feet.

One Saturday morning after breakfast, Pam, Paul, and I sat in front of the TV, watching *H.R. Pufnstuf,* when Rosalie breezed into our kitchen. She had on a plain white dress, white stockings, plain white shoes, and a stiff white hat that looked like a bunched-up petrified handkerchief.

"*HelllllOOOOoooo!*" She added an extra syllable to the word as she swiftly drifted through the door.

"How was work?" Mom asked.

"Fantastic," Rosalie said as she removed a Marlboro Red from its pack, wrapped her lips around one end, and lit it with a struck match. She took a long drag and exhaled. "Everyone died," she added gleefully.

I was pretty confused about why a nurse would be happy that all of her patients died. Weren't nurses supposed to take care of sick people?

"Why are you happy that everyone died?" I asked earnestly.

"Rosalie works in the ICU. That's the place where patients go when they are so sick, they are very close to dying," Mom explained.

"And we've been very full for the last two weeks. I haven't had a break," Rosalie said, then added, "The place finally cleared out," as if the hospital were like a restaurant after the lunch rush clears.

She sat down at the table, her arms and legs bent this way and that, and her knees and elbows jutted out at strange angles. It was as if her tall sticklike body were the wrong size for our kitchen chairs.

Paul got up from the living room floor and turned, standing, to face the kitchen table. "Can I go play with Chris?" he asked.

"Sure!" said Rosalie. "He's home with Ted."

Paul ran out of the trailer in his pajamas and bare feet.

"Can we go too?" Pam and I asked in unison.

"Go ahead," Mom said.

We didn't bother to change out of our pajamas either.

When we got to Christopher's trailer, we found him sitting on his couch, eating cut-up carrot sticks and more dry Froot Loops from a Dixie cup.

"Can I have Froot Loops?" Paul asked, even though he already had eaten one breakfast.

"No!" Christopher barked. "They're mine!"

Christopher was not good at sharing, and Mom said it was because he didn't have any brothers or sisters and that's why he never learned how to share anything with anyone.

Paul hung his head for a moment, then suddenly perked up and said, "Let's play G.I. Joes!"

Christopher sprang from the couch and ran to his bedroom, calling after Paul.

"Come on!" he squealed. Paul followed him.

"Let's play outside," Pam suggested.

I said OK, but that I had to pee first.

I walked into Rosalie, Ted, and Christopher's bathroom, closed the door, and sat on the toilet. I looked around the place, and there on the floor by the vanity sat a pair of those same ugly sandals!

I wiped myself, flushed the toilet, and walked over to the sink to wash my hands, which Mom told us was important so we didn't spread germs.

I looked around the vanity, and on the right side of the sink, I spotted a handheld blow-dryer, a set of strange-looking curlers that were neatly lined up in a row, covered with a clear plastic lid and had a cord with a plug at the end that you put into an outlet. On the left side of the sink, I saw a yellow bottle with a black top that looked like a large black marble. The bottle had the words *Jean Naté* written up the side. I grabbed it, unscrewed the lid, and took a whiff. It smelled like old lemon and the stinky cedar chest that Pop-Pop-with-the-Screwdriver kept in the upstairs bedroom that we slept in. I stuck my head out of the bathroom and whisper-shouted with urgency to Pam. Whenever I found something important, she was the first person I told.

"Pam!" Then after a moment or two, "*Pam!*"

"What?" She sounded annoyed.

"C'mere, hurry!" I urged, afraid that Ted would emerge from the master bedroom and tell us to keep it down.

Pam approached the bathroom, still looking annoyed. "What do you want?"

I grabbed her arm and pulled her into the bathroom, shutting the door tight behind her.

I grabbed the open bottle of *Jean Naté* and shoved it under her nose.

"Smell this," I said. She stuck her nose down in the opening and sniffed.

"So?" she said.

"What does that smell like?" I asked, already knowing the answer.

"I don't know," she said, as if to say, *What are you asking* me *for?*

"Smell again," I instructed. She stuck her nose in the opening and gave it another whiff. Then she sniffed once more and closed her eyes to concentrate.

"Kinda like Mom?" she guessed.

"Yes, and look." I pointed to the ugly sandals.

Pam peered down at the Dr. Scholl's footwear, waited a beat, and then looked at me.

"So? Ms. Patton and Mom have the same shoes and the same perfume. What's the big deal?"

I stared at her, considering her apathy. Finally, I said, "I guess."

Pam walked out of the bathroom, and I stood there feeling confused.

I didn't know why things always had to change just when I felt like I could count on them. In only three months, we had moved from Birch Street to Aunt Sadie's to Pop-Pop-with-the-Screwdriver's to the trailer, where we just wanted to stay.

Dad had definitely changed. He was only thirty-one years old, but after spending months in the belly of the flood zone—hauling, hosing, and scraping mud, saving what little he could, and throwing away almost all of what he had built for himself and his family, he seemed decades older. He hadn't played with us since before the flood, hadn't made pancakes for us or given us a sack of potatoes either, and it seemed like he was always tired, because he sat in that black recliner most of the time he was home.

And now Mom seemed to be changing. It didn't seem to bother Pam at all, and I felt stupid for being concerned about it. I made a vow to pay attention to more habits of Rosalie Patton's that Mom might pick up. If I saw Mom pick up Rosalie's habit of smoking Marlboro Red cigarettes, I just didn't know *what* I would do.

Mom was spending more and more time with Rosalie and Marty, who weren't like Mom's old friends. Mom's old friends had hairdos piled high on their heads, held in place with Aqua Net hairspray. They spent their days at home cooking and cleaning and taking care of the children. Those old friends had names like *Marion* and *Donna* and *Barbara*. Mom met them at Meyer's High School, and like Mom, they all married their high school boyfriends, who had names like *Tom* and *Lee* and *Jack*. The boys all played together on the high school basketball team. Mom and her friends wore their letterman jackets.

In high school, all the couples hung out together after school, playing pinball at the back of the Luna Rossa Pizzeria on Carey Avenue, which was now torn down because of the flood. They all got married right after high school graduation and had babies right after that.

The women held Tupperware parties and got together for something called *card club*. They talked about keeping house and raising kids and shared recipes with one another.

Rosalie and Marty were different. Mom called Marty and Rosalie *independent women* because of their macramé wedding dresses like Rhoda from *The Mary Tyler Moore Show*. They used curse words that were worse than *Jesus Christ* or *son of a bitch*, which were the curse words that Mom used when she got mad. She called them independent women because they had *minds of their own* and opinions of their own, and they didn't wait until their husbands were around to make plans or go places, and especially Rosalie because she had a real important job that didn't even stop when the flood filled up the hospital where she was a nurse.

I heard Dad tell Mom that Marty and Rosalie were *rubbing off on her*, and he didn't seem too happy about it. Rosalie was not a homemaker, and cleaning and cooking and doing laundry were less important to her than helping sick people in the hospital, which now I knew she wasn't much good at either because it didn't make her sad when they all died.

Rosalie's favorite thing was doing fun stuff like shopping and going on adventures with her friends, and now Mom was one of Rosalie's friends.

When Rosalie wasn't wearing her white nurse's uniform, she dressed like she had stepped right off the pages of a Ralph Lauren ad. She breezed into any room with a lit cigarette and her bouncy hair, as if she were passing through on her way to a yacht or a riding stable. She usually wore a string of pearls.

Rosalie was what Dad called *a sun goddess*, because when the sun was out, she set up a lawn chair outside her trailer and held a reflecting silver piece of cardboard with three panels under her face so that she could get a really brown face.

Rosalie didn't much dote on Christopher, and she wasn't the kind of grown-up that talked to kids in a funny voice like some grown-ups did, and even though Mom and Dad and even Aunt Sadie and Uncle Ray called us Suzie and Pammy, Rosalie always called us Suzanne and Pamela because she was too sophisticated to call us by those kid names.

We heard Christopher's trailer door open, and Pam and I scrambled out of the bathroom.

"Get your bathing suits on, kids! We're going to Moon Lake!" Rosalie sang, and before we could even collect Paul and head to our trailer to change, Rosalie had changed into her strapless brown one-piece bathing suit. She looked a little bit like a Tootsie Roll with toothpicks sticking out of the bottom, but she even made that look *classy*.

Once Pam and Paul and I went back to our trailer to change into our bathing suits, Mom piled us all into the car, and we headed out for an adventure without the dads, which wasn't typical.

Mom wore her usual bathing suit. It was a sturdy red-white-and-blue one-piece bathing suit with a built-in bra that looked like the ones in the Playtex Cross Your Heart commercials, but it had an anchor stitched in black on the front. Instead of her normal teased-and-sprayed style, Mom wore her long black hair parted in the middle and pulled back in a tight ponytail, secured there by a small stretchy band that had a ball on each end that looked like jawbreaker candies. She normally used those ponytail holders on me or Pam, when she brushed our hair and pulled it back into a ponytail. It felt weird that Mom was wearing kid things in her hair. I decided to start paying more attention to the choices Mom was making.

Mom and Rosalie set up low-to-the-ground fold-up beach chairs on a small knoll next to the lake, which gave them a good view of what was going on down there. They slathered themselves all over with Johnson & Johnson's baby oil, and when they had it all over themselves, they extended their arms and legs as long as they could, exposing as much skin as possible to the summer sun. Rosalie's arms were so long they extended beyond the arms of the chair, and her hands dangled down from her wrists, the way that Frankenstein holds his arms out and dangles his hands when he walks.

We swam in the lake and played on the sandy beach for hours. The midday sun had reached its highest point in the sky and began to descend, but there was plenty of daylight left.

"I'm hungry," I said to Pam.

"Let's go ask Mom for something to eat," she suggested.

All four of us ran to the top of the knoll where Mom and Rosalie were sitting.

Paul wrapped a towel around himself and shivered. His teeth chattered together, and his lips were blue. The skin on our fingers was white, pruny, and soft. It seemed as if you could easily scrape a few layers off with a dull knife.

"We're hungry," Pam said, speaking for all of us.

"And *thirsty*," I added.

"Do you have any money?" Rosalie asked Mom.

"Let's see," Mom said, reaching for her new, large macramé satchel that she had bought on a recent shopping trip with Rosalie. Rosalie reached for her matching macramé satchel, and they both began to rummage around in the bags.

Mom's old purses were small enough so that she knew where things were and could find them quickly, but Mom kept *everything* in that macramé bag, which always made it hard to find anything, especially the car keys. There were hairbrushes and crumpled-up papers and lipstick and loose credit cards with *Mrs. Robert Jones* written on them. There were loose bills and jingling change and sometimes half-eaten apples or open, empty packets of Planters Peanuts—the contents scattered on the bottom of the bag with everything else that she might have tossed in there along the way.

From the bottom of their bags, Mom and Rosalie gathered

crumpled-up loose bills and change. They poured what they had scooped up into our hands as if it were precious gold.

"Go and get yourselves and the boys a snack," Mom said.

"Careful not to drop any of that, or we'll have to go *hayome*," Rosalie added.

Pam and I ran to the snack bar with our fists full of tattered dollar bills and loose change. Pam, being more shy than I was, turned to me and said, "Ask what we can buy with this."

"*You* ask!" I protested.

"No, you're better at that!" Pam fired back.

"I don't wanna," I said.

"Fine," Pam flatly stated. "We'll go home, then."

Pam somehow always got me to do what she wanted because I was less patient than her, and when I wanted something, I wanted it *now*. Pam, on the other hand, took great pleasure in drawing out the time it took her to eat something delicious. She enjoyed *delaying gratification*, which made her seem superior, and made me feel like a *greedy little snot*. After I gobbled down a piece of candy or a cupcake, I would look to Pam, who took tiny little bites of her treat and smacked her lips together as if to amplify the enjoyment that was sadly over for me.

Pam saved her Halloween candy for months, eating just one piece every day or so, which seemed completely impossible to me. I immediately scarfed down every piece of candy and felt jealous and angry because all of my candy was gone and Pam still had a bag full. One time I found Pam's hiding place for her Halloween candy, and when she wasn't around, I raided her stash and ate some of her candy every day until she figured out what I was doing and told on me.

Here at the snack bar of Moon Lake, it was clear that Pam had no problem walking away without something to eat, but I was too hungry, so I looked at her angrily and said, *"Fine!"*

Behind the counter, we saw burgers cooking on the flat grill. The smell made my mouth begin to water. A boy who was behind the counter approached us. He wore a blue-and-white-striped shirt and a little white hat on his head that looked like a smaller version of Rosalie's nurse hat.

French fries being dunked into a vat of hot oil crackled as the boy looked at us and said, "Can I help you?"

We poured the contents of our fists, the bills now wet and soggy from our hands, onto the counter in front of the boy. He looked down at the pile of coins and bills and then back up at us as if to say, *You're joking, right?*

"What can we get with this?" I asked.

The boy began separating all the quarters into one pile, all the dimes in another, nickels in another, and pennies in another. Then he straightened out the crumpled, soggy bills and put them in a pile. He began counting all the loose change in his head as he used his fingers to move one coin at a time away from the pile that it was in and off to the side. He then counted the bills and said, "You have two dollars and forty-seven cents here. That will buy you a hamburger or a hot dog, one order of fries, and a drink."

Since I was in charge of buying the food and because there were four of us kids and because I wasn't practical or patient like Pam, I asked, "How many ice creams can I get for this much?"

They boy did a little silent tallying in his head and said, "You can get four small cones, with a little left over."

*Genius!* I thought and told him we wanted two vanilla cones and two chocolate cones and a Coke if there was enough money left over.

Pam and I carefully carried the ice creams and one drink in both hands back to the rest of the kids and distributed them among the four of us while Mom and Rosalie kept their eyes closed and continued soaking up the sun. Mom didn't say anything about the fact that we came back with ice cream, so I kept my mouth shut and hoped this trend of buying us sugar cereal and letting us eat ice cream for lunch would continue. Mom just kept her face turned to the sun. I wondered if she was becoming a *sun goddess* too.

Halfway through eating our ice-cream cones, Christopher started crying. He had vanilla ice cream dripping down his chin onto his bare belly. His ice cream was melting faster than he could eat it, and his hands were covered in sticky melted ice cream. He toddled up to Rosalie and held out his melted ice-cream cone, which was hard to distinguish from his hands because everything was white with melted vanilla soft serve.

"Not a problem, not a problem," said Rosalie. "Give me that," she said as she held out her hand for Christopher's ice-cream cone. "Go wash off in the lake," she then instructed.

Christopher ran to the shore and began washing his hands and face while Rosalie quickly licked all the drips around the cone and licked the ice cream enough so that it wasn't dripping all over the place anymore. We saw Christopher playing in the water and raced down to join him. We returned to the knoll much later, after getting distracted by a game of Marco Polo. Christopher's ice cream was long gone.

We spent the rest of August doing fun things with Mom and Rosalie and sometimes Jamie's mom, Marty, and playing and exploring and discovering treasures in our fantastic outdoor playground. Dad said our trailer was so small that you could open the windows on either end and let the wind blow the dust out, and Mom seemed to take that seriously because she did a lot more hanging out with Rosalie and a lot less scrubbing and cleaning. After the flood, Mom was sad and quiet like Dad most days. But once we moved into the trailer and she had a new best friend in Rosalie, who told her, "Whatever was gonna happen was gonna happen," we noticed that Mom didn't worry quite so much about so many things.

I guess she wondered what the point was of working all day to clean and keep a home pristine so you could host Tupperware parties and card club, when you could be having fun with your new best friend and not worry about things that could be ruined overnight anyway.

Us kids felt wild and free living in the trailer, and now Mom seemed to feel better too. I added wishing that Dad would start feeling that way to my list of things to pray for.

# 14

# *Early September 1972*

In September, Pam and I started going to our new school. Pam was in the third grade, and I was in the second. We had to take a bus every day, which meant that instead of walking to school with my best friend, Lowri, I walked with Pam down the hill to a dirt road where the bus picked us up, drove us to Hoyt Elementary School, and deposited us on the tarmac recess area in front of the building.

Taking the bus every day meant that I didn't have to worry about being scolded for being late, and because for me it was a brand-new school, I also didn't worry if anyone knew that I had accidentally pooped my pants in kindergarten.

The school building wasn't modern looking like Lafayette Elementary School, which Mom told us had been torn down because of the flood. It was made of red brick, had big drafty windows, and was hot on the inside in the summer and cold on the inside in the winter.

When the bus dropped us back off at the dirt road just below our trailer, we wasted no time finding Paul, Christopher, Jamie, and Patrick so we could resume playing house and preparing for disasters and going on carnival rides in the woods.

One day after school, Pam and I found a nearby ravine. We became very excited when we discovered fossils of ferns on flat pieces of shale, because we were sure the discovery would make us all rich! I silently told myself that I would share my riches with the other kids but didn't say it out loud just in case I changed my mind.

Suddenly, we noticed that Jamie was standing over us, gasping for breath again, because he always had exciting news to share with us and always ran to tell us, because when something is so exciting to share, you can't just walk. We hadn't heard him approaching. We looked up at him as he bent over and panted.

"Want to explore the golf course?" he said through his huffs and puffs. He hunched over and rested his flat palms on top of his thighs. Just up a hill at the back of the dirt patch was the golf course belonging to the country club where Dad, Ted Patton, and Patrick Koons's dad, Pat, were members.

We had never gone up there. It was a place for the dads. Dad had taken us all on golf cart rides from time to time, but as far as we could tell, it was not a place for kids to run around and play.

"Are we allowed to?" Pam asked, a lilt of worry in her voice.

"It's almost dinnertime! No one will be up there," Jamie assured us. It made a lot of sense to me.

Just then, Paul, Christopher, and Patrick came running over from the edge of the woods where they were catching frogs.

"I don't know," said Pam. "We could get in trouble."

"I'll go!" I shouted and jumped to my feet, ready to abandon my pile of fossils and geodes for a new and exciting adventure.

"Where're we going?" Paul asked excitedly.

"Yeah, can we come?" Christopher added.

Jamie didn't answer but shouted, "Kids! Let's go!" and Paul and Christopher and Patrick shouted, "Yeaaah!" even though they had no idea where we were going. If Jamie was excited, then so were we.

The golf course was rich with green manicured grass, glassy ponds, and tamed woods. We followed Jamie up and over the crest of the hill and walked on to the fifth green. We removed our shoes and felt the cool carpet of grass under our feet, and we began to feel so free, we started to run around with our arms outstretched like airplanes.

It was just after dusk. All the golfers had returned to the clubhouse for the evening to drink amber-colored and bad-smelling drinks and play cards. Suddenly, the sprinklers came on, and we steered our airplane-like bodies toward that fantastic water and ran around and around in circles over and over, passing under the sprinklers so many times that we got soaked through with water. We didn't care.

The spicy odor of the fresh-cut grass and the musky scent of the nearby pond with its lily pads and algae mixed with the cool and crisp metallic smell of the sprinkler water was a hedonistic assault on the senses that made us feel deep down in our bones the meaning of joy. We felt like the luckiest kids in the world that we had this enormous and intoxicating place that we could go whenever we wanted to feel wild and alive and free.

The air was warm and humid. Our bodies were wet and cool, and after we exhausted ourselves from running through the sprinklers over and over, Jamie fell to the ground and laughed and laughed like he did when the feeling of fun wanted to bust out of his body. "Ha ha ha ha ha ha ha!" he laughed in his rat-a-tat-tat laugh, and we all fell to the ground and rolled around and laughed right along with him.

Jamie stopped laughing, pointed into the air, and squealed, "A firefly!"

All six of us kids sprang up to our feet and began running around again, catching fireflies in the dusk of early autumn until it was dark and we could hear our moms calling our names from the doorways of our trailers.

"I'll get a jar!" Jamie shouted when we landed at the bottom of the hill on the dirt patch where our trailers sat.

Jamie came out of his trailer with a jar. We had continued to catch fireflies and carefully closed our fingers around them so they didn't escape.

"Here," he said as he screwed off the lid. We put our few fireflies in the jar, and Jamie replaced the lid, before continuing to chase and catch more.

We saw Rosalie walking toward us. Next to her was a teenage girl dressed in a green Catholic school uniform. The girl had white knee socks and black-and-white saddle shoes. Rosalie and the girl went inside our pea-soup-green trailer.

"Who's that?" Jamie asked, holding the jar full of fireflies.

"How should *I* know?" Pam said. She sounded a little snotty.

"C'mon," I said. "Let's go and see." I began walking toward our trailer. No one followed me.

"Are you guys coming?" I yelled back at them.

It looked as if they were discussing the issue; then Jamie answered, "Here we come!" and all five kids began running to catch up to me.

When we walked through the door of the trailer, we saw Mom, Rosalie, and the girl sitting around the kitchen table.

"Charlene!" Christopher yelled and jumped into her lap.

Charlene gave him a little tickle on the sides, and Christopher began giggling.

"This is my babysitter," Christopher informed us.

Mom said, "And now Charlene's going to babysit *all* of you kids!"

I wondered what Mom was so excited about. We had never had a babysitter before, unless you counted Nana and Momo. I wasn't sure I wanted one, and I *definitely* didn't want one who was a teenager. I eyed Charlene suspiciously.

Charlene was fifteen years old and a sophomore at Bishop Hoban High School. She wore glasses on her round, friendly face, had long and thick chestnut brown hair, and was what Mom called *a little chunky*.

"Whaddaya got there?" Charlene asked, pointing to the jar in Jamie's hand.

"It's for lightning bugs," Pam said indignantly.

"If you pull off their lit-up part and put it on your finger, it looks like an engagement ring!" Jamie shared excitedly.

"Ooh!" yipped Charlene. "Let's go get some!"

She sprang from her chair with Christopher in her arms, jutted her arm out toward Jamie, with her hand open, and said, "First we need to put holes in that lid!"

My mouth dropped open. I could not *believe* this teenager was as excited to catch lightning bugs as we were. Charlene opened and closed a few of the drawers in the kitchen until she found an ice pick. She took the jar from Jamie's hands, poked a bunch of holes in the lid, and shouted, "OK, we're ready." Then her face got serious, and she said, "But no pulling off their lit-up butts, OK?"

Jamie frowned, but we all said *OK*.

We ran out of the trailer with Charlene, who was running and screaming right along with the rest of us kids.

"We have to act fast!" Charlene shouted. "Our mission is to catch as many lightning bugs as we can before they stop flashing! It's urgent! Hurry! We don't have much time!"

Charlene's challenge made catching the bugs feel like a race against time, and I felt adrenaline rushing through me as we all laughed and ran around screaming, "I got one! I got one!" before running over to Charlene, who removed the lid for us to plop our bug in the jar.

When the bugs stopped flashing their lights and the jar was as full as it could be with them, Charlene triumphantly yelled, "Mission accomplished!" and then, "Line up single file."

Charlene began to march like a soldier toward our trailer, punctuating each step with a singsong chant, *Your left . . . your left . . . your left, right, left, right, left . . . left . . .*

We all followed her in single file, first Pam, then Jamie, Paul, Christopher, Patrick, and finally me as we sang along, *Your left . . . left . . . left, right, left, right . . .* all the way across the dirt patch until we reached the trailer and continued that marching song all the way inside, down the hall, and into the bathroom.

Charlene grabbed a bottle of Palmolive dish soap from the kitchen, piled every one of us kids into the tub, squirted the green liquid under the running faucet, and didn't turn the water off until the tub was filled to the top with bubbles.

Jamie, Pam, and I put the bubbles on our heads and pretended that we had white curly hair. Jamie played with the bubbles on his head until they were just so, then informed us that he was a winter fairy and did we want some winter-fairy dust sprinkled on us so that we could make a wish and have it come true? We said yes, and I didn't mention that I was already praying to God and Santa and everyone else, so I didn't really need to make wishes to a pretend winter fairy with hair made of bath bubbles.

I used the bubbles to pull my hair straight out on either side so it looked like I had long, pointy pigtails. I chimed, "I'm Pippi Longstocking!" which made me happy because Pippi Longstocking was adventurous and fun, and I felt like I was adventurous and fun, except Pippi Longstocking never got in trouble for all of her adventures because she didn't have an older sister who tattled on her.

Paul and Christopher and Patrick tried to slip and slide up and down the tub, sloshing past the rest of us and spilling water up and over the sides, splashing water all over the floor. Charlene didn't yell or get mad. Instead, she grabbed all the towels she could find and put them all over the floor to catch the water so that the boys didn't have to stop their game. She rolled the towels up into log-like shapes and began to make a sound like the one we heard at Aunt Sadie's the day that we arrived. "*WhooooOOOooo! WhoooooOOOOooooo!* Alert!" Charlene yelled. "It's a flood! It's a flood! Get the sandbags! Hold back the water!" she yelled as she pushed the rolled-up towels between the tub and the floor, all the while continuing with the *whooooOOOooo* sound.

I had never had so much fun at bath time in my whole life, and none of us wanted to get out of the tub, even when all the bubbles were gone and the water went cold.

I hadn't wanted to leave Aunt Sadie's when we did. Her house and family gave me a feeling inside that I wanted to hold on to forever. But when we moved into the trailer, and the gang of us kids started exploring and discovering our woods and ravine and golf course, I didn't want to leave there either, and I wished Aunt Sadie could come live there with us. But the night we met Charlene was the first night I didn't think of Aunt Sadie once.

The next day, Charlene came to babysit all us kids while the adults were out.

Charlene gathered us outside our pea-soup-green trailer and said, "OK, kids, what adventure are we going to get up to today?"

*What kind of teenager is she?* I thought to myself.

"Can we go to the golf course?" Jamie asked.

"The *golf course*?" Charlene answered, as if it were the most magical and exciting thought in the world. "Abso-*lute*-ly!"

"Yaaaaayyyy!" we all yelled and jumped up and down.

After a few seconds, we stopped jumping and were silent.

"Where is it?" Charlene asked.

"This way!" we all yelled and started running toward the hill, but we never made it to the golf course.

The hill was what separated the dirt patch where our trailers sat and the green of hole #5 and the lush green fairways of the golf course beyond that. The hill was covered with soft, overgrown brush, and when Charlene saw that hill, she let out a squeal of delight. She screamed, "It's Marshmallow Hill!" as if she had discovered a long-lost treasure. "Let's go!" she shouted, and we excitedly followed her as she scrambled through the overgrown brush, holding on to the tufts of tall grass to help her get to the top of the hill. We weren't scared, and we didn't question Charlene because there was always an amazing adventure when she shouted things like *follow me* or *let's go*.

When we got to the top of the hill, Charlene told us to lie down one next to the other like sardines. We smooshed together side by side at the top of the hill, laughing and giggling. Charlene started singing "There Were Ten in the Bed." When she got to the part about one falling out, she pushed Paul, who was the kid closest to the edge of the hill, like a log until he rolled and rolled and rolled down the hill. We all started singing the song. And one by one, the kids rolled down the hill until we were all at the bottom; then we climbed back to the top of the hill and sang the song again and then again and again.

We didn't care that we got brush in our hair and nettles on our clothing and dirt all over. It felt good to sing and roll and roll and sing, and we were all together, laughing and feeling free, so we did it as many times as we could until it got too dark to see where we were rolling and had to go home.

Marshmallow Hill become one of our favorite places to play, and sometimes we went to Marshmallow Hill without Charlene and lined up like sardines and sang and rolled, and as much fun as that was, it just wasn't the same without Charlene because there was something special about her that we felt when she was with us and missed when she wasn't.

## 15

# *Late September 1972*

Richard Nixon and Bob Hope had come and gone. Mom and Dad still watched the news. People were starting to move back into their homes. The Koonses moved out of their trailer, taking Patrick with them. Dad was still cleaning out our Birch Street house, and the valley began to look a little better but still smelled bad. After the news, Dad watched *Laugh-In*, or some other variety show, and sometimes he even chuckled, which we liked. And much later, after our bedtime, Mom and Dad watched Johnny Carson, but we didn't much care about any of it because it didn't matter because we were kids and now we had Charlene and everything we saw or heard was an idea that could be turned into a game.

One day when Charlene was babysitting, I thought it would be a great idea to pretend that I was Olga Korbut—the Russian gymnast and sweetheart of the 1972 summer Olympics with her blond pigtails and plucky little dances over the balance beam and her graceful loop-the-loops over the parallel bars, by attempting my own loop-the-loop on the shower-curtain rod. I grabbed the rod with both hands and lifted my feet off the edge of the tub, and that stupid rod folded right in half and sent me crashing down into the tub with a thud. I wasn't hurt, but I was terrified and began crying. I locked myself in the bathroom, sure that I would get a spanking for breaking that curtain rod.

There was a knock at the door. It was Charlene.

"Suzie?" she asked as if she weren't sure it was me in there.

"I'm not coming out!" I said between sobs and gasps for air.

"What happened?"

"I can't tell you!" I said through more sobs. "I'm gonna get a spanking!"

"Let me in. I promise you won't be in trouble," said Charlene. And since Charlene was half-adult and half-kid and had never been mean to us and had only been the most fun teenager I'd ever met, I believed her.

I opened the door to the bathroom. Charlene looked at the shower-curtain pole, which was bent almost clean in half and had crashed down into the tub, taking the shower curtain with it. I sat on the toilet and looked at Charlene, panicked. I was sure this was the end.

"Oh my," she said. "Looks like this stupid rod was cheaply made. We should get our money back."

I stopped crying, not entirely understanding what she was saying and fully expecting the other shoe to drop, because whenever we broke something, we got in big, big trouble.

But Charlene didn't tell me that I was in trouble or that I was going to get a spanking. Instead, she promised me that I would not get a spanking for folding that curtain rod in half under my weight because how could I know what worked for Olga Korbut wouldn't work for me?

"How do you know?" I asked her, suspect.

"Because I am going to talk to your mom and dad and tell them that it was the shower-curtain rod's fault for being cheap and not your fault for doing gymnastics."

I didn't for one minute believe that Charlene could get me out of a spanking, but she promised and crossed her heart and hoped to die that she would talk Mom and Dad out of giving me one, and I trusted her because she did have a kind of magic that none of the other grown-ups had. Not even Aunt Sadie.

I never knew what she said to Mom and Dad that day, but for once I did not get a spanking for breaking something.

# 16

## Early October 1972

Soon Charlene babysat every Saturday night because every Saturday night Mom and Dad started going to the movies because Mom told Dad it would be good if he *got out at least once a week.* Dad loved movies, and before the flood, if there was a movie that he especially loved, he took everyone he knew to see it, even if it meant that he saw the same movie six, seven, or eight times.

Dad hadn't been to the movies since the flood, but now that Mom told him it would be good for him, they never missed a Saturday night. Sometimes it was just the two of them, and sometimes they went with Ted and Rosalie, who were by now their best friends just like Lowri had been my best, best friend. When they went out with Ted and Rosalie, it was especially great because Charlene was the most fun when all us kids, including Jamie, who played with us even if his parents didn't go to the movies with Mom and Dad, were together.

We completely lost ourselves in the incredible imagination games that Charlene created; it was as if we entered a completely different world where cleaning up houses and building new buildings and driving down streets that still stunk to high heaven with flood mud didn't exist.

One Saturday we were outside collecting fossils when we heard Charlene's voice shouting "Waterfence! Waterfence!" That was our signal to head straight to the trailer for some important news.

Charlene had named our group meetings *Waterfence* because of the Watergate hearings that they had been showing on the news since early summer. We didn't know what Watergate was all about, and it looked really boring, but when Charlene shouted *Waterfence!* we knew that we had better get our behinds to the trailer quick and whatever it was she had to tell us was most definitely not going to be boring. We didn't hesitate a second but jumped up and ran from whatever ditch or tree or hill or pond we were playing near to hear what Charlene had to tell us because she was now our favorite person in the whole wide world and always had a surprise for us.

We walked the last few yards to the trailer, huffing and puffing. Charlene was already standing outside the trailer door, and when she spotted us, she said, "I discovered a special land! Come quick!"

She began marching toward Marshmallow Hill, singing, "We're going to the Land, the Land of Magic Doors . . . ," and we all started marching behind her and repeating, "We're going to the Land, the Land of Magic Doors . . . ," even though we had no idea what that meant.

Charlene led us up to the top of Marshmallow Hill, across the #5 green, past the pond on hole #4, and up the hill to hole #6. It was almost dusk, and there were still some golfers on the course, so Charlene led us to the edge of the fairway, turned to face us, and pronounced, "Welcome to the Land of Magic Doors!"

"Yeeeeaaaaahhhh!" we all yelled, even though we hadn't the faintest idea what the Land of Magic Doors was. We just knew it was going to be great, just like everything else with Charlene was.

"Jamie, come stand in the middle here," Charlene instructed.

Jamie sauntered over to Charlene with a swing in his hips as if to say, *Would you get a load of me! Aren't I something now!*

"Now, close your eyes and point your finger straight out in front of you."

Jamie did as he was told.

"We"—Charlene paused for dramatic effect—"are surrounded by a circle of magic doors!"

All of our eyes got as big as saucers in anticipation.

"Each door leads to a magic land!" Then she said to Jamie, "I'm going to spin you around; then when I let go, you are to stop and keep your finger pointed straight out in front of you. The magic door that you point to will be the one we go through. And *don't drop your arm* or else the magic won't work!"

Charlene taught us that magic was like that. You had to do everything *just so*, or it wouldn't work.

Our excitement was almost too much to contain. I felt like I might burst.

Charlene began spinning Jamie, who began giggling, rat-a-tat-tat. "Oh my! Oh my!" he shouted between his giggles.

Charlene stopped spinning Jamie, and two seconds later, he stopped spinning and stood with his feet planted on the ground, his body swaying this way and that as he stumbled a bit and continued to say, "Oh my!"

When Jamie finally stopped swaying and stumbling, Charlene instructed him to open his eyes. She walked around to where his finger was pointing, faced all of us kids, and held her arms out wide as if to say *May I present to you* . . . but instead she said, "Door number two! Welcome to *Animal Land!*"

She waved us through in a *follow me* fashion. The moment we passed through the imaginary door, we all instantly turned into animals. I chose to be a lion because my birthday was in August, which meant that I was a Leo. Pam chose a kitty cat; Paul chose a tiger; Christopher, a horse; and Jamie strutted around the land, crowing, "I'm a *peacock!*"

Charlene shouted out commands: "Dance!" "Sing!" "Race!" and finally, "Scream!" And we all started roaring, meowing, growling, neighing, and because Jamie didn't know what kind of sound a peacock made, he started *cuckawing* and prancing around and giggling in his rat-a-tat-tat laugh in between cuckaws.

We really and truly felt like we had turned into animals, and we really and truly felt like we had passed through a magical door that was one of many magical doors leading to magical lands, and we were the only kids on Earth that knew that this incredible place existed because

Charlene was ours, and she was letting us and *no one else* into her magical world.

We played in Animal Land until it started to get dark. Charlene told us to line up shoulder to shoulder; then she walked up and down and up and down the line, inspecting us and murmuring *mmm hmmm, mmm hmmm* to herself.

We nudged each other and stifled our giggles until Jamie's infectious laugh made it impossible and Paul fell on the grass and laughed in an uncaged way while he held his belly and rolled around on the short, manicured grass, which made us laugh even more.

Charlene yelled, "Last one to Marshmallow Hill is a rotten egg!" and we took off running like our lives depended on it. I knew I was the fastest runner of all of us, and I wanted to win, so I dug the balls of my feet into the grass and concentrated on getting ahead of everyone. Charlene, who was at the back of the group, shouted, "Stop before the pond if you want to live through the night!" I stopped short, and the rest of the kids nearly piled into me. The pond was just ahead. We fell onto the grass, gasping for breath.

Charlene gathered us in a huddle and began speaking in an urgent, hushed tone. "Kids," she said, sounding very serious, "it's getting dark, and you know what that means, don't you?" She said it as if we knew what she was about to tell us. Which we never did.

We looked at each other; then Jamie said, "Bath time?"

"No, not that," said Charlene.

"Dinnertime?" Pam offered.

"Not that either."

Then Charlene pulled us all really close and said in a whisper, "It's Ishkabibble."

No one said anything. Then Christopher, who was almost never the first to speak, asked, "What's Ishkabibble?"

*"Shhhhhh!"* Charlene shushed. "Ishkabibble is a *who*, not a *what*."

We silently waited for more.

"She's a horrible monstrous witch who lives in the lake and comes out at night when there is a full moon." Then Charlene looked up and pointed to the bright yellow, round full moon that was just coming visible in the night sky.

"I'm scared!" said Paul, seeming as if he might cry.

I was scared too, but I didn't say anything. I knew that if you could pray for good things to come true, you could also make bad things happen if you thought about them in your head. Like bridges crashing down, or the Wicked Witch of the West. And now I had another thing to try not to think about, and I definitely made a note to never come to the golf course without Charlene at night when the moon was full.

"Don't worry," Charlene assured. "We only have to recite a poem while we walk past the pond, and Ishkabibble will stay under that water until we have passed. But . . ." She got very serious. "We have to keep reciting the poem until we are all the way home. Inside the trailer with the door shut."

She looked around at all of our faces, then added, "*All* of us. Or the poem won't work."

She looked at Christopher the longest because he didn't talk very much, and then she said, "OK, Christopher?"

Christopher didn't say anything; he just nodded his head.

Charlene taught us the poem, and when she was sure we all knew it by heart, she said in a whisper, "OK, follow me. And remember, *everyone* has to say the poem, and you can't stop until we are in the trailer and the door is shut!"

Right then, I felt like I could probably run faster than a speeding bullet. I imagined I would be just a blur as I sped right past that pond, down the hill, across the trailer park, through the stand of trees, and into the trailer, where I would shut the door behind me before running to my bedroom and hiding under the bed where I always thought monsters hid, but I didn't care.

But we *had* to listen to Charlene, so as we approached the pond in a huddle, she started quietly reciting:

> When the moooooon is full,
> And the skyyyy is black . . .

We all joined in.

> Ishkabibble prepares to attack.
> She waits in the pond,

As the kids come near.
But we know this poem,
So there is nothing to fear!

Our volume increased as we felt the evil of the pond on our right.

Try as she might,
She's unable to roam,
From her lair in the pond,
Until we are safe at home!

We recited that poem over and over as we ran as fast as we could once we got past the pond. We shouted the poem louder and louder as we approached Marshmallow Hill because Charlene kept commanding *Louder!* And we wanted to make darn sure that Ishkabibble heard us and would stay under that water until we were safe at home.

We slid down Marshmallow Hill without skipping a word of that poem. Even Christopher was shouting.

At the bottom of Marshmallow Hill, we took off running and shouting, *"Try as she might! She's unable to roam!"* And we didn't stop running and shouting until we were safely inside the pea-soup-green trailer and had closed and locked the door.

Charlene triumphantly yelled, "We did it!"

"We did it!" we all yelled and hugged each other in a big group and began jumping up and down, still clinging to one another and chanting, "We. Did. It! We. Did. It! We. Did. It!" before Charlene piled all of us kids in a tub full of bubbles so that we could squeeze out every last ounce of play that we had in us until we collapsed in whatever bed we happened to be nearest to.

# 17

# *Late October 1972*

One Saturday morning, Dad asked us if we wanted pancakes instead of cereal. Dad hadn't made us pancakes since before the flood, so we said *yes we did* and tried not to act too excited in case it was another few months before he would make pancakes for us again.

After he slid our pancakes on the plates he had set, and we slathered them with butter and drowned them in Log Cabin syrup, Dad sat down at the table with us. Mom looked at him, and he looked back, hesitating. Finally, he said, "Girls, how would you like to come take a look at the house on Birch Street today?"

Pam and I looked at Mom and gave her an *Is this OK with you?* look. We had overheard Mom many times telling Dad that she didn't want us to see the house.

"I want their last memories of the house to be the way it was before the flood," she had insisted. But now it seemed they had reached some sort of arrangement, because Mom nodded her head as if to say, *Yes, it's OK.*

I wasn't sure that I wanted to miss a Saturday morning of watching cartoons, because it was the only day that *good* cartoons were on TV.

"I wanna watch cartoons," I finally said.

"What about you, Pamela?" Dad asked Pam.

"I don't care," Pam said.

"Tell you what," Dad said. "How about you watch a few cartoons and then we go down? Let's compromise."

We hadn't spent all that much time with Dad since we left our Birch Street house because he had been gone every day cleaning up the mess. Now Dad was asking to spend time with us, and we felt excited, and we didn't want to miss the opportunity even if it wasn't *exactly* what we wanted to be doing.

I thought about the time before the flood when Dad took me and Pam to see his favorite movie, *West Side Story*. I wanted to be with Dad, but I was worried about seeing what was in that movie because I remembered seeing *Old Yeller* one Sunday night on the *Wonderful World of Disney*, and I was so sad when Old Yeller died and I couldn't stop myself from thinking about it. Every time I thought about it, I had a heavy feeling that I didn't like in my heart, but I just couldn't put it out of my mind, and it lasted for months and months.

Before we walked into the cinema, I asked Dad if anyone was going to die in this movie.

"No, no one dies," he lied.

In the end, I wasn't mad at Dad for telling me that no one died, because I was happy to be at the movies with him, and I could overlook the bad so I could take in the good—and being with Dad was very good.

Pam and I decided that being with Dad was worth missing a few cartoons. So we didn't complain or make cow eyes, and as soon as *Josie and the Pussycats* was over, Dad turned off the TV and said, "OK, let's head down."

We climbed into the car, and Dad popped an eight-track cassette into the eight-track player.

Neil Diamond began singing "Cherry, Cherry."

As we headed down the Sans Souci Parkway, back over the bridge and down into the valley, the pungent smell of flood mud hit our nostrils with a smack.

"What's that smell?" Pam asked, pinching her nose. "It stinks!"

"Blech!" I punctuated, then added, "It smells like a fart!"

"That's the smell of the flood," Dad told us. "Most people think the river water would just make things wet, but the river was full of mud and garbage and lots of other toxic stuff."

"Does our house smell bad?" we asked hesitantly.

"Not anymore!" Dad said, and he looked into the rearview mirror and smiled at us. Then he added, "I took everything out of the house. Even the walls."

I wasn't sure I believed him, because as we drove through the streets of town and looked at all the other houses that were all emptied out and finally turned down Birch Street, we could see piles and piles of trash heaps with everything in them from couches to TVs to smashed-up piles of wood to toys and kitchen cabinets and rolled-up rugs, and it smelled like someone had taken a big vat and piled in fish and dirt and the stinkiest fart ever, mixed it up, and poured it over everything. I pinched my nose too.

When we pulled up to the curb in front of our house, ahead of us was a white truck with a red cross on the side of it. Neil Diamond was singing "Sweet Caroline."

Dad told us to get out of the car, then lifted me up and sat me on the hood. He lifted Pam and sat her next to me. We looked toward the house and could see that the driveway was ripped up and smooshed into the side of the house. I could see that the front door and all the windows were wide open, their screens removed.

"Why are all the windows and doors open?" Pam asked Dad.

"To air the place out," Dad said.

I peered into a window and could see that the house was completely empty, and all of the walls and ceilings and floors had been torn down so that it definitely did *not* look like the house I remembered, and it didn't *feel* like our house anymore. By that time, I had lived at Aunt Sadie's and Pop-Pop-with-the-Screwdriver's house and now the trailer. It felt like years since I had even been there.

"Can we go in?" Pam asked.

Dad told us it was still too dangerous because the house had *structural damage*.

He spun around and walked over to the white truck with the red cross. "Two sandwiches, please," he told the lady inside the truck. She handed him two cheese-and-yellow-mustard sandwiches on spongy white bread, each one wrapped in wax paper.

Dad returned to the car and handed me and Pam our sandwiches. We each took a bite.

"Is anyone going to live here?" Pam asked.

"Well," Dad started, as if gearing up for a long explanation. "Someone will buy this house and fix it up for themselves." He paused to examine our faces.

"And *we* will be moving into our brand-new house in Mountain Top as soon as it's finished being built."

I wanted to tell Dad that I wanted the trailer to be our home. And if the trailer couldn't be our home, I wanted to live with Aunt Sadie. Instead, I said, "What if we don't like Mountain Top?"

"Oh, we will," Dad assured us. "It's a beautiful place with lots of trees and grass, and it's way up on the side of the mountain where even the biggest flood can't reach us." We thought that Dad would be acting happy about living in a house on the mountain, because he would never have to clean it up after a flood. But Dad wasn't smiling. He was just quiet for a while, then said, "It's going to feel good to be in a brand-new house."

Pam and I were silent. I wasn't sad that we weren't moving back to Birch Street, because we were having much more fun in the trailer, especially now that Charlene was there almost every day and had invited us into her magical world of imagination. We were in no hurry to leave, no matter how new and fancy our house was going to be.

"What about Christopher and Jamie? Are they building a house in Mountain Top too?" I asked.

"Well, they are building new houses up on the mountain, but not in the same neighborhood."

Dad looked at me and Pam and seemed to know from the frightened looks on our faces that what he told us was most definitely *not* what we wanted to hear.

"But they will be close enough to us, and you'll have lots of opportunities to play with them," Dad assured.

We weren't convinced.

"How long before our house in Mountain Top is done?" Pam asked. I figured she was thinking the same thing as me: *How much time do we have left in this wonderful place of exploration, imagination, and wonder?*

"At least a year," Dad said. "Maybe two," he added. He suddenly seemed lost in thought as he looked at the gutted Birch Street house. His face looked tired.

"Ready to head back?" he finally said.

Pam and I nodded our heads. We looked at each other with expressions of relief. We wouldn't mind if we *never* moved to Mountain Top.

# 18

# November 1972

Jamie's dad, Al, had moved out of the trailer. Mom told us that Jamie's mom and dad were *separated*. So after Patrick Koons and his family moved out of the trailer park, and we lost him as a husband in our games of house, we just pretended that Patrick was a dad who was also separated and we didn't see him anymore just like we didn't see Al Oliver anymore.

Jamie told us that his dad moved out because Jamie had asked for an umbrella for his birthday so that he could dance around and sing and pretend to be Mary Poppins and that his dad didn't want Jamie pretending to be a singing and dancing nanny or playing with *Goddamn dolls for Christ's sake* unless they were G.I. Joe dolls. But when we asked Mom if Jamie's dad moved out because Jamie wanted to be Mary Poppins, she said it had nothing to do with Jamie and that his dad loved him very much, but he just couldn't live with Marty anymore. I figured it was because Marty was vulgar and used curse words that were much, much worse than anything we had ever heard.

When the weather started getting colder, Pam, Paul, Jamie, Christopher, and I began playing indoors a little more. Charlene had brought us a new machine that she called a tape recorder. You popped open a little compartment, slid in a small reel-to-reel type of cassette, pressed two buttons at the same time, and spoke into the recorder, then played it back to hear it. We all thought this was the most fantastic thing we had ever seen, and soon we began to make up all sorts of things to record, like game shows and news bulletins reporting on tornadoes and hurricanes and floods that had hit the valley and devastated homes.

I made my voice real low and pretended to be Walter Cronkite, the old man who read the news on TV, except we called him Walter-Not-So-Bright, which made us laugh until we couldn't breathe. Pam was always *Jane-the-On-the-Spot-Reporter*, who was on the scene to interview the victims of the disaster that had struck the town.

One of the women that *Jane-the-On-the-Spot-Reporter* interviewed was always Mrs. Jones, a role that we all knew without question or debate belonged to Jamie. Jane asked Mrs. Jones what she did when she heard that there was a flood coming and that everyone had to evacuate. Jamie said, "Well, my husband put me and the kids into the car and drived us up to Mountain Top."

And when Jane asked Mrs. Jones how she felt when she went back into her house after the flood, Jamie described perfectly what we had seen and heard every day from the grown-ups everywhere around us.

"I didn't feel too good," Mrs. Jones explained. "This is how I sounded." Then Jamie let out a long, heavy sigh, expelling the word *nooooooooooooooo* out through his breath, which was the sound of hopelessness and helplessness that we had heard over the summer as the grown-ups around us went back down into the valley to face the monumental task of cleaning up and rebuilding their lives.

Christopher was a little too shy to talk into the tape recorder, so Paul did most of the talking for him because he was what Dad called a *ham* and liked to make us laugh by being really silly.

One day Paul took the tape recorder and hid himself somewhere that we wouldn't find him and spent hours talking a bunch of nonsense into the machine. When Mom found the tape and listened to it, she said *out of the mouths of babes* and laughed until tears ran down her cheeks. She told us to make sure we kept the tape and said we would want to listen to it when we grew up. We didn't much care about growing up or thinking about what we would want to listen to, but we didn't want to get rid of any of the tapes anyway because we were sure that our made-up skits and shows and new stories would be another thing that would make us rich and famous someday.

Since moving into the trailer, I hadn't played with anyone but Pam, Paul, Christopher, Jamie, and Patrick, before he moved away. These were kids who were *from the flood*. We could have fun with anything that we found, no matter how ordinary it might have seemed. And now that Charlene was our babysitter, hills, trees, and golf course greens and fairways became fabulous lands of fun and imagination. Ravines, rocks, and ditches became lands of treasures. And a stand of trees was our neighborhood community with families working together to prepare for a coming disaster.

But one day I decided to invite a kid who wasn't *from the flood* to the dirt patch of trailers to play. His name was Bobby Skipalas, and I called him my boyfriend because he teased me in a nice way that made me giggle and called me *Bones* instead of Jones because I was skinny. Other than that, I wasn't exactly sure what a boyfriend was supposed to be, but he seemed interested when I asked if he wanted to come to my house to play.

"This is where you live?" Bobby asked when we stepped off the school bus and walked up the hill to the dry patch of dirt. Bobby lived near Hoyt Elementary School, which wasn't *from the flood*, which meant that Bobby and his house weren't *from the flood* either.

"Yeah," I said. "It's really fun," I assured him.

I showed him Marshmallow Hill and the woods with our make-believe amusement ride. I showed him the stand of trees where we played house and the ravine where we dug for geodes and fossils.

"What's down there?" Bobby asked as he pointed to the dirt road down below, near where the school bus dropped us off.

"We don't play down there," I informed him. "My sister and I once found a broken beer bottle, and I cut my finger and needed stitches."

It was a half lie. Pam and I *did* find a broken beer bottle, and I *did* cut my finger. As Pam walked me up the hill to find Mom, I screamed hysterically, "Am I gonna die? Am I gonna die?" and Pam wrapped her arm around my shoulders and assured me that I would not die, which made me feel very relieved because she knew a lot of things that I didn't. But I didn't get stitches even though Mom said I probably should have.

"Cool!" exclaimed Bobby. "Let's go play down there!"

I wasn't much interested in going back down there, but I wanted to play with Bobby, and I didn't want to seem like a scaredy-cat, so I said, "OK, let's go."

We walked down the little hill to the dirt road, then continued down the road until we saw a dirt ditch that looked like it could be a fun place to play. Bobby began sliding down the sides of the ditch on his butt, and I followed him.

"Look! What's that?" Bobby yelled, pointing his finger to a spot ahead of him.

I could see in the distance there was something lying in the dirt, but I couldn't quite make out what it was.

"Let's go see," I encouraged, hoping that Bobby would think I was as cool as a boy because I liked discovering treasures. I was sure whatever it was we'd spied was a fantastic treasure.

We both began running toward the unidentified thing. When we got close enough, Bobby squealed, "It's a baseball glove!"

*It* is *a treasure!* I thought, convinced that Bobby Skipalas would be bragging about playing at my amazing trailer park and all the cool stuff we did to all the kids at school.

We raced over to the baseball glove, and I hurried to be the first one to grab it. I picked up the glove and held it triumphantly over my head. "I got it!" I yelled.

"Let me see," pleaded Bobby. I held the glove out to him so he could take a look without me having to hand it over. Bobby's face crunched up, and he said, "Eeeeeeewwwwww! There's dog poop on it!"

My stomach suddenly felt like I'd swallowed rocks. My face turned hot. I dropped the glove on the ground in front of me and took off running as fast as I could toward the trailers.

I didn't look back. Bobby ran after me, yelling, "Wait up! Wait up!" but I didn't wait up. I didn't want to see Bobby ever again because I was so embarrassed that I picked up a baseball glove and didn't even see that it was covered in dog poop.

Along the road that led to the trailers was a bank of mailboxes. One for each family. The boxes were lined up one next to the other, and the whole thing stood on posts so that you could check your mailbox without getting out of the car. I knew that mailbox #4 was our mailbox because it had the name *Jones* on it. I could see that something was sticking out of our mailbox. It was too big to close the door. It was a large book, larger than a phone book, that had been folded in half and stuck in there. I immediately forgot all about the baseball glove and the shame I felt when I discovered dog poop on it because there, stuffed in that mailbox, was the Sears mail order catalog.

Bobby caught up to me, huffing and puffing to catch his breath. "You're the fastest girl in the class!" he exclaimed.

I stood there looking at Bobby. I decided that I didn't like him anymore. I decided that maybe only kids who were *from the flood* were fun to play with because all the kids in the trailer park could make a game out of anything, probably even a baseball glove covered in dog poop.

"You should go home now," I suggested.

"OK," Bobby agreed, and we headed back to the pea-soup-green trailer so that he could call his mom to pick him up.

When we got back to the trailer, I found Pam sitting at the kitchen table, eating a peanut butter and jelly sandwich.

"Look what came today!" I said as I put the Sears catalog down on the table in front of her with a thud.

"Yeeaah!" Pam said and immediately began tearing through the pages until she got to the toy section.

I wanted to flip through the pages with Pam because when the Sears catalog came, it meant that Christmastime was coming, and Pam and I had hours of work ahead of us leafing through the pages and circling all the toys and sometimes clothes that we wanted Santa to bring us that year.

But after Bobby's mom came to pick him up, I heard the boys' voices outside and suggested to Pam that we go see what they were playing.

*"Pleeeaaasssee!"* I begged when she told me she was busy with the catalog, but she just said, "Suzie, no," and whenever Pam said *Suzie, no,* I knew that I was not going to be able to change her mind.

I walked out of the trailer alone and followed the voices until I found Paul, Christopher, and Jamie digging for fossils and geodes in the ravine. Paul said, "Wife, I bought you beautiful jewels because I like you so much."

As I approached, I saw Jamie put his hand on his heart and exclaim, "Oh, sweetheart! These are just so beautiful that I think I might *die!*"

"She's *my* wife!" Christopher protested. "You're supposed to be the baby!"

"That's stupid," Paul retorted. "I don't wanna be the baby."

"I don't wanna be the baby either!" Christopher complained. "I always have to be the baby!"

Jamie extended both of his arms out in front of him, turned both of his palms to face Paul and Christopher, and said, "Boys . . . *boys.*"

Both boys stopped arguing and waited for what Jamie had to say. We always listened to what Jamie had to say because to us he had as much wisdom as any of the adults in the trailer, but he was more fun.

"You can *both* be my husband," Jamie offered. "I'll have *two* husbands!"

Paul and Christopher looked at each other, shrugged their shoulders, and said in unison, "OK."

"Hey!" I yelled as I approached the boys.

They stopped and looked in my direction.

"Guess what I found?" I yelled.

"What?" They yelled back.

"I found a baseball glove!" I informed them.

"So?" Paul said. "I have one of those."

"It's covered in dog poop!" I added excitedly.

"*Cooooll!*" Paul and Christopher shouted as they sprang to their feet. "Where?" Paul asked. "We wanna see it!" Christopher added.

Jamie, who wasn't really into things like baseball gloves or dog poop, crinkled up his nose and said, "That sounds *atrocious!*" Then he added, "I wanna see too!"

I waved for the boys to follow me as I turned and took off running back to where Bobby Skipalas and I had found the glove. As the boys ran to keep up with me, Paul yelled, "Get a stick!"

When we arrived at the spot where I had thrown the glove, it was still there right where Bobby and I had left it. Christopher came running from behind, carrying a long stick.

Jamie looked at the glove, then took a step back. *"Lord have mercy!"* he gasped. "I'm not going near that thing!"

Paul grabbed the long stick off Christopher and caught the edge of the glove with the stick. He flipped it over, revealing the large smear of dog poop.

"Ewwwww!" Paul yelled. Then he inched closer to the glove, bent down cautiously, and took little sniffs with his nose so that he could get a whiff of the dog poop. He suddenly recoiled and yelled, "Oh, man!"

Christopher then did the exact same thing, catching a whiff of the poop and confirming, "That's dog poo all right!"

"Let me see!" I said, approaching the glove. I bent down and took a whiff. The smell pierced my nose the way Vicks VapoRub did when Mom smeared it on my chest at night to help me breathe better when I was sick. But it did *not* smell like Vicks VapoRub, and I tried to expel the smell from my nose with several short, sharp puffs of breath out of my nostrils.

Jamie started laughing his contagious laugh. Paul, Christopher, and I started laughing too. Paul used the stick to flick the glove in Jamie's direction. Jamie squealed a high-pitched scream and began hopping on one leg at a time backward away from Paul and the baseball glove, as if he had stepped on a bed of hot coals and was trying to hop his way backward off them.

"Oh! Oh!" he yelped with each step backward while he waved his hands around frantically. The more Jamie screamed and laughed, the more we laughed, and the more Paul and Christopher tried to flick that glove closer to him.

We laughed ourselves to exhaustion, and when we had had enough of the baseball glove with the dog poop on it, I didn't feel embarrassed anymore about finding it in the first place. I knew then and there that Paul and Christopher and Jamie, and even Pam when she wasn't being a snot, were the best kids to play with because all of us had lost all of our toys and things in the flood, and we just had fun with anything we could find.

I never invited Bobby Skipalas back to my house, and I told myself not to even bother being friends with kids who weren't *from the flood* because they were definitely not the same as kids who were.

# 19

# December 1972

That Christmas, Mom said we were going to have an *arts and crafts* holiday. The flood destroyed all of our Christmas decorations, our Christmas tree ornaments, our fake Christmas tree, and all of the tinsel and lights that we used to decorate it. We had to start from scratch.

After Dad came home with a real Christmas tree that smelled like the pine cleaner that Mom used to clean the kitchen, Mom gathered all us kids around the kitchen table and gave us each a pair of safety scissors. She spread different colors of construction paper on the table and placed a bottle of Elmer's Glue in front of each of us. She cut the construction paper into strips with a pair of safety scissors, and I watched her small hands, paying careful attention to her thin nails as she took one of the strips of paper and glued the ends together, making a loop. She then showed us how to pass the end of a strip of paper through that loop she made and glue the ends together.

"We're making a chain, so keep adding loops and we can make it as long as we want! Then we'll wrap it around the tree," she told us.

We spent the rest of the afternoon working on our construction-paper chain until it was all piled up in a big mess next to the table. When we were done, we helped Dad hang the chain all around the tree. We stepped back and took a look at it, feeling pretty proud of our work.

Not long after that, we had another arts and crafts day. Again, Mom gathered us around the kitchen table and brought out three little paint sets and about a dozen paintbrushes. She gave us each a glass of water for rinsing our brushes.

"What are we painting?" Pam asked.

Mom told her we were making Christmas ornaments for our tree. She pulled out a box that had a stack of rectangular sheets of thin balsa wood pop-outs. There were candy canes and rocking horses and Santa Clauses and fancy balls and candles. Mom popped each one out of the sheet and gave us each a few.

"After you paint these, we'll let them dry, and then we can hang them on the tree!" Mom explained excitedly.

I chose a brush, dipped it in the water, and started moistening the paint so I could paint my wooden ornaments.

Pam and I paid close attention to staying within the lines, carefully filling Rudolph's nose and Santa's sack full of toys. We were both very good at that. But Paul made a *damn mess*.

"Paul's are ugly!" we complained to Mom. We told her we didn't think we should hang his ornaments on the tree. But Mom told us that we shouldn't judge Paul's ornaments because they were his *artistic expression* and we were going to hang all of the ornaments on the tree.

So that year for Christmas, our tree was decorated with the paper chain and the nice ornaments that Pam and I painted and the ugly ornaments that Paul and his *artistic expression* had painted. I didn't get *all* of the things that I prayed to God and Santa for, even though I also circled them in the Sears catalog to increase my chances. I got a record player, and a Beauty Parlor Hairstyling and Makeup Set. Pam got the one thing that I prayed the hardest for—a Barbie Dream House. She also got a gumball machine, and even though I was mad and jealous, I knew that God and Santa were very busy replacing all the toys that all the kids who were *from the flood* lost, so that was probably why they couldn't give me everything I wanted for Christmas that year.

## 20

# *April 1973*

Mom still made us kids go to church and Sunday school every Sunday, and Dad still never came with us because he was a Protestant. On Friday nights, we ate fish, and if we were lucky, we ate pizza because Jesus didn't like Catholics to eat meat on that day. Even though Dad wasn't Catholic, he didn't eat meat on Friday either, and that was about the extent of his religion as far as I could tell.

Instead of church, Dad went to the golf course, which he said was *his church* when we asked him if he would come to church with us one of these Sundays.

I wondered, if Dad's church was the golf course, why couldn't my church be the dirt patch that I loved so much. But Mom said I had to have my First Holy Communion that year, and I couldn't do that unless I went to church every Sunday and then to catechism after that. The only reason I looked forward to my First Holy Communion was because I got to wear a brand-new beautiful white dress, because as much as Dad tried to clean Pam's First Holy Communion dress, it still stunk like flood mud, and I refused to wear it.

I felt happy that I didn't have to wear a hand-me-down for once and looked forward to my First Holy Communion day with nervous anticipation, but I didn't like all the things I had to do in order for me to be able to take communion at church.

The thing I hated most was going to confession, which we learned in Sunday school was what you had to do if you wanted to take communion during Mass because you couldn't put the body of Christ on your tongue if you still had sins inside of you. I wasn't very good at confession because even though I knew I had probably done a lot of bad things, whenever I entered that dark room, my mind froze up, so I would just make a bunch of sins up.

Kneeling in that dark little room on the maroon puffy kneeler, I pressed my sweaty palms together and interlaced my fingers while I listened for the raspy open-mouthed breathing of the old priest on the other side of the screen. When he finally spoke, he was quiet as he blew his words out on his breath, like we were telling secrets.

Even if I didn't remember getting mad at Mom and Dad or yelling at Pam or telling lies, I said I did anyway. You could never be too careful when it came to getting rid of your sins, because if you forgot to whisper a sin to the old man on the other side of the screen before taking communion, God would know.

The nuns told us that we had to stand in line and fold our hands in front of us as we shuffled toward the altar where the priest was standing. They told us that he would hold up the wafer and say, *The body of Christ*, and that we should say, *Amen*, and then stick out our tongues so the priest could place the wafer on top of them. And because the wafer really was the body of Christ, we had to be very careful not to bite the wafer because if we did, we might not even be able to talk our way out of it in confession because it was a big, big sin to bite Jesus Christ, who was so kind and never hurt anyone and who would forgive all of my sins and would make me a good kid so that I could go to heaven. But I wasn't concerned about going to heaven as much as I was concerned with God answering my prayers, and since Jesus was God and God was Jesus, I needed to make sure that I didn't bite Jesus and make him mad and blow my chances of getting what I was praying for, which was still a Barbie Dream House because playing with Pam's wasn't the same as having one of my own.

Mom said that after my First Holy Communion, we were going to have a big dinner at Perugino's, which was Uncle Ray's favorite restaurant because he said their sauce was as good as Aunt Sadie's. I was *very* excited that I would get to wear my beautiful white dress at Perugino's because everyone would see that it was my special day, and I would be the center of attention for once. I was also excited because Aunt Sadie would be there, and I hadn't seen her since we left to go live with Pop-Pop-with-the-Screwdriver, which meant that it had been a long time since anyone had called me *Ya Habibi* or kissed my forehead or folded me into their arms for a hug that felt like being wrapped in a fluffy blanket.

On the day of my First Holy Communion, I wore my beautiful white First Holy Communion dress. I didn't think it was as beautiful as Pam's First Holy Communion dress, but at least it didn't smell like it was from the flood, so even if I was a little mad and jealous that Pam's dress was more beautiful than mine, I was still happy about that. And at least I didn't wear the crown of my veil upside down on my head and look stupid like Valerie Geist, but that was something that she probably did on purpose, because Mom called her a *troublemaker*.

Mass at church was boring, and sometimes Pam and I got a fit of the giggles that we had to hide, which made us laugh even harder. But on this day, I didn't get the giggles because I was too nervous about coming face to face with the priest, saying amen, and sticking out my tongue so that the body of Jesus Christ could be placed on it.

When the time came, we lined up in two lines. The boys stood in one line, all dressed in their navy or black suits and ties. The girls stood next to them in a second line, all wearing white dresses and beautiful veils. I folded my hands in front of me as I shuffled forward. I could hear the priest mumbling something as he held up each wafer. My heart began beating very fast. If I blew this, I definitely wouldn't be getting a Barbie Dream House, or *any* of my prayers answered for that matter.

When I got in front of the priest, my mind went blank. "Body of Christ," he whispered as he held the wafer up in front of my face. He waited. "Body of Christ," he said again. I said nothing. Val Geist, who was directly behind me, gave me a shove on the back of my shoulder and loudly whispered, "Say amen, dummy!"

"Amen!" I shouted. The kids near me giggled.

"Open your mouth and stick out your tongue," the priest whispered to me.

He placed the wafer on my tongue, and that dry piece of what tasted like Styrofoam stuck to the roof of my mouth, where my teeth couldn't bite down on it if they wanted to.

When I returned to my pew and knelt down next to Pam, she nudged me with her shoulder. I turned to face her, and she mouthed, *You did it.* That made me feel good inside, like I felt when Aunt Sadie hugged me and when Charlene kept me from getting a spanking.

For the rest of the mass, I fiddled with the wafer that was stuck to the roof of my mouth with my tongue until it was small and soft enough for me to swallow whole.

After the mass, the nuns told all the kids to get together for a big group photo. All the girls in their pretty white dresses were in the front; all the boys in their dark suits in the back; and there in the middle of the group was Valerie Geist with her upside-down tiara stuck to her head. She was crossing her eyes, sticking out her tongue, and making an ugly face.

When we got to Perugino's, Aunt Sadie was already there. *Ya Habibi!* she squealed when she saw me. She had a large tray of her homemade baklava in her hands, but she put it down on the hostess stand and rushed toward me with her arms open.

"I'm so proud of my Suzie!" she said, squeezing me tight. When she let go, she knelt down so her face was at the level of mine. She held me by the shoulders and said, "God lives inside of you now, Suzie. You will feel him. He will take care of you." I could see that her eyes were getting wet.

But I didn't feel different after that day. I didn't feel closer to God, and I didn't feel like he took care of me at all because I never saw him and he never hugged me or told me he loved me or called me *Ya Habibi* like Aunt Sadie did. But I wanted to believe Aunt Sadie, so I told myself that God was watching and God would take care of me and God would answer my prayers. But I also told myself that if I did not get a Barbie Dream House next Christmas, either God wasn't so great at taking care of me, or I had missed whispering a few sins in the dark little room to the priest who whispered on the heavy breaths.

After that day, I was allowed to take communion every Sunday during Mass, but I felt sick to my stomach with worry that there were some sins left in me that I had forgotten about. I was afraid to stand in front of the priest, who held up the wafer and reminded me every time about the *body of Christ*, and even more afraid of going to hell if I touched it with my teeth.

There were so many rules and so many things to think about and so many things that could make God stop listening to my prayers or stop loving me all together. It felt like a lot of work just to try to get a Barbie Dream House for Christmas. I started to think that playing with Pam and Jamie, and even Christopher and Paul, and being baby-sat by Charlene were more fun that a Barbie Dream House anyway, and they sure were a whole lot less work.

## 21

# *June 1973*

It was one year after we left our Birch Street house in the middle of the night and never went back. We had lived with Aunt Sadie, Pop-Pop-with-the-Screwdriver, and now in the pea-soup-green trailer. Our house in Mountain Top was finally starting to be built, and Dad was done cleaning up businesses and houses destroyed by the flood.

Even though Dad wasn't putting on his boots and going down into the valley every morning, we didn't see him any more than we did when he was busy cleaning up all the flood mud. Instead of cleaning, Dad spent all of his days going to work in the morning, then going to the club after work and staying there into the evening. On the weekends, he went straight to the club in the morning, and we didn't see him until it was dark. Dad even went to go *hit some balls* over the winter if there wasn't too much snow. If there was snow, he went to the club anyway and played cards with his golfer friends.

Mom and Rosalie started calling themselves *golf widows* because Dad and his best friend, Ted, spent so much time on the golf course, so they said *to hell with the men* and started doing more and more things with more and more women.

Rosalie introduced Mom to her nursing school friends and to Linda, her high school friend, who she knew from the girls' field hockey team.

When Mom met Rosalie's lifelong friend Linda, she seemed instantly captivated by Linda's intelligence and critical thinking. Up to this point, Mom had never had a chance to exercise her intellect or use her brain for much other than focusing on the house and us kids, but something seemed to awake in her as she started to get to know Linda more and more, and it began to change her on the inside.

Linda, who was what I imagined people meant when they called a woman *handsome*, had short black hair and a masculine face. She never wore dresses, and she drove a little red sports car. Mom told us that she was a doctor, but Linda wasn't like any doctor that I knew because she didn't take care of sick people. Linda taught women's studies and philosophy at a local university and was also an amateur photographer.

Mom was becoming better friends with Linda, and sometimes Mom and Linda had coffee together in the trailer even when Rosalie was working at the hospital. One day, Mom asked Linda if she would take photographs of her and us kids because the flood destroyed every last photograph of us except for that single photo of Paul playing golf in the basement in his footie pajamas. Mom thought this was a great way for us kids to spend some time with Linda and to also start recording our lives in photos again.

Linda took us all up onto the golf course, where she was also a member. We found a group of white birch trees that Linda said would look great in black and white. I wore my favorite top, a pink knit button-down top with ruffled cap sleeves and little delicate flowers painted on each button. I felt *fantastic* in that top and paired it with some snug bell-bottom jeans that had a built-in belt with a big black anchor as the buckle.

Pam wore a blue-and-white-striped T-shirt that looked very *sensible*. Even though I thought Pam's shirt was plain and boyish, she still looked sophisticated and beautiful in those photographs because there was just something about Pam that was quietly alluring.

I wanted to strike a sassy pose, so I leaned the back of my shoulders against a tree, jutted my hips out in front of me, twirled a long blade of crabgrass in my hands, and looked into the camera as if I had a secret. Pam looked like the Mona Lisa, with an angelic hint of a closed-mouth smile on her face, the corners of her mouth turned up slightly. Paul, who was only four years old, just wanted to climb the tree and make silly faces and cried every time he was told to stay still and look into the camera.

Mom enjoyed spending time with Linda more and more. We often overheard Linda sharing her thoughts on religion and race and especially Linda's passion on equal rights for women. We listened as Linda challenged Mom's acceptance of how things were with questions like, "Why isn't your name in the phone book? What if someone wants to call you?" and "Doesn't it bother you that you can't get a credit card in your own name?"

When Mom said *Mrs. Robert Jones* was her name, Linda challenged that by saying that it wasn't her name, and it was a way to keep women oppressed and financially dependent on their husbands.

Mom must have thought about Linda's questions because before long we heard her telling Rosalie she wanted to do "something more" with her life.

Mom spent more and more time with Linda, who didn't have children, and Rosalie's friends from nursing school who mostly did. Together they all talked about kids and camps and school, and they started planning group vacations with all the kids and just the girls and also trips without the kids. Before Mom met Rosalie and Linda, we never went on a vacation without Dad.

When Mom was with Rosalie and Linda and Linda's "life partner," Jenny, they talked about work and travel and art and history and feminism and "personal goals" and "professional goals"; this was very, very different from what Mom talked about when she was sitting around the kitchen table on Birch Street talking with Peggy Koons.

One day Mom opened the morning paper, then grabbed a pen from the pen jar and drew a big circle around something. She folded the paper back up, tucked it under her arm, and said, "I'll be right back." She sounded urgent.

"Where are you going?" Pam asked.

"Just over to Rosalie's."

"I wanna come!" Pam said.

"Me too!"

If Pam was going, I was darn sure going.

"I won't be long," Mom said, and she walked out.

Pam followed her, and I followed Pam.

Mom walked straight over to Rosalie's trailer and opened the front door without knocking, which we were getting used to by now. Pam and I followed her in.

Rosalie was sitting at her kitchen table, still in her pajamas, a lit cigarette in her hand. Rosalie looked like a praying mantis, all pointy elbows and bony knees sticking out in every direction even though she was sitting on a chair.

Pam and I went to the corner of the kitchen and pretended to leaf through a stack of magazines that were piled on the counter. We were quiet as could be so we could hear what Mom and Rosalie were saying.

Mom put the paper down on the table in front of Rosalie, opened to the page with the notice, and stabbed at the spot she wanted Rosalie to see with her index finger.

"Look," she instructed Rosalie.

Rosalie looked at the paper and said, "OK, so the community college is offering an RN program."

"I think I wanna do it," said Mom. Then she added, "What do you think?"

Rosalie paused for a moment; then she said, "I think you can do it."

"Really? You think?" asked Mom.

"If you want to do it, you can do it," encouraged Rosalie. Then she listed all of the reasons why right now was the perfect time for Mom to enroll in college and become a nurse.

"The kids are in school. You have Charlene. When the kids are on break from school, so are you. We can take the kids on those adventures we talked about!"

Mom considered Rosalie's rationale. "I guess I could take just a couple classes at a time. And I *would* have my summers off." Mom looked up at the ceiling, as if she were thinking everything through.

"You can do it," Rosalie said.

I had never heard of anyone going to school when they were so old, but Rosalie seemed really sure that Mom could go to school and become a nurse. She didn't say *anything* about Mom being too old.

The next week, Mom submitted her application for the nursing program at Luzerne County Community College.

By the time the summer of 1973 finally came, we had spent every Saturday playing, exploring, and losing ourselves in the world of imagination that was the dirt patch and golf course that surrounded us. Sometimes Charlene, who we now just called Char, came over after school on the weekdays just to sit around the kitchen table and talk with Rosalie and Mom because she was a young woman who was in high school now, and she told us Mom and Rosalie were her "idols," her "role models," and "mentors." But even though she sometimes spent time with the grown-ups, she never lost her fun or her magic when she was babysitting us kids.

This was the summer that Rosalie and Mom decided to start taking us kids on summer adventures without the dads, and they decided to bring Char along with us, which made us kids very excited because it meant that we could continue our fun and magical games even when we weren't at home.

The first adventure was in June. Rosalie, Char, and Mom packed up all the camping gear and piled us in the car to begin *our great camping trip adventure to the Jersey Shore*. To prepare for our great adventure, Rosalie brought a few IV bags that Mom could fill with warm water in case we needed to take a "shower" and wash our hair. She packed that along with the Coleman stove and lanterns, the sleeping bags, and the giant canvas tent with metal poles that was so heavy, it took at least two grown-ups to carry it, and all of us to hoist it up.

Mom didn't care and said that *women can do anything men can do*, and so we were going camping without the dads because all they did was complain anyway, so why not just leave them at home?

We arrived at midafternoon the first day, regardless of the predictable Philadelphia traffic. We hastily set up camp, taking the last spot left in the campground. We all helped put up the heavy canvas tent and spread the sleeping bags inside because Char said *all for one and one for all*. We started arguing about who got to sleep next to Char, but before we could declare a winner, we could hear and then see two white pickup trucks with large clouds of what looked to be smoke trailing behind them. As the trucks drove their way along the dirt road, making their way closer to our campsite, we could see that they each had some sort of machine in the bed of their trucks, and the smoke was coming from those machines in a spray.

Rosalie told us that it was a *bad year for mosquitoes* and the trucks that sprayed huge clouds of insecticide were meant to reduce the mosquito population and make vacationers like us more comfortable. The problem was that the plumes of insecticide were so thick that we couldn't breathe or see the person next to us. It made us cough, and our eyes stung, and we all started choking and waving our hands in front of our faces to try to thin out the poison that we were inhaling.

Rosalie was coughing just as much as any of us, and she suddenly sputtered, "Grab your suits, kids; we're going to the beach!"

Char helped us find our suits and told us we could put them on in the car.

Mom piled some beach toys, towels, a beach umbrella, sunscreen, and beach chairs into the car, and we all hopped in and sped out of there as fast as we could.

"Well, that solves *that* problem," said Rosalie. "Now when we return, we won't be bitten alive by mosquitoes!"

Paul said, "I didn't like that!"

Mom replied, "Mosquitoes carry disease. They have to spray."

Char said, "Next time they come around, we'll have a breath-holding contest!" which cheered Paul up.

The sun was still high in the sky when we arrived at the beach. Having changed into our bathing suits in the car, we were eager to find a spot on the white sand beach, which seemed to go on for miles in either direction. To the right, in the distance we could see a roller coaster and a Ferris wheel.

"Where is that?" I wanted to know.

Char said, "*That . . .* is the Wildwood Boardwalk, and it is the most fun place in the whole world! We can go there tonight."

Paul, Pam, Christopher, and I all yelled in unison *yeeeeee-aaaaaaah!* while Mom and Rosalie got busy setting up the umbrella, opening the beach chairs, and slathering baby oil all over themselves in preparation for an afternoon of tanning.

Char took us to the water's edge and drew our attention to a tall white lifeguard chair. Perched high on top of the white chair was a girl in a red one-piece bathing suit. She was standing up and spinning a string with a whistle on the end of it around and around and around. A boy in red bathing suit trunks sat next to her, with the same type of string around his neck. He was gripping the whistle between his teeth and tooting it every now and again.

"See those lifeguards?" Char said as she pointed to the chair behind us. "Don't go in the water above your knees, and *always* stay directly in front of this lifeguard chair. The current will move you, so keep checking."

We said OK and asked Char if we could bury her in the sand, to which she replied yes. We spent about an hour digging a hole big enough for Char and considered that maybe we should have buried Paul or Christopher instead because we wouldn't have had to dig such a big hole, which was a lot of work.

Once the hole was big enough, we buried Char up to her neck in sand, making sure that every inch of her was covered, and we became irritated when she wiggled her fingers or toes and knocked the sand off them.

When we had Char good and buried, she furrowed her eyebrows and said in a low and gravelly voice, "I'm Ishkabibble's sister, the sand witch *Ishkabobble*! And I smell children!"

Then she began to break out of her sand sarcophagus and chased us as we ran straight for the crashing waves while we screamed our heads off.

We spent the rest of the day making sandcastles and drip castles, eating Good Humor ice cream bars and Bomb Pops from the ice-cream truck that came by, ringing its bell every hour, and we played in the waves. Mom and Rosalie and sometimes Char, who had bought the same red-white-and-blue bathing suit with the built-in bra and the anchor on the front of it as Mom wore, sat in their beach chairs with their arms and legs stretched out in front of them. They kept one eye open so they could watch us in the water, and every once in a while, one of them would stand up, walk toward the water, and wave us back in the direction of the lifeguard chairs.

We were happy and tired by the end of the day, but when we climbed into the car to head back to the campground, we reminded Char of her promise to take us to the Wildwood Boardwalk, so Rosalie said we would clean up at the campsite and could have cheesesteaks for dinner on the boardwalk.

Christopher asked, "Can I get cotton candy?" and Paul immediately added, "Me too?" I chimed in with "Me too?" and Pam said, "I don't like cotton candy."

Mom said we could get cotton candy after we ate our cheesesteaks, and we all cheered. Paul said, "Mom, I *love* this place!" and we laughed because sometimes we thought Paul was annoying, but sometimes we thought he was pretty funny.

When we got back to the campsite, the thick fog of insecticide had cleared and the disgusting smell of burning rubber was almost gone. We were made to use the outhouses and took IV bag showers, which took a long time because the water came out very, very slowly, even when the tube that ran out of the bag was opened as much as it could be.

Even though they came around with those trucks and sprayed that horrible spray, the mosquitoes buzzed around our ears, eye, and noses in annoying clouds, so Mom made us spray Off! bug spray all over our clean clothes.

Rosalie said, "Let's hang a line so we can hang the clothes to dry." Mom added, "Let's air out the sleeping bags too; they smell like insecticide." So, before we left for the Wildwood Boardwalk, Char and Rosalie hung a long clothesline, and we all helped hang the sleeping bags and wet clothes over the line to dry and air out.

The town of Wildwood was full of people. There were lots of families with kids walking down the sidewalks eating ice cream or carrying big stuffed animals that they had won playing games at the boardwalk. Rows and rows of hotels with several stories and balconies overlooking the central pool were busting at the seams with teenagers who were hanging off the balconies, playing chicken in the pool, and walking around with big red plastic cups. They were laughing and shouting, and all those teenagers scared me because they had a wildness to them that we didn't see in Char, and it seemed dangerous and unpredictable. I wondered if any of them had been in a flood like we had.

"Can I stay in the car?" I asked after seeing all those teenagers acting like wild animals.

"Why would you want to do that?" asked Char.

"I don't like those teenagers," I admitted.

Char thought a moment; then she said, "Oh, don't worry about them. They won't be at the boardwalk; they are too busy partying at their hotels."

I was quiet. I hoped she was right.

As we approached the bright colored lights and the big amusement park rides of the boardwalk, Paul and Christopher started bouncing up and down in their seats, chanting, "Cotton candy! Cotton candy!"

Mom said, "Cheesesteak first," but Paul and Chris just kept right on chanting, "Cotton candy!"

Pam barked, "Stop it! You're *disturbing* me!" which only made them chant louder.

"Mom!" Pam pleaded.

Mom said, "We're almost there."

Thirty seconds later, we pulled into the parking lot of the boardwalk, piled out of the car, and ran as fast as we could toward the lights and sounds of the boardwalk.

After we ate our cheesesteaks, everyone got cotton candy except for Pam, who asked for a vanilla ice-cream cone. As much as we couldn't wait to eat that cotton candy, we only took a few mouthfuls before begging and pleading, "Can we please go on some rides!"

We went from one ride to another, riding on the Tilt-a-Whirl, the Ferris wheel, the Chair Swing Ride, and the roller coaster. Once Paul saw the bumper cars, he absolutely insisted that he drive one, but Mom told him he was a little too small.

"I am not!" Paul screamed. "I wanna drive a car!" and he began to have a meltdown, which embarrassed Mom, so she told him he could go on the bumper cars if I went too.

"OK, fine," I said, and we handed our tickets to the kid at the gate, and each of us got into a bumper car of our own.

I didn't like the bumper cars, and I didn't get the point of riding around smashing and bashing into each other, and I think what Paul really wanted to do was drive the car around in peace, because when the other kids started bumping into him, he stopped his car dead right there in the middle of everything and pretended that he was asleep.

I called out to him, but I guess his plan was to pretend to be asleep until the end of the ride because no matter how loud I yelled at him, he sat there with his car parked and his head slumped down and eyes closed as if he had fallen asleep sitting up.

I drove my bumper car toward the barrier where Mom was, though it wasn't so easy getting there because all the other kids were smashing their cars into me, smiling venomous grins and laughing. I got very irritated. When I finally made it over to Mom, I could see that she was laughing so hard, tears were streaming down her cheeks.

"*Mom!* Paul is pretending to be asleep!" I reported.

"I know . . . ," she said through her laughter. "What a character this kid is!" She continued to laugh, so I laughed too and let Paul stay in his parked bumper car and pretend to be asleep until the ride was over.

Before we left the boardwalk, Pam, Paul, and Christopher wanted to go to the haunted house, and Char said she would go with them. I did not want to go into the haunted house, whether Char was with me or not, but I felt like a baby, so I lied and said that I felt sick to my stomach.

For one thing, I didn't like being scared. But I also knew from seeing *The Wizard of Oz* that if I saw something scary, I kept scaring myself by thinking about it every time I was alone in the dark, and I *definitely* didn't need more scary things to think about. On top of that, there were parts of that boardwalk that were directly over the ocean water, and you could see and hear the waves crashing beneath. That almost scared me more because just like I was scared of going over bridges, I was convinced that we would all collapse into the water and die.

It felt like forever before the others came out of the haunted house, proclaiming that it was *no big deal* and telling me that I should have come with them. I hoped that maybe I wouldn't feel like such a scaredy-cat next time.

The rain began coming down just as we were about to head back to the car.

"Quick! We better head back," said Mom. "All our stuff is hanging on the line."

"Let's run!" shouted Char, and we raced to the car but had to wait there in the rain for Mom and Rosalie to catch up.

By the time we got back to the campground, what had started as a sprinkle was now an out-and-out downpour, like the one in the days before we left our Birch Street house.

We could barely see through the windshield of the car, and the streets were starting to almost look like the way our street looked the night we left Birch Street, with streams of water almost high enough to spill above the curbs.

"*Son of a bitch!*" said Mom.

Rosalie felt sure that the line was under a tree canopy and the clothes and sleeping bags would be shielded enough to keep them fairly dry. "It'll be fine," she said.

But when we got to our campsite, everything was not fine. Mom yelled, "Everyone grab something and head into the tent! Quick!"

We all piled out of the car, laughing and screaming because even though we knew this was serious, it still felt like fun. Each of us grabbed whatever we could off the line and ran into the tent, dripping from the downpour that had by then soaked through all of our clothes.

Mom lit a flashlight and began to help all of us change into the dry clothes that she had stored in the tent, while Rosalie and Char spread out the sleeping bags, inspecting each one and picking out the driest of the bunch. Mom piled our wet clothes in one corner of the tent and said, "We'll deal with these tomorrow."

As Char surveyed the sleeping bags, she said, "These four here are the driest. I think we can sleep two to a bag for tonight."

Rosalie said, "Great idea, Char," and we paired up. Rosalie and Christopher, Charlene and Paul, Mom and me, and of course, Pam got a bag to herself.

The sound of the rain on the tent was so loud that Mom said it was like a *freight train*.

"Don't touch the side of the tent!" she warned, wearing a very worried look on her face. Mom explained that if we touched the sides of the tent, it would stop being waterproof, and the rain would come inside.

"Well, this is *cozy*," Rosalie said with a half-smile.

"Can we go to the beach and build sandcastles tomorrow?" Christopher asked.

"We'll see," answered Rosalie. "Now, go to sleep."

We knew enough by now that when a parent said *we'll see*, it usually meant *no, and don't ask again*, so we didn't.

We all drifted off to sleep in our damp sleeping bags, listening to the rain pound down on the tent and wondering what tomorrow would bring.

At around 3:00 a.m., I woke up to Mom shouting, "Jesus Christ!"

She was frantically wriggling out of our sleeping bag and demanding that I *get out! Get out!*

I scooted out of the bag and noticed a puddle of water inside the tent. The others woke up, and Rosalie said, "There's a river in the tent! Move over! Move over!"

We all shoved our sleeping bags to one side of the tent, scooching together tightly in one corner. Char turned on the flashlight, and sure enough, the middle of the floor of the tent was almost completely submerged in water. Rosalie grabbed another flashlight and went outside with Mom to see *what the hell was happening.*

*Here we go again,* I thought. I wondered if I would be woken up in the middle of the night every time there was a rainstorm.

Mom and Rosalie aimed their flashlights toward the ground near the tent and could see, clear as day, a river of water rushing down a small incline that our tent happened to be right in the middle of, and the water was rushing directly through our tent.

When Mom and Rosalie came back into the tent, they were real quiet for a minute or two. Mom shined the flashlight toward where we were all smooshed by the side of the tent and began yelling, "Don't touch the side of the tent! What did I tell you!" But we couldn't help it because we were squeezed so far to one side to avoid the river running through the middle, there wasn't any way we *couldn't* touch the sides.

Pam, Paul, Christopher, and I sat in a huddle and wrapped our arms around our knees, which we had pulled tight into our chests. We were wet and shivering and looked toward Mom pleadingly. The light was too bright for us to make out her face, but we knew that this was not good at all. I thought about suggesting that we go back to Aunt Sadie's, but I kept my mouth shut.

Mom, Rosalie, and Char huddled together and talked in whispers. Finally, they said, "OK, kids. Let's get into the car. Grab the driest sleeping bag you can find and follow us."

We grabbed two sleeping bags and a couple of pillows that were moist but not soaked through. We piled into the station wagon and opened the sleeping bags so that we could use them like blankets. We took off our now wet clothes down to our underwear. We piled the wet clothes in a corner and tried to get warm under the sleeping bags. The rain pelted and pelted against the roof of the car. The sound reminded me of the night Pam and I played gin rummy with Dad on the screened-in back porch, and I got a good feeling and a bad feeling at the same time because it was the last time I remembered playing with Dad.

Pam looked like she might cry. She asked, "Are we gonna be all right?"

Rosalie said, "Yes, Pamela. Don't worry; we have a plan." I was just glad she didn't say anything about a *precaution*.

But Pam wasn't convinced, and she kept me awake all night, poking me every few minutes and asking me if I was scared and what I thought was gonna happen.

For once I felt more brave than scared, so I told her to shut up and to go to sleep, which felt pretty good.

The next morning, after not much sleep at all, we were told to stay in the car. It was still raining, and our whole campsite was flooded, including our tent and everything in it.

"What are we doing?" Pam asked.

Mom said, "There is a coin-operated laundry here. We're going to dry as much as we can." And with that, Mom and Rosalie ran from the car to the tent with their pockets jingling with quarters. They grabbed all the wet clothes and sleeping bags from the tent, piled back into the car, and drove us a few yards to the laundry building, telling us to find the driest clothes we could and go get dressed. We put our wet clothes back on.

We spent the morning in the laundry building, playing games of I spy and hide-and-seek to pass the time. Paul and Christopher asked Mom for a flashlight so they could go look down the toilets of the outhouses.

"That's gross!" Pam said, wrinkling up her face.

"Not right now," said Mom, but within all the commotion, they somehow snuck out of the laundry room and into the outhouses with a flashlight before Rosalie could notice and ask, "Where are the boys?"

Charlene went to find them, knowing exactly where to look. By that time, they were all soaking wet again from running through the still-driving rain. The boys stripped down to their underwear, and Mom told them to *just stay put.*

By 4:00 p.m., Mom and Rosalie had dried most of the sleeping bags, pillowcases, and towels. They had run most of the clothes through the washer and had started drying them in the dryers. The dryer ran for ten minutes for each quarter, but we were all out of quarters and the clothes were still wet.

Then Mom started laughing. I didn't know what was so funny. Then Rosalie and Char started laughing too. The three of them were laughing so hysterically that tears began streaming out of their eyes. Mom, still laughing, looked at Rosalie and said, "Well, you wanted an adventure!" which made all three of them laugh even more.

Through her laughter, Rosalie said, "Next time let's take a cruise!" and by then all of us were laughing and laughing.

Even Pam was laughing as she said, "This is the worst camping trip ever!"

And Paul echoed, "This is *terrible!*" which made us all laugh even more because he was only four and it just sounded funny.

When our laughing quieted down and everyone was wiping tears from their eyes, Mom said, "Woo, at least we can laugh about it."

Rosalie said, "If we weren't laughing, we would be crying."

We were all quiet for a moment, with only the sound of other people's dryers spinning their wet clothes around and around.

"Let's get something to eat," suggested Char.

We were all hungry, having only eaten Pop-Tarts and raw hot dogs up until then.

"Yeah! I'm starving!" shouted Paul, and I said, "Can we go to McDonald's?"

Rosalie said, "McDonald's it is! I think we've earned it."

We pulled into the McDonald's parking lot, and Mom said, "Just follow us, and don't draw attention to yourselves."

We did as we were told and followed Mom and Rosalie through the side door and into the women's bathroom. Char followed behind, dragging a black garbage bag full of the clothes that remained damp because of running out of quarters.

Rosalie instructed us to each grab something out of the bag and hold it under the hand dryer. We got to work drying our clothing one article at a time under the automatic hand dryers in the McDonald's bathroom. Char was the lookout, and anytime someone came to use the bathroom, she popped her head inside the door and whispered, "Incoming!" Then according to what we had planned out, Mom grabbed all our clothes and locked herself into one stall. Rosalie pretended she was helping us wash our hands, and we waited until the person left the bathroom. Eventually, Char ordered hamburgers and french fries for us kids, and we sat in the dining room, thoroughly enjoying our hot and delicious meals while Mom and Rosalie finished up drying the clothes.

By 9:00 p.m., all the clothes were dry. We ducked into the women's restroom one at a time to change into our newly dried clothes. Paul emerged with his green Toughskin jeans and his Incredible Hulk shirt. He puffed out his chest and strutted toward our table, having what seemed to be a conversation with himself or some imaginary friend.

When Mom and Rosalie joined us at the table, they looked like they might fall asleep right then and there. Mom picked at some cold french fries. Rosalie lit a cigarette, took a long drag, and let it out with a big, big sigh. She pulled a small aluminum ashtray closer toward her on the table.

The rain started tapering off. We all sat there finding ways to have fun. We grabbed a bunch of straws, tapped one end on the table so the paper coverings accordioned together tightly, then dripped some Coke on it and watched it writhe open like a worm. We played more I spy and thumb wrestled and arm wrestled and got *rambunctious* until we were told to *settle down.*

We finally left McDonald's because they started shutting off the lights and a boy behind the counter said, "We're closing," so we knew it was time to go. We drove back to the campsite and slept in the car, but this time with dry clothes and sleeping bags.

The next morning, it didn't matter how clear and sunny it was; it was time to leave the Jersey Shore. Dad told us that after the flood, the bright sunshine made the flood mud *stink to holy heck* and bake into everything in a way that made it ten times harder to clean out, so I figured that even though we spent the whole day at the laundry room and drying everything under the McDonald's hand dryers, there was probably more cleaning to do and probably some mud and dirt that needed to still be washed out.

So Mom and Rosalie packed up all our camping gear while Charlene kept an eye on us and Paul and Christopher headed to the outhouses with the flashlights again.

On the ride home, Rosalie said, "Well, that was *some* adventure!"

Charlene added, "Hopefully the first and last of its kind."

Mom said, "Don't tell your father. As far as he's concerned, we had a great time."

There was a pause. We watched all the cars with suitcases strapped to their roofs and bikes attached to the backs, heading in the opposite direction as us, toward the Jersey Shore.

Finally, Paul said, "Can me and Christopher play outside when we get home?"

Mom said, "Sure."

That July, after our rained-out camping adventure at the Jersey Shore, Rosalie convinced Mom, Dad, and Ted to take a family vacation together at a place called Ortley Beach. Ortley Beach was also at the Jersey Shore, but in a place called Seaside Heights, which was not near Wildwood or the Wildwood Boardwalk. I was relieved we didn't have to stay in tents or in a campground and risk more flooding, and Dad said he *wouldn't be caught dead* camping, so instead, we stayed at a place that we called George's.

George's was a cluster of little pastel-colored rental cottages, situated in a semicircle around a kidney-shaped pool next to a tarmac parking area and owned by a man named George, which was why we called it George's.

George's was next to an expanse of white sand beach that was so crowded with different-colored blankets and beach chairs and umbrellas and bathing suits that the only way we could find where we had put our blanket and chairs was by locating the nearest tall lifeguard chair as a landmark and remembering where we were in relation to that.

Mom, Dad, Pam, Paul, and I stayed in one cottage. Christopher, Rosalie, and Ted stayed in the cottage next door. Char went back and forth between cottages.

The adults went out at night to drink gin and tonics because it was summer and even though by that time everyone's house from the flood was cleaned up and the new houses were starting to be built, the grown-ups still needed *to take their minds off things.* And not just because of the flood, but because building a house wasn't easy and general contractors were *lazy sons of bitches,* so why not bring Char so she could play magic games with us at George's just like she did in the trailer?

We had a great time at the shore this time because we didn't get soaking wet and have to dry all of our clothes under the hand dryers at McDonald's, and we only had to walk across the parking lot area and around the hotel to get to the beach.

There were other kids at George's, staying in other cottages, but they weren't from the Wyoming Valley, and they weren't *from the flood.* Instead, they were from New York and New Jersey, and they had names like Joey and Gerard, which they pronounced *Geraaaad.* We tried to play our favorite games about hurricanes and tornadoes coming to destroy our homes, but Joey and Gerard said those games weren't fun and instead could we play freeze tag or have races on the tarmac.

Unless it rained, we spent our mornings at the pool with Char and waited for the grown-ups to finish their coffee and be ready for the beach. We spent the rest of the day, every day, at the beach making drippy sandcastles, eating snacks, lying in the sun, buying ice cream from the ice-cream truck, and being clobbered by the crashing waves.

When the lifeguards left for the day at 5:00 p.m., there was still plenty of daylight, so we climbed on top of those tall wooden chairs and felt like we were on top of the world because we could see all the way up the beach and all the way down the beach and far, far out into the ocean, which was important, because if you were a lifeguard, you had to be able to see if someone was drowning and needed saving.

At dusk, the adults put on their sweatshirts and mixed up a pitcher of gin and tonics and arranged their beach chairs in a circle. They laughed some and talked in hushed tones while we played tag in the sand or flew kites, and as long as Char was around to watch us, they let us swim in the ocean as long as we didn't go in past our knees.

Even though we were still kids and didn't drink gin and tonics, Rosalie told us that you didn't drink gin and tonics or wear white until after Memorial Day, and you had to stop after Labor Day. Pam and I were pretty sure that this was very important information, so I kept a list of important things to remember, like how to keep my cereal from getting soggy, not to touch the communion wafer with my teeth, and what not to drink or wear before Memorial Day and after Labor Day.

There was one rule at George's that no one was allowed to break, and that rule was that absolutely no one could enter the cottage before they washed the sand off in the outdoor shower. So, at the end of every day at the beach, we walked from the beach up the path lined with a rickety, weatherworn, gray wooden fence, which was meant to keep people off the dunes, around the side of the hotel, across the tarmac parking area, and along the side of the cottage, crunch-crunching up the stone pathway that led to the outdoor shower.

But no matter how much we showered and scoured and rinsed between our toes and took our bathing suits off and rinsed and wrung those out too, we still had sand in our beds at night, and our parents still had to sweep up and complain about *so much Goddamn sand* every day.

When we crawled into bed at the end of the day, we could feel the scratchy, gritty sand that had sluffed off our bodies the previous night and stayed trapped between the sheets. No matter how many times Mom yanked down the bedspread and tried to swipe all the sand off with her hands, she couldn't get it all. We just tried to get used to sleeping with sand in our beds.

One night, Pam and I crawled into bed with all the sand. Pam pushed the sand toward my side of the bed using a sweeping motion with her legs.

"*Stop!*" I warned.

"I don't want all this sand," Pam said in an annoyed tone.

"Well, I don't want it either!" I snapped back.

"Ugh!" Pam sighed, then sprang out of bed and ripped all the covers and top sheet off the bed.

"Hey!"

"I thought you didn't want sand in the bed," she said sarcastically.

"I don't wanna sleep with you anymore," I said, and I meant it too.

Sometimes Pam could make me feel like punching or throwing something, but I always got in trouble for that, so I made myself be still.

"Fine. I don't want to sleep with you either," she said as she turned and walked out of the room. "Baby," I heard her mumble under her breath.

I hoped Pam would come back to sleep in the room with me because even though she could make me so mad, she also made me feel safe.

I was relieved when, a few minutes later, she came back and said, "*Don't* push sand on my side."

"*Fine!*" I said, pretending to still be mad. But secretly I was very glad.

We loved the Jersey Shore because it felt like a real vacation. The smell of low tide was a little bit like the smell of flood mud, but when that sulfuric smell hit our noses as we crossed over the Bay Bridge, it made us feel excited that we were almost there.

The air of the Jersey Shore, thick with humidity and saltiness, made our hair wild with curls and waves. The sun turned our skin the color of a perfectly cooked pancake, and dried salt water and sand coated us like the sugar frosting on a glazed donut.

Mom brought a family-sized container of Vaseline Intensive Care and told us to slather that stuff all over our body after a full day in the sun and sand, but not until we took our outdoor shower and hung our wet towels and bathing suits on the clothesline behind the cottage.

The shore felt exotic, with the sound of seagulls, the arcades full of blinking lights, and the carnival sounds of the Seaside Heights boardwalk, which was just like the Wildwood Boardwalk except better because it didn't jut out over the crashing waves of the ocean, so I wasn't constantly worried that it would collapse and we would all be swallowed up by the churning water and die.

The shore was full of kids from places that made them sound funny when they shouted, "Get ovah heeeya!" to us—kids who weren't *from the flood*, but who we liked playing with anyway because it was the shore, and for that one week, we could forget about the flood.

The shore was a sound and a feeling and a smell that represented the fleeting freedom of the beach in summer. I was worlds away from the dirt trailer park or the green golf course. The sound of waves crashing on the beach, the smell of Coppertone suntan lotion, and the feeling of climbing the lifeguard chairs at dusk while the grown-ups sat nearby, drinking clear and citrusy-smelling gin and tonics, were reminders of the preciousness of time. One moment here, the next gone.

## 22

# *September 1973*

One day, we returned home from school to find a black dog in our trailer.

"Where'd we get the dog?" I asked.

"Can we keep him?" Pam immediately began pleading.

Mom told us that he was a sweet dog but not to get too attached to him because he was also probably a lost dog and his owners would eventually see the ad she put in the paper and come to pick him up and take him away. I was used to not getting attached to things after having to leave Birch Street, then Aunt Sadie's, and now I knew we were going to eventually leave our trailer. So not getting attached to this dog didn't seem so hard.

"What if no one comes to get him? Can we keep him?" Pam asked again. Then she added, *"Pleeeeeaasse?"* and folded her hands in front of her, the way we learned to do in Sunday school before we went into the small dark room to tell the priest about all of our sins.

Mom was silent. She just looked at Pam for a few seconds, considering what to say. How much to promise. Pam got down on one knee and again begged, *"Please!"*

"We need to give it a few days. Let's call him Licorice for now," Mom said.

I hoped that a few days would be enough time for Pam to stop being attached to stuff.

Mom named the lost dog Licorice because he was all black like black licorice. Licorice had black curly fur like a poodle, except he wasn't a poodle even though Mom said he had some poodle in him. Mom loved Licorice because he was a sweet and well-behaved dog. She could let him out to *do his business*, and he came right back in without any trouble. Sometimes he stood by her side when she watched us kids leave on the morning school bus. We could see Mom waving to us, with Licorice sitting beside her like a good boy.

Dad didn't want Licorice to be our dog, and he definitely didn't want Licorice to be treated special, but Mom let Licorice sleep in the bed with them, and even though Dad kidded about being treated like a *second-class citizen*, we could tell he was warming up to Licorice.

The first Sunday night that we had Licorice, Mom decided to give him a bath after Pam, Paul, and I had ours. She brushed our hair in front of the television, then brushed Licorice's hair too. She put a little blue bow on his collar and said, "There, he's all freshened up!"

We knew that Mom was getting attached to Licorice, even though she told us not to get too attached ourselves. She started calling Licorice *our dog*, and that made us very happy. The next day, Mom said, "I guess I'll take the ad out of the paper. Seems like he might be a stray after all."

We secretly prayed that Mom was right, but I remembered how I thought we might live with Aunt Sadie forever and reminded myself not to get too attached until we knew for sure.

The next day, Mom got a phone call. It was Licorice's owners. They saw Mom's newspaper ad and told Mom it was *the answer to their prayers*. When Mom told us that Licorice was going to live with his original owners, she cried and cried, which made me and Pam cry and cry because I had never seen Mom love anything as much as she loved the lost dog Licorice.

When Licorice's owners came to get him, they told us that his real name was Teddy. Mom held back her tears as they told her how grateful they were that Mom had found Teddy and had taken such good care of him, even putting a blue bow on his collar.

Mom gave Teddy a hug and buried her face in his fur. We could see her shoulders shaking up and down.

After Teddy and his owners left the trailer, Mom closed the door and didn't say anything. Instead, she walked directly into her bedroom and closed the door behind her. We could hear Mom crying, but it sounded muffled, like she had her face buried in a pillow. Pam and I looked at one another blankly because Mom didn't cry very often and we had never heard her cry *this* hard, so we didn't know what to say or what to do, and we just didn't know what would happen next.

Just then, Paul came in from playing outside in the dirt with Christopher.

"I want Mommy," he said.

"She's busy," I said, then asked, "What do you want?"

Paul said, "I want a marshmallow."

Pam and I didn't say a thing. Paul repeated, this time more slowly, *"A maarrshmaalllooww?"*

"Why?" Pam finally asked.

"Me and Chris want to see it get covered with ants," he said, as if it were the most normal thing in the world.

Pam grabbed a chair from the kitchen table, moved it over to the upper cabinets, climbed on top of the chair, and grabbed the bag of marshmallows from the cupboard.

"Here," she said, tossing the entire bag into Paul's chest.

"Hey!" Paul protested.

"Sor-*ry*!" Pam yipped back.

Paul grumped, then spun on his heels, clutching the bag of marshmallows, and ran out the door, as if he were afraid that lingering would cause Pam to reconsider and grab the bag back from him.

If he heard Mom's sobs coming from the bedroom, he didn't seem to care.

Mom cried for days. Dad said Mom *got too attached* and reminded us that nothing was permanent. By then I already knew that, and I was glad that I managed not to get too attached.

"Things come and things go, kids," Dad continued. "Remember

that," he told us. I didn't tell him that it was something I wasn't going to forget.

One week after Teddy left our house, Mom finally stopped crying and woke us up on a Saturday morning.

"We're going to find a dog of our own!" she told us. "Get dressed."

Mom took us to all the shelters in town. Pam and I found a lot of dogs that we just loved, and we begged Mom to bring this one or that one home, but Mom seemed to have a very specific dog in mind. *"Pleeease!"* we begged her, but she just said, "Maybe," and then, "Let's keep looking."

Finally, after what seemed like the entire day of looking at dogs, we saw a dog that looked just like Teddy. Mom's face brightened, and a smile spread across her face as she shouted, "This is the one!"

Pam and I were relieved because we were sure this new dog, who looked like Teddy but didn't have any owners who would come and take him away, would make Mom happy. We were really tired of Mom being sad.

We named our new dog Licorice, but it didn't take too long to discover that Licorice was *not* a good and well-behaved dog like the lost Licorice/Teddy was. New Licorice would not sit obediently next to Mom while she waved goodbye at us as we rode away in the school bus. Instead, he had to be tied up outside of the trailer because if he wasn't tied up, he would bark and bark and chase people and bikes and cars, and he *especially* wanted to chase the school bus.

Every morning when our school bus came to pick us up and take us to school, Licorice ran back and forth and back and forth because he was tethered to what looked to me like the longest clothesline in the world, so there was only one direction he could run.

He wanted to chase our bus more than anything in the world, and I knew that because of how much barking he did. One day our school bus came as usual, only this time Licorice pulled so hard on that clothesline that he snapped right off it and ran like a rocket after our bus. That dog never stopped barking even when he caught up to the bus and tried to bite the tires like it was some kind of giant monster that he was trying to rescue us from.

Dad hated Licorice and always called him that *Goddamn dog*. When Licorice got off his line, he ran *all over the creation*, and we had to form search parties and walk around yelling, "Here, Licorice! Come, boy!" When he finally did come back, he smelled like garbage or skunk or God know what else, and he was covered in burrs that Dad had to cut out with a pair of scissors. Under his breath, Dad muttered *Goddamn dog* as he hacked away at Licorice's fur, leaving some bald spots in places, which made Mom tell Dad he was making Licorice look like he had mange.

I remembered when Dad told us that things come and go, and I prayed every day that one of those things wasn't Licorice because I thought it was safe to get a little attached to him since we got him from a shelter and he really was ours.

One day, new Licorice got off his line, and we all screamed and chased him because he was barking and nipping at a man on a bicycle who, no matter how fast he rode that thing, couldn't get away from Licorice. When we finally got him on a leash, that man started yelling and screaming things like *Your dog could have killed me!* and *You need to control your dog!* And I guess that Mom realized that just because you're sad about losing one thing like Teddy the dog, replacing it with something that kind of looked the same, like Licorice the dog, didn't really make the sad go away.

The next day, when we got home from school, Licorice was gone. Mom said they took Licorice to live on a farm where he would be much happier because he could run around as much as he liked. Pam and I and even Paul cried because Licorice might not have been like Teddy, but we loved him anyway, and we wanted him to stay with us and not at some stupid farm.

But Mom seemed happy, which confused me, because I thought she got Licorice from the shelter so that she could feel better about having to give Teddy away. Dad was definitely happy and told us to stop crying. He said we would never ever get another dog because they were just too much work and the work always fell on him eventually.

## 23

# *October 1973*

I was now eight years old and had just started third grade. Pam was nine, and Paul would turn five that coming March. We had been living in the trailer for just over a year, and Dad told us it would probably be another year before our house in Mountain Top was done, which was fine by me.

One Friday evening after we finished our dinner of pizza, Mom and Dad told us to *come and sit on the couch.* We were sure we were getting into trouble for one thing or another, but when Mom and Dad sat on the black La-Z-Boy recliner *together,* we knew something different was happening.

"Your mother and I have something to tell you," Dad said.

*What? What?* I wanted to know. *You're getting divorced? You decided not to move us to Mountain Top? We're getting another dog?*

We waited while they were quiet. Dad looked at Mom, who smiled. They both looked so happy. It was weird.

Mom looked at us and said, "You're going to have a new brother or sister."

"Now?" Paul asked.

Mom chuckled. Dad said, "No, bud, the baby will be here around your birthday."

Paul protested, "I don't want a baby on my birthday!"

"Be quiet!" Pam scolded.

"Where is the baby now?" I asked, noticing that Mom didn't look any different to me.

"It's in here." She pointed to her stomach. "It's still very small, about the size of an orange."

We all stared at her blankly.

"Where does it come out?" Pam asked.

Mom said, "A special spot."

I imagined that Mom's belly button would open up like elevator doors, the baby would be lifted out of there, and the doors of that *special spot* would close right back up.

"Can we name it this time?" I asked Mom. The disappointment of Paul not being called Jonny Quest still stung.

"We'll see," said Mom.

"Pleeeeaaaassse?" begged Pam.

"Let's see how it goes," Mom said. Which didn't leave us feeling hopeful.

Having all the information we felt we needed, we asked if we could please go outside to play and could they please let us know when our baby brother or sister had arrived.

## 24

# December 1973

We thought our new baby might arrive as a Christmas present that year, but Mom told us it was too early even though her belly looked like it definitely had a baby inside of there. So instead of asking Santa for our baby, I asked him for some Sea-Monkeys that I had seen advertised in an *Archie* comic book.

The Sea-Monkey ad showed a dad, mom, baby, and kid Sea-Monkey family. The ad promised *A bowl full of happiness*, and *instant pets* and said they could *even be trained*. I thought Sea-Monkeys were a great alternative to the dog that we would never ever get, because I would take care of them myself and Dad wouldn't have to do a thing.

The mother Sea-Monkey had blond hair and a red bow tied to what looked like three little antennae, each topped with little red balls that looked like fireball candies. She wore red lipstick. Each Sea-Monkey had scales down the back and a tail.

I wanted Sea-Monkeys so badly, even though Mom said they didn't look anything like the picture on the advertisement and instead were tiny little shrimp that did not have hands and feet and blond hair and bows and lipstick. I didn't care what she said. I wanted to see it for myself.

But along with not getting a baby that year for Christmas, I also didn't get Sea-Monkeys, and for a second year in a row, I did not get a Barbie Dream House or an Easy-Bake Oven, and I made a note to myself to have a conversation with the priest or at least Aunt Sadie about the fact that God was doing a really bad job of taking care of me and answering my prayers.

Instead, Pam and I got matching bikes that were pink and blue with banana seats and fringe that came out from the end of the rubber grip of each handlebar. Paul got a big wheel. We were excited to ride our new bikes, but it was winter, and we didn't have anywhere to ride them, and so along with waiting for the baby, we also had to wait for warmer weather to ride our bikes.

That night, Pam and I lay in bed trying to fall asleep. Pam rolled over to face me, gave me a very serious look, and whispered, "Guess what?"

"What?" I asked, excited that Pam was going to confide in me. It made me feel special and good inside.

"Last night I woke up to go to the bathroom, and guess what I saw?"

"What?" I could tell this was a very serious secret.

"Well, I heard a noise, so I hid behind the black recliner," she continued.

*And? AND?* The suspense was killing me.

"And I saw . . ." She looked me dead in the eye, then raised her eyebrows as if to say, *If I tell you this, you better promise not to tell a single soul.*

"What did you see?" I whispered, desperately wanting her to spit it out already.

She continued to just look at me, pausing dramatically. She seemed to enjoy seeing me squirm with anticipation.

"Tell me!" I shouted through a whisper.

"I saw . . ." She paused again. I felt like I might explode.

"Santa's *boot!*" she finally said.

It took my breath away. I just *knew* Santa was real.

"Why didn't you come get me?" I wanted to know. Why did *Pam* always have all the luck? I missed out on everything!

"I didn't want him to see me," she said, adding, "I was afraid I would scare him and he would leave without putting our presents under the tree."

I wouldn't have thought of that, but Pam was very practical and sensible, and what she explained to me made sense even though I was still mad that she got to see Santa's boot and I didn't.

"Did he see you?" I asked.

"I don't know. He looked in my direction, but I don't think he saw me hiding."

I paused and thought about what she was telling me. It seemed like a fantastic stroke of luck.

"Are you telling me the truth?" I finally asked, considering that maybe she was making the whole thing up.

"Yes, I swear!" she promised. I was silent. "Suzie, I saw his boot. I'm *telling* you!"

"OK, I believe you," I said, then made a note to set an alarm next Christmas Eve so I could sneak into the living room and hide behind the recliner and see Santa for myself.

The next morning, after breakfast, Mom went over to the couch to put her feet up because she said her ankles were swollen. She called all us kids over to sit next to her on the couch.

"Wanna feel something?" she asked us, and she took my hand and put it on the side of her round belly and said, "Here."

Nothing happened for a few seconds, but it felt good to be that close to Mom because it didn't happen that often, so I didn't really care *what* I was supposed to be feeling. What I was feeling right then was enough for me.

Finally, I felt a hard bump rise up into the center of my palm and sweep across it.

"Is that the baby?" I asked, not wanting to sound too interested.

"Yes," she said. "Isn't that neat?"

"Mom?" I asked, "Where is the special spot exactly?"

"Let me feel!" Pam insisted. Paul wriggled and writhed around on the couch, singing "Do You Know the Muffin Man" quietly to himself.

Mom ignored my question and guided Pam's hand onto her belly.

"Does it hurt to have a baby?" Pam asked.

"No, it doesn't hurt. It's more like pressure," Mom said. Then she added, "I had all of you naturally."

I wondered what the alternative was. Unnaturally?

"What was I like as a baby?" I asked.

"You cried a *lot*," she said, looking like just the memory made her tired. "Your dad used to walk you back and forth in front of the big mirror in our parlor in the middle of the night for hours and hours. That was the only way to quiet you down."

I sat there quietly, thinking how strange it was that I couldn't remember doing all that crying.

"Did I cry a lot?" Pam asked.

Mom said, "Not so much. You were all very different as babies."

Paul stopped singing and protested, "I'm *not* a baby!"

Mom laughed and said, "You had a perfectly round head. Like an egg."

Paul busted out laughing. Then we all laughed, because when something cracked Paul up, his reaction was so big, it felt like we could feel what he was feeling, and so we all laughed right along with him.

"A head like an egg!" Paul repeated, as if it were the most ridiculous thing he'd ever heard.

Then Mom looked at me and said, "Pam was so curious about you when you were born. She pulled your bassinet right over, trying to get a look at you! You were all wrapped up in so many blankets that you bounced off the floor and rolled once or twice. You weren't hurt at all."

"I don't remember that," said Pam.

"Did she get a spanking?" I wanted to know.

"No. She was only a baby herself," Mom said.

I didn't think it was very fair that Pam made me fall out of a bassinet and roll on the floor as a baby and didn't get a spanking, when I got spankings for things like digging a hole to China in the backyard of Birch Street. And I didn't think it was fair that Pam got to see Santa's boot and I didn't, and I didn't even get Sea-Monkeys or an Easy-Bake Oven or a Barbie Dream House for a second year in a row, and I hoped and prayed that when this new baby came, it was a girl so I could be the older sister and feel a little bit special for once in my life.

# 25

# *April 1974*

On April 2, 1974, we woke up in the morning to find Nana in our kitchen, preparing coffee. Mom and Dad were gone.

When we walked out of our bedrooms that morning and saw Nana, we were surprised. It was a Tuesday morning, which was an unusual day to have a babysitter, and because Char was in high school on the weekdays, she couldn't be our babysitter during the weekdays unless it was summertime.

"Good morning," Nana said when we emerged from our bedrooms, rubbing sleep from our eyes.

"Where's Mom and Dad?" Pam asked Nana.

"Your dad took Mom to the hospital very early this morning. The baby is coming!" She smiled broadly.

"Can I have Count Chocula?" I wanted to know.

"You can have whatever you want," Nana said.

*In that case, I want a Snickers Bar,* I thought.

"I want Lucky Charms!" Paul shouted.

"Don't give him that," Pam told Nana. "He only eats the marshmallow pieces and leaves the rest."

"Hey!" Paul shot Pam an angry look.

"It's a special day," Nana said. "You can have Lucky Charms, honey," Nana said, looking at Paul, who wore a grumpy expression on his face.

Nana took several cereal boxes out of the cabinet, the milk out of the refrigerator, and collected three bowls and spoons. She set it all on the table in front of us. Then she poured herself a cup of coffee from the stainless-steel percolator that moments before had hot brown liquid bubbling up inside a clear knob on the lid.

She sat at the table with us as we poured large mounds of sugar cereal into our bowls. We added milk and began crunching. Paul strategically scooped up and ate all the marshmallow shapes from his bowl of Lucky Charms, leaving the rest of the cereal soggy and uneaten.

"See?" Pam reported to Nana.

"Let him eat his cereal however he wants," Nana said calmly. I really loved Nana at that moment.

After that, we only heard the sound of our own crunching for a while.

Finally, Nana said, "It's a very exciting day!"

"Do we have to go to school?" I asked, thinking that if it was so exciting, we should at least be able to stay home from school.

"Yes, you still have to go to school," Nana said.

*How exciting of a day can it be?* I thought.

At school that day, I told my third-grade teacher, Miss Vasile, that Mom was in the hospital having a baby, and that I hoped the baby would be a girl and that us kids were maybe going to pick out the name. Miss Vasile said she had always wanted to have a little baby, but it wasn't in *God's plan*, but if she did and if it was a girl, she would name her Jessica.

Miss Vasile was the most glamorous teacher of all. She had dark curly hair piled up on her head in a messy mess and black-lined almond-shaped eyes. She had a long nose with a bump in the middle, and she wore red lipstick. Mom said she looked like Sophia Loren, but that didn't mean much to me.

Miss Vasile had been Pam's third-grade teacher the previous year and was her favorite teacher of all time, and that was how I heard all about the book *Jonathan Livingston Seagull* and how Miss Vasile read aloud to the class every day from that book. Pam told me how she always got to sit in the front row like she was Miss Vasile's favorite girl in the class, which didn't surprise me because Pam was *everyone's* favorite girl.

So, on the bus ride home from school that day, I told Pam that Miss Vasile had always wanted a little baby girl named Jessica. Pam took a big gasp of air in and screamed, *Oh my gosh, yes!* like she had just been given the secret to everlasting life. This time, if that baby was a girl, we would not take no for an answer because Jessica was the most beautiful and glamorous name for a baby girl that we could imagine.

The next morning, Nana was still there, but so was Dad. Dad quietly tapped us awake and whispered, "You have a new baby sister!" Dad smiled wider than he had since our house on Birch Street filled up with water.

"Let's sneak you in to see her!" he suggested. Then he said, "Be quiet, though, so you don't wake your brother."

On the way to the hospital, before we even saw our new baby sister, we begged Dad to please, please, *please* let us name her because, after all, they promised we could name Paul and took back that promise, which we didn't think was fair at all.

Dad said that we had to *take it up with Mom* and warned us that children were not allowed in the hospital, so we had to be really quiet and try to stay as close to him as possible so that we wouldn't draw attention.

I was very, very nervous about being snuck into the hospital and imagined if we got caught, we might be put in jail, so I stayed glued to Dad's side and was as quiet as I could be.

The hospital was quiet and clean, but it felt cold and lonely too. The only place that felt nice was the hospitality shop, where we stopped to buy balloons and flowers to bring to Mom. Pam and I saw a collection of figurines on a shelf in the shop, and we insisted on each picking one to give to Mom as a present.

The figurines were creatures that looked half-human and half-ogre, with tufts of hair on their heads in different colors that you could touch and feel. Each figurine held a sign with something written on it. Pam picked out one with blue hair that held a sign reading, *I Love You.* I was immediately drawn to a figurine that looked mischievous like me. He had bright orange hair and was winking at me. He held a sign that said, *You're Sexy!* And that was the present that I wanted to give to Mom.

When I handed the figurine to Dad and said, "This one," he looked at me and said, "Are you sure?"

"Yes, I'm sure," I confirmed.

"Maybe you should look again. There might be another one you like better," Dad suggested.

But I told him *no*, this was the figurine I wanted to give to Mom. I was sure of it.

We brought our balloons and flowers and our figurines up to Mom's hospital room that Dad told us was on the *maternity floor.* When we gave Mom her figurines, she looked at Pam's and said, "That's very sweet, Pamela, thank you." When she saw mine, she laughed out loud and said, "Suzanne, do you know what *sexy* means?"

I told her that it meant that she was very pretty like the girl in *I Dream of Jeannie*, to which she replied, "Well, thank you. It's nice to know you think I'm very pretty."

I wanted to tell her that she didn't look very pretty at the moment, but when Mom put on her makeup before going out with Dad, I thought she was the most beautiful woman I had ever seen. More beautiful than *I Dream of Jeannie*, and even more beautiful than Miss Vasile.

"Where's our new baby sister?" Pam asked.

"Oh, they took her for a nap. You can go see her," Mom said.

Pam and I excitedly told Mom about Miss Vasile and that *God's plan* made her not have a baby and how she loved the name Jessica. We insisted that we should name this baby because we didn't get to name the last one, and we'd had to put up with a dumb name like Paul for five years now.

Mom said, "It's a nice name." Then she added in a slurred, dreamy voice, "I'll think about it," before closing her eyes and dozing off. She was still sitting up.

Dad snuck me and Pam around the corner to the nursery. We had just seen the movie *Peter Pan* on the *Wonderful World of Disney*, but this nursery wasn't anything like the nursery that Wendy, John, and Michael slept in.

Dad took us up to a big glass window. We looked through, and on the other side, there were rows of metal bassinets that looked more like food carts than baby cribs. Each bassinet was topped with a clear plastic bin, and lying in each bin was a swaddled-up baby. The babies were wrapped in either pink or blue blankets, and other than some babies with dark skin and some babies with light skin, they all looked pretty much the same to me. Small, sleeping, and boring.

Dad pointed to one of the bassinets on the right and said, "There she is. Second from the end and third row from the back."

"Can I hold her?" Pam asked.

"Maybe when we take her home," said Dad. "It's up to your mother."

Most things were.

When we got home and told Paul that Dad snuck us into the hospital to see Mom and the new baby, he was madder than I'd ever seen him.

"That's not fair!" he shouted. "I wanna get snuck in too!"

I doubted that Paul really wanted to see the new baby. He just wanted to break the rules along with me and Pam.

"Dad said you're too little," I said.

"No I'm not!" Paul insisted.

Pam said, matter-of-factly, "You're too much of a loudmouth."

"Am *not*!" Paul screamed.

"See?" Pam said. She had a point.

For a whole day and a half, Paul wouldn't shut up about how mad he was that Dad didn't take him to the hospital. So Dad said he could come with us to pick Mom and the baby up from the hospital, and that got him to shut up.

On the ride home from the hospital, Pam got to sit in the front seat and hold the baby in her arms, of course. We pressed Mom to tell us if we could give our baby the name Jessica, and she said that she gave it some thought and that *yes*, we could name our baby sister Jessica as long as she could give the baby the middle name of Lynn, and so our sister Jessica Lynn Jones was finally home with us in the pea-soup-green trailer on the dirt patch below the golf course and above the shop.

Our baby Jessica, who was born into the world perfect and brand new and without mud and without the smell of being *from the flood*, made Dad smile again. Dad gave her the nickname of *Bumper Schnooks*, and when Dad was with Baby Jessica, he had a big, wide smile on his face and he made his voice sound all goofy and happy and he blew raspberries on her belly.

We could tell Dad was happier than ever that Baby Jessica was born because he started smiling more and spending more time at home with us kids and Baby Jessica and less time at the shop and the golf course. And even though Dad didn't go to church with us or pray the rosary like Aunt Sadie did, he was included in *God's plan* to give us a baby sister. I wondered why *God's plan* was to give me a baby sister but not any of the presents I asked for. And I wondered why he didn't give Miss Vasile a baby even though it was what she prayed for.

I really didn't understand God or his plan at all.

# 26

# *June 1974*

We weren't too interested in Baby Jessica for the first few months that she was home because she didn't do much but cry, sleep, and eat. But because Mom had started taking two night classes at Luzerne County Community College to become a nurse, she had to go back to school the week after we brought her home with the baby, so Dad was home a lot more because he had to make us dinners or get us pizza. He spent a lot of time burping and rocking our new baby, and we liked that because he smiled a lot and sang to the baby, and it just felt good to have him home and feeling happy about something.

I told Miss Vasile that we did name our baby Jessica. That made her smile, and she said, "Well, Baby Jessica will always be a very special baby to me!" but what I really wanted her to say was *Thank you for giving your baby the name that I love, and now I like you better than Pam, and you are my new special girl!* But she didn't say that.

One day, Miss Vasile told our class that we were going to read the book *Jonathan Livingston Seagull*. I knew about Miss Vasile and this book because Pam had told me all about it the year before. I wanted to sit right up front and feel special like Pam.

Miss Vasile announced, "Class, for the rest of the school year, I will be reading from this book each day until we finish it. Everyone will write a book report for your final project, so no sleeping!" She smiled and winked at us.

"Let's push the desks to one side. I'll sit here in the middle." She pulled a chair to one side of the room. "You all sit around me in a semicircle."

I always loved when we moved our desks around because I thought sitting in rows facing the front of the room was boring.

All the kids started talking and moving the desks, and it got real loud, and Miss Vasile said, "Quietly!" in a loud voice.

I found my third-grade best friend, Christy, and said, "Let's sit in the front!" But Christy was very shy, and she said she didn't want to sit in the front. So instead of sitting in the front row, where Miss Vasile could see me and I could feel as special as Pam, I sat in the back with Christy because I didn't want her to feel lonely, and that's what a best friend does.

When we were all situated, Miss Vasile started reading. "'It was morning, and the new sun sparkled gold across the ripples of the gentle sea.'" My mind drifted to the summertime and the Jersey Shore and ice cream and the little cabins at George's and the seagulls that tried to grab our sandwiches right out of our hands and how Christopher's dad, Ted, called them *rats with wings*.

Each day we moved the desks and circled around Miss Vasile for her readings from *Jonathan Livingston Seagull*. Each day I sat in the back with Christy, daydreaming about playing on the golf course and laughing with Jamie or being a famous movie star who everyone adored. I never listened to Miss Vasile reading because I thought a book about a seagull was just about the dullest thing there was, and I didn't know why anyone would bother writing it.

One particular day, I daydreamed that Miss Vasile and all the kids in the class came to our trailer park and I showed them Marshmallow Hill and Ishkabibble's Pond and the ditch where we found our treasures and the tree in the woods that we rode like an amusement park ride and our stand of trees where we played house, and they would be so amazed by all the wonderful things like the dirt patch and the golf course, and everyone would think that I was the luckiest kid in the world.

But I couldn't think of any reason why the whole class would come to see our trailer neighborhood, so I decided that I would ask Miss Vasile if she thought it would be a good idea to bring the whole class to Bedwick and Jones to see how books were made, and that might be almost as good.

That night, I asked Dad about it, and he said, "That sounds fun," which made me very happy because Dad hadn't been all that fun since the flood. When I shared my idea with Miss Vasile, she smiled really big and said, "Wonderful!" and after that, every day felt like a year because I just couldn't wait to show all the kids around the shop and for them to think that I was *just great*.

The shop wasn't as much fun as our trailer neighborhood, but sometimes Pam and I played there, and it wasn't so bad. It was full of loud machines that spit out large printed sheets of paper one after another after another. The rhythmic sounds of the printing presses felt soothing and familiar. The loud *kablim, kablim, kablim, kablim, kablim* of the printing presses meant that you had to shout at one another just so you could be heard.

All around the machines were thick piles of very large sheets of paper stacked up high on wooden pallets. The whole place smelled like magic marker ink. Dad had dark stains on his fingers and under his fingernails. Dad smelled strongly of that ink when he got home from work, and every time we used magic markers in school, I removed the top and took a sniff of the marker and thought of my dad.

Junior, one of the guys who worked for Dad, carried big piles of paper that smelled like that same ink over to the biggest knife I had ever seen, which wasn't like a knife you used in a kitchen, but a machine almost as big as the machines spitting out the big printed pieces of paper.

Instead of spitting out paper, this machine had a giant guillotine-style blade that came down when you pressed a button and ka-chunked that huge pile of paper in half, then in quarters or eighths until they started to look like pamphlets, brochures, or booklets. Junior or sometimes Kenny, another one of the guys who worked for Dad, took the cut pieces of paper to another machine that folded them or stapled them into books, and sometimes Pam and I helped out by collating pieces of paper together before they got stapled or folded.

But the best part about helping out in the shop was the thousands of thin strips that were left in giant trash barrels after the piles of paper were trimmed. When we saw them, piled high and spilling out of the trash cans, Pam and I could not resist grabbing handfuls of those long, thin strips and pretending to be cheerleaders, waving our pom-poms, jumping up and down, and feeling like we were really something.

The day came when my whole third-grade class, plus my favorite teacher in the world, Miss Vasile, arrived at the shop to learn about printing. Dad met our class at the door and invited everyone into the front of the shop, where it was quieter than the back with all the presses. It still smelled like ink.

"I'm gonna teach you all about printing today," Dad said. Then he asked, "Is everyone ready?"

All the kids shouted, "Yeah!" and I felt like I might just die right then and there of happiness.

Dad took us into his office and showed us his giant calendar that was the size of one entire wall. He told us that he was in charge of scheduling the printing jobs, and the giant calendar kept track of every job that was happening in the back.

The words were color coded to indicate which stage of the job was happening. He could take one look at that giant calendar and see if something was on the printing press or if it was being sent to the giant knife, or if it was being folded and stapled, and he would always know when it was ready to be packed up and shipped to where it was going. Everything was written in erasable marker so that Dad could change colors as a job went from prepress to press to packing and shipping, keeping everything up to date. Dad was very neat and organized, unlike Mom who he said was *loosening her standards* ever since she started school and hanging around with Linda. Linda told Mom that cleaning the house shouldn't be all up to Mom just because she was a woman, so Mom stopped being as much of a housewife, which meant that the trailer wasn't quite as neat and tidy as it used to be.

Dad's handwriting was neat and orderly just like Dad. It wasn't cursive and hard to read, like Mom's. His handwriting was more like printed letters, all unified, all slanted at the same angle, and it evoked a feeling of safety and predictability in me. I wondered if the kids had the same feeling when they looked at Dad's handwriting on the big calendar. I liked that Dad's handwriting was always the same and I could count on that, because lately there were just a lot of things that weren't staying the same, no matter how much I wanted them to.

After the calendar, Dad let us peek into Uncle Ray's office that had a fancy modern desk made of wood and chrome and glass and had no sharp corners, only curved lines. Facing the desk were two matching chairs that Mom said were very fancy and designed by an architect. They looked like they were made of bicycle handlebars with brown leather straps stretched across them to make the seats and the back. Whenever I went into Uncle Ray's office and sat on those chairs, I thought, *Who cares who made these stupid chairs?* because I thought they were ugly and uncomfortable.

Uncle Ray was on the phone. The handset of the phone had a weird vinyl-covered foam piece attached to it, which Uncle Ray used to sandwich the whole thing between his ear and shoulder so that his hands were free. He picked up a pen, scribbled some numbers, then put the pen down and began twirling his diamond pinkie ring around and around his finger, saying, "You tell him that's the best quote he'll get. He can come back to us when he finds that out for himself, or he can go to hell!" Then he looked at all of us and gave a little nod of acknowledgment.

Dad said that Uncle Ray was the *business side* of the printing business, and his job was to deal with the customers. Uncle Ray spent his days on the phone, writing down a bunch of numbers on a pad of paper with his pen, or going out at the exact same time every day to get a cup of coffee.

Mom said that Uncle Ray was a good salesperson because even though he was *rough around the edges*, he only had to take a tray of Aunt Sadie's baklava to a customer and he got the job.

Dad said, "Now, let's go to where the fun stuff happens. The back of the house!" and as we all started walking away, we heard Uncle Ray shout, "That's *bullshit!*" A few kids giggled, to which I replied, "That's my uncle Ray. He's really rich," as if that were some sort of excuse for his bad language.

I knew Uncle Ray was rich because of his diamond pinkie ring, the expensive presents he always got for us kids at Christmas, and his car, a Lincoln Continental. Uncle Ray's Lincoln Continental was the biggest car I had ever seen. It had a bump in the back, right in the middle of the trunk, and for a long time, I thought that it was some sort of clock or sundial until Mom told me it was where the spare tire was kept.

The adults called the Lincoln Continental a *smooth ride*, but riding in that car made me feel carsick because I guess it was a little *too* smooth, so I didn't think a smooth ride was a very good thing, and I tried not to ride in Uncle Ray's car if I could help it. Even so, I made a note to point out Uncle Ray's Lincoln Continental to my classmates before we all left on the bus.

Dad led us all through the door to the back and directly to my favorite things in the shop, the giant camera and darkroom.

Before anything could be put on the presses for printing, a plate needed to be made by taking a picture of what was to be printed, and because the papers were so giant, so was the camera.

The camera was so big, it went right through the wall of the darkroom, so half of it was inside the darkroom, and the other half was outside the darkroom. Dad showed us a big paper with letters and pictures and page numbers, and everything was glued down with rubber cement so it would stay put in the exact place it needed to go. Dad said it was called a *layout*.

"Come in a little closer," Dad said as he gathered us around the part of the camera that was outside the darkroom. He grabbed what looked like a window but was actually two panes of glass sandwiched on top of each other. There were hinges on one side so you could open the thing up, separating the panes of glass. The whole thing could be tilted into a vertical position or tilted down to a horizontal position. Dad tilted the apparatus into the horizontal position and separated the panes of glass.

"We need to make a negative of this layout next," Dad said.

Carl Schimmer, a weird-looking kid with blond hair, buck teeth, and a cowlick at his forehead, said, "What's a negative?"

I rolled my eyes at Christy, who was standing next to me. She snickered.

Miss Vasile asked, "Does anyone know what a negative is?"

Christy, who didn't usually speak up, raised her hand. "It's what you need to make a photo. You shine a light through it onto photo paper, then develop the photo with chemicals."

Christy's father was a pastor at a local church that was for Protestants, so we never went there. But Christy's dad was also an amateur photographer, *and* he owned the Gateway Cinema, a local movie theater in town that had been in the flood but was all cleaned up now.

When I went to Christy's house, we hung out in her basement, where they had a darkroom. The whole basement, including the darkroom, was decorated with movie posters from the Gateway Cinema. There were posters of *The Godfather* and *The French Connection*, which were movies that I didn't see because I wasn't allowed to see R-rated movies.

There was also a poster of *Paper Moon*, which Dad took us to see but I didn't much like because even though there was a kid in the movie, I thought it was boring. There was a poster of *Willy Wonka and the Chocolate Factory*, which I thought was a terrific movie. But the poster that left the biggest impression on me was from a movie called *Ben*, which was a horror movie about a rat. I felt like a baby and a scaredy-cat, but I was as sure of never wanting to see that movie as I was about never wanting to go into the haunted house at the Jersey Shore boardwalk.

"Very good," said Miss Vasile, and Christy got shy again and looked down at the floor.

Dad said, "That's right, and that is what we are going to make right now. And because we have a very big layout, we need a very big negative. That is why the camera has to be so big!"

Dad placed the layout in the center of the glass, hinged the top pane down on top, creating a glass sandwich with the paper in the middle, just like my favorite sandwich that had a piece of bologna in the middle of two pieces of white bread. Once he fastened it all together, he tilted it back up into a vertical position.

"Let's head in!" Dad said.

This was my favorite part, and I was so excited, I felt like I might scream.

*Oh, the kids are gonna be talking about how great this field trip is for weeks!*

"We're going to have to squeeze in," Dad said.

"Line up and don't push!" Miss Vasile instructed. The kids formed a single-file line and entered the darkroom one at a time. There were *oohs* and *aahs* and a few exclamations of *neat-o!* and *cool!*

Inside the darkroom, against the wall was the inside part of the camera. It had a door that was pulled down on hinges from the wall, kind of like the door to an oven. On the inside of the door were hundreds of tiny holes.

Dad said, "This is where we put the photo paper." He removed a giant sheet of shiny white paper from a big flat box sitting on a shelf and centered it on the back of the door. "It's gonna be a bit noisy for a few seconds because see these holes?" and he pointed out the hundreds of tiny holes on the back of the door. All the kids strained their necks to see. "This is a vacuum, so when I turn it on, all of these little holes will suck the paper onto the back of the door and make it stick there," Dad said before flipping a switch that turned on the vacuum and sucked the paper to the door.

Dad turned off the lights, and the room glowed red. There were more *oohs* and *aahs* from the kids. Each one confirmed for me that every kid in the class from this day forward would understand how great I was!

Dad set the hands of a big timer with glow-in-the-dark numbers and turned it on at the same time as the camera. When the timer buzzed, Dad shut off the camera, opened the door, and turned off the vacuum. We all shifted around, bumping against one another as Dad grabbed the negative with a pair of rubber tongs and carried it from the door to a long, shallow sink lined with a row of plastic pans. Each pan had a different-colored liquid in it. Dad put the paper in the pan farthest to the left and said, "These are the chemical baths. The chemicals process the image."

Dad let some of the kids lift and lower one corner of the pan, helping the liquid slosh over the paper. The image appeared like magic, even more *oohs* and *aahs* came from my third-grade class. I was so happy, I thought I might throw up.

After the darkroom, Dad took us into the noisy part of the shop and showed us all the big printing presses and the gigantic knife and the machines that folded and stapled. I showed the kids how to make pom-poms with the thin strips of paper stuffed into the giant garbage barrels. Some of the girls tried it, and some of the boys grabbed handfuls of the paper strips and pretended they were their hair. Everyone was laughing and having a great time until Miss Vasile sternly warned, "Children! This is not a playground," and everyone put the paper back in the bin and got real quiet.

Before we all left, Dad handed each of the kids a scratch pad printed with the words *Miss Vasile's Third-Grade Class* on the bottom.

Miss Vasile pressed her pad into her chest and said, "Thank you so, so much!" like it was the most wonderful thing anyone had ever given to her.

The kids were flipping through their pads saying things like "Cool!" and acting like a notepad with something printed on the bottom was the most amazing thing in the world.

It felt like Dad was magic.

As we headed outside to climb into the bus, I pointed out Uncle Ray's Lincoln Continental to the class. Then I pointed toward the back of the shop and up the hill and said, "That's where I live," and added, "It's the coolest place to live *ever!*" No one seemed particularly impressed, even after Bobby Skipalas said, "It's pretty cool."

When I got into bed that night, I thought about the day at the shop with Dad. I decided that I liked the new shop much better than the shop Dad had before the flood at Kingston Corners, even though I had thought that place was really great before the flood.

I considered how great I had thought the Birch Street house was before it filled up with water. And the fact that I had thought Aunt Sadie's house was even better than the Birch Street house, and now I thought the trailer was the best of all of them. And that made me think that even though I didn't want to move to our brand-new house in Mountain Top when it was finished being built, I should change my mind about that, because Dad built a new shop that was so terrific, so he probably would build a new house that was also terrific.

Before I fell asleep, I felt so proud that I had a dad who built such a great shop, even though it meant that we didn't see him all that much.

And I felt happy that all the kids in my third-grade class got to see how great my dad was and how great the new shop was, but most of all I was happy that for once I didn't have to share anything with Pam. The day of my class field trip was all mine.

# 27

# *August 1974*

By the time August came, we were the only family still living in the trailers. Jamie and his mom had moved to their permanent home, a second-floor apartment in Kingston. Kingston was a town in the flood zone, and Dad said Marty was nuts for moving back there. But it was now two years after the flood, and the towns and all the houses had been cleaned up and rebuilt and moved back into. Mom reminded us that we would never have to be afraid of another flood because our new house was up in the mountain where the river water would never reach.

Christopher and Ted and Rosalie had moved out of the trailer park too, but Dad said they *had some sense* because they bought a brand-new house up on the side of the mountain that would not get filled with water in another flood. I didn't care what kind of sense they had; I was very unhappy that we didn't have Jamie or Chris around to play with anymore even though Mom said we could make plans to see them.

*Make plans*, I thought. *Who wants to make plans just to play?* That just sounded dumb.

Our house in Mountain Top was almost ready for us to move in, but Dad said it would be at least one more month, so Pam and Paul and I resigned ourselves to playing together when we were bored. Now that we had to *make plans* if we wanted to play with Christopher and Jamie, we didn't see them as much and we fought a lot more, which gave Mom a headache and made Dad *aggravated*. Mom kept reminding us that we would see everyone at the Jersey Shore that month, and as great as that felt, it didn't stop all three of us from fighting.

By this time, Baby Jessica was starting to coo and make babbling noises, and even though she couldn't walk or even crawl yet, we could make her laugh, and that lightened the mood some because when Baby Jessica laughed, it made us feel like we were being tickled on the inside.

Mom put Baby Jessica on the floor on top of a blanket on her stomach and said it was good for making her neck strong because that baby just wanted to look up, up, up even though nothing very exciting was happening up where we were.

One time Dad got right down on his stomach to come face to face with Baby Jessica, so Pam and Paul and I did too. Dad looked right at Baby Jessica and stuck out his tongue. Baby Jessica stuck out her tongue.

"Did you see that!" Pam squealed with delight.

"Yeah," I said, playing it cool because I didn't want Pam to get too fond of Baby Jessica. I was starting to feel like she was a very special little baby sister to me, and if something was special to me, it usually meant that Pam wanted it too.

Dad stuck out his tongue again and made it vibrate, the way you would if you were trying to say *na na na na boo boo* to someone. Baby Jessica did the same thing right back.

I gasped and exclaimed, "Let me do it!"

Dad made room for me, and I came face to face with Baby Jessica. She was smiling and bobbing her head like the Joe Namath bobblehead figurine that Paul got for Christmas that year, along with a New York Jets jersey that had since replaced his favorite Incredible Hulk shirt.

I looked at her clear blue baby eyes and the dimples on her cheeks, and for the first time, I could see that she was a miracle. Right then I realized that life before Baby Jessica was like a bad taste left in your mouth, like the disgusting stuff that tasted like earwax that Mom had recently put on my thumb to help me stop sucking it. I remembered the taste, but only so as never to repeat the experience.

I concentrated on the fact that a baby can suddenly be there, *poof,* in an instant. I drew that miracle in like a sharp, deep breath. It hit my chest like a sledgehammer. It was a beautiful miracle that kind of hurt.

Dad nudged my shoulder, and I stuck out my tongue, making the *na na na na boo boo* sound. Baby Jessica did it back, and we all laughed, and suddenly all of us were making the sound, and Baby Jessica just kept doing it back to us, and just then I wanted to pick her up and squeeze her as tight as I could because she was so cute that I just didn't know what to do with myself. I knew that Dad felt the same way because I could feel how happy he was when he was with Baby Jessica. It felt like his whole body smiled.

So even though Jamie and Christopher were gone from the trailer park, and that made me have an empty sort of feeling inside, I looked forward to being with Baby Jessica more and more every day, which meant that I was also with Dad more and more every day, and the feeling I had when I took my third-grade class to the shop stuck around because of that.

The excitement of stepping outside our trailer and into a world of play and imagination and kids and Charlene and Marshmallow Hill and Ishkabibble and the Land of Magic Doors and games of house was not something we had to *make plans for.* Now, seeing Baby Jessica every day was the only exciting thing we didn't have to make plans for because she did something new every day, and every day we would discover something new about that baby and yell, "Mom, look! Look!" and for now that had to be enough.

God had let me down by not letting me live with Aunt Sadie, but when we moved into the trailer park, I forgot about how great Aunt Sadie's house made me feel because for two whole years, the trailers on the dirt patch felt like one giant family too, with lots of kids and Charlene and all the grown-ups all together.

Mom told us that everyone would be at the Jersey Shore that year and this time we were going for two whole weeks instead of one, and instead of separate little cottages at George's, we were all going to stay in one big house. We were so impatient for the vacation at the shore, where Pam and I would celebrate our ninth and tenth birthdays, that Dad had put a calendar on the refrigerator and wrote, *The Shore!* with his lovely handwriting on the day that our vacation would start. Every day he let us draw an $X$ on the calendar until all the days were filled up with $X$'s and it was time to pack up the car and get on the road.

Dad and Ted didn't like the shore anymore because they didn't care about getting a suntan and they didn't like the sand, and most of all they had both gotten sick on a deep-sea fishing boat the previous year. Mom and Rosalie said it was their *own damn fault* because they drank too many gin and tonics the night before, but Dad and Ted said they didn't care *whose* fault it was and they would never set foot on another boat ever again.

All us kids were so excited about our vacation together that it was pretty much all we talked about once school got out. When Dad told us that he and Ted would come for the first week, I figured it was probably because Dad loved Baby Jessica so much that he didn't want to be away from her for two weeks, and I couldn't wait to be at the beach with everyone including Dad and Baby Jessica. So the second week, after Dad and Ted left, it would just be Mom, Rosalie, Marty, Charlene, and us kids, which was just fine with us.

From the day we arrived at the Shore, we went to the beach every day, but this time we got to bring Baby Jessica, which meant that we brought a lot of other stuff too, like her portable playpen, extra coolers with baby food, a diaper bag with extra diapers and wipes, baby blankets, and a giant umbrella. I didn't care because by this time I loved being around Baby Jessica, so even though Paul complained about how long it took to get to the beach in the morning, and Charlene needed to take the boys down before the rest of us, I stayed at the house with Mom and Baby Jessica. That baby kept surprising us every day by doing something new like rolling over and trying to crawl, and I didn't want to miss anything.

I loved spending all day every day on the beach playing in the sand and water together while Mom and Rosalie and Char worked on their tans. We still had to stay in front of the lifeguard chair, but now Rosalie had bought a whistle of her own to blow at us, so she didn't have to get up from tanning herself to wave us back in front of the lifeguard chair. Sometimes she did stand up to blow the whistle, and sometimes she just stayed seated in her beach chair, but either way when we looked back toward our umbrella, we saw Rosalie's long tentacle-like arms waving us over, while she gripped the whistle between her teeth just like the lifeguards did.

The house we rented was much bigger than the cottages at George's, but it had the same knotty pine walls that were familiar and made us feel good. Unlike the cottages at George's, this house had three floors and two staircases and lots of bedrooms, and we didn't have to walk out the door to see what the other kids were up to because we were all in the same house.

At night we sometimes slept on the floor of the living room with pillows and blankets just because we wanted to drink up every last minute of being together. We talked and giggled past our bedtime and made fart noises with our mouths and hands, which made us laugh so hard our stomachs hurt. Every now and again, the voice of Mom or Rosalie would come down from somewhere upstairs, with a stern warning of *kids!* But after the first week, the dads went home, so we weren't all that worried about getting a spanking.

Dad said he didn't like being *on top of each other* like that, but Mom liked being together with Rosalie and Marty and Charlene because if a kid needed something, there was always one adult or another around to help. I liked all being together in one house too and thought about asking Mom if we could *all* move into the Mountain Top house because that just made sense to me.

One morning, Charlene was making a breakfast of toaster waffles for us kids. We all sat around a large table and laughed at Jamie because he was eating and fidgeting in his chair and at the same time humming the theme song to *Hong Kong Phooey*. Paul started singing the song but replaced the word *Phooey* with *Pooey*, which made us laugh even harder.

Mom came into the kitchen, holding Baby Jessica.

"Maybe you guys want to skip the boardwalk this year?" she suggested, as if her power of persuasion could keep us from the mecca of fun that was the Jersey Shore boardwalk.

"No way!" Paul protested.

Pam confirmed, "No, Mom, we wanna go."

Then I said, "You *promised*," which may or may not have been true, but it sounded like a good thing to add.

Mom looked at Charlene with a pleading look in her eyes and said, "How do you feel about supervising the trip to the boardwalk this year?"

"Yeah!" we all yelled because we loved Charlene so much, and we knew that we would have much more fun at the boardwalk if Charlene was there and our moms stayed home.

"Sounds fun!" Charlene smiled, and we all started pounding the bottom of our forks that we held in one hand and the palm of our other hand on the table, chanting, "Board! Walk! Board! Walk!"

Then Paul, in a fit of uncontrolled excitement, leapt up from his chair, clenched his hands into fists, and started trembling his arms as if the excitement were too much to contain in his body. He blurted out, "We're gonna take Jamie to the haunted house!" which made my stomach drop because every year I pretended to have a stomach ache as an excuse not to go into the haunted house, and every year Paul, Pam, and Christopher emerged from the haunted house laughing and holding their bellies and telling me that *it wasn't scary at all*, and every year I told myself, *maybe next year*, but next year was here, and I was just as scared as ever.

We could not wait until our trip to the boardwalk with Char, and we whispered in anticipation how we just *knew* that Char would come on all the rides with us and buy us anything we wanted to eat like snow cones and cotton candy and she would make every minute of the boardwalk so much fun because she just had that kind of magic that no other grown-up or even half grown-up like Uncle Mark had. We fell asleep dreaming of the night we would finally go to the boardwalk with Charlene.

One day, I left the beach around noon to come back to the house with Mom and Baby Jessica, who we called Jessie. Mom said Jessie needed a break from the sun and needed her nap, but I thought that maybe Mom came to the house to take a nap herself because she always slept when Jessie slept.

I turned on the television and saw a black-and-white movie with people who were singing and dancing, and all of the clothes looked so beautiful and glamorous that I was utterly captivated. When the commercial came on, the announcer said, *We'll be right back after this commercial break for more of Fred Astaire Week.*

I had never heard of this *Fred Astaire*, but if this was *Fred Astaire Week* and it meant that every single day I could watch a movie with Fred and a glamorous woman singing and dancing and wearing beautiful clothes, it gave me a feeling that was almost but not quite like the magic I felt when we were with Charlene, so I came back to the house every day after that to watch a Fred Astaire movie before going back to the beach.

The night finally came when we were going to the boardwalk *alone* with Char. Mom and Rosalie and Marty stayed home, so us kids anticipated having even more fun than usual at the boardwalk because no one would be around to tell us to eat cheesesteaks or hot dogs before snow cones and cotton candy, and no one would be around to tell us to wait until our food digested before going on the Tilt-a-Whirl, and best of all, unlike the grown-ups, Char was going to come on every single ride with us! Every ride but one.

We approached the haunted house, and I felt my usual feeling of dread. I just hadn't gotten up enough courage for the haunted house because I still couldn't stop my mind from thinking about scary things at night when it was dark, and I didn't need more scary things to think about, even though Paul, Pam, and Christopher told me the haunted house was more funny than scary.

We all stood outside the haunted house, and Pam, Paul, Chris, and Jamie jumped up and down pleading with Char, "Come with us! Come with us!"

Char knew that I didn't want to go into the haunted house because I was very quiet and pale and was sweating a little bit.

"I'm going to stay outside with Suzie," Char said. "She has a belly ache," which was something that I hadn't said this year, but she knew it was the excuse I always made for not going into the haunted house.

"She has a stomach ache *every* year!" Pam stated. "Just come on; she'll stay outside like always!"

I felt like a real baby.

*"Please?"* pleaded Jamie. "It's the only time I'll be here!" And he stuck out his lower lip and turned it down so we could all see the inside of his lower lip, which I noticed for the first time was very large.

Charlene thought a moment, then said, "Tell you what. How about you kids go in the first time; then maybe someone else could stay out with Suzie, and I'll go in with you a second time."

The kids all looked at her blankly. Why would someone stay outside with *me* when they could go through the haunted house with Char? That was like telling a kid to stay home while the other kids rode on the sleigh with Santa and his reindeer!

After what felt like a long silence, Pam said with just a slight hint of irritation, "I'll stay." And Paul, Chris, and Jamie jumped up and down with jubilance before Paul shouted, "Let's go!"

Just like every other year, I watched the kids run into the haunted house and felt like a dumb little baby and wished I didn't have the kind of mind that just couldn't get scary stuff out of it. But I felt happy that Pam would stay outside with me while Char went in. It made me feel a good feeling inside, like Pam could make me feel safe just by being with me, and that was something that big sisters were for. I made a note to remember that good feeling and was happy I got to be a big sister to Jessica, who I thought probably needed more protecting than Paul, who didn't seem to ever be scared about anything except loud noises.

Charlene led me to one of the built-in wooden benches that lined the railing of the boardwalk, and we sat down. She said, "You know, I'm kind of scared of things too."

"You are?" I said, looking up at her and feeling a warmth in my heart that was replacing the dread that I had felt when we first got there.

"Yes, and I think it's perfectly fine for you to skip the haunted house until you are ready to give it a try. And it's OK if you never want to go inside the haunted house!"

"I like the Fun House," I said. If I was ever going to go into any kind of house at the boardwalk, it made much more sense to go into a house that had the word *fun* in the name, as opposed to a house that had the word *haunted* in the name.

"Me too," Char said. We sat for a minute or two in silence, and I anticipated being left out because that was how it was after the kids emerged from the haunted house, going over all the fun they had in there.

"You know what?" said Char.

"What?"

"There is a very, very scary movie out right now that is so scary it is rated X. It's called *The Exorcist*, and even though all my friends have seen it, I'm too scared," she told me.

"Do you feel like a baby?" I asked.

"A little bit," she said.

"Do you feel left out?" I asked.

"I do, kind of," she said.

We sat again without talking. We didn't need to because Charlene always made me feel better inside.

A few minutes later, we heard a bloodcurdling scream and saw Jamie running out of the haunted house, flailing his arms all around as if he didn't have any control of them. He wasn't laughing but was screaming and crying and looking frantically all around like a wild animal trying to locate Charlene.

For a split second, I thought he was trying to be funny, but just then, Pam and Paul and Christopher came out running, and they were also screaming and crying and running faster than I had ever seen any of them run, including when we had races and the point was to run as fast as you could and beat everyone to the finish line.

Charlene stood up, and the kids ran to us and collapsed in tears and sobs, saying things like "Thank God we made it out!" and "We almost died in there!" and "They tried to kill us!" before breaking down and heaving sobs that were so big, they couldn't get any more words out.

They all huddled together and hugged each other and cried until Jamie pulled himself together a bit and said, "It's over, kids. It's OK. We're safe now."

The sobs turned to whines and moans and finally petered out into whimpers and occasional start-and-stop gasps for air. Char, who seemed stunned and frozen, finally crouched down closer to the heap of collapsed kids and asked, "What on earth happened in there?"

Jamie, who seemed to be the spokesperson for the group, explained that this was not a haunted house but rather a "death chamber" with real people that had horrible, disfigured faces and carried axes and knives and chain saws. From the moment the kids entered the haunted house, it was pure terror, as they were startled around every corner and chased by the monsters. Jamie spoke for all the kids when he said, "We were sure we wouldn't make it out of there alive!"

Charlene hung her head, but I could see a little bit of a smile on her face before she said, "That sounds absolutely terrifying." Then she added, "Let's go get some ice cream and see if that helps."

Paul, Pam, Christopher, and Jamie all slowly got up from where they were crouched, acting as if the haunted-house experience almost crippled them. They put their arms around one another and hobbled along behind me and Char. We heard them still whimpering behind us, and for once in my life, I felt perfectly fine about being left out.

By the time we got home that night, Paul and Christopher had concocted stories of courage and bravery in the face of those monsters. They told Mom, Rosalie, and Marty that they stood their ground and put up their fists and karate kicked those monsters like the Bruce Lee movie they had seen on the television. They reenacted the scene, and both strutted around the house with their chests puffed out, looking very proud of their made-up story.

Pam said, "It was scary, Mom," to which Jamie added, "Terrifying!" Then he fanned his face and added, "I fainted!" even though he hadn't.

It didn't matter to me what kind of fake stories the kids were making up about the haunted house; I was just glad that I didn't go in. And for once I considered that maybe it wasn't that I was a baby or a scaredy-cat that made me stay out of the haunted house, but maybe it was something else. Something bigger. Maybe even though God didn't answer my specific prayers for specific toys and specific places to live, this was what Aunt Sadie meant when she said *God will take care of you*. And if that was true, then I wouldn't be so mad at God for not answering my prayers and giving me all those other things.

# PART III

# *Mountain Top*

# 28

# *September 1974*

In mid-September, Mom and Dad told us it was time to move into our brand-new house in Mountain Top. I didn't feel as sad about leaving the trailer as I thought I would, because since everyone else had left, it wasn't the same. Instead of a land of play and imagination and magic, it was just quiet, dusty, and lonely.

The only piece of furniture we took to the Mountain Top house was Dad's black La-Z-Boy recliner. Mom and Dad packed boxes with clothes and dishes and our arts and crafts Christmas decorations and the toys and bikes we had accumulated over Christmases and the black-and-white photos that Linda had taken and Mom had framed and hung around the walls of the trailer.

They packed up all of Jessie's things, like her playpen and her automatic swing and all of her diapers and toys and baby wipes and baby lotions and crib and high chair.

I wanted to go back in time. I wanted all the families to be living in the trailer like before and to feel the magic of that place like before, but I decided that it wasn't in *God's plan* just like Miss Vasile not having a baby of her own wasn't in *God's plan*. But ever since considering that God had kept me safe by keeping me out of the haunted house on the boardwalk, I accepted the plans he had that weren't my first choice.

As we drove down the dirt road, away from our pea-soup-green trailer, which was now the only trailer on the dirt patch, I thought of how lucky I was that us kids got to live there and have such a great time with one another and with Char. I felt happy that Jessie was born there and Mom started going to school there and Dad started to feel happy again. And I remembered the feeling that I had when we left Aunt Sadie's, but the feeling I had when we drove away from our trailer wasn't quite the same because I learned that it wasn't the place that gave me the feeling; it was the people that were in that place.

I folded my hands and said one more prayer to God, hoping he could include it in his plan. *Dear God, please let our new Mountain Top home have the same feeling as Aunt Sadie's house and the trailer neighborhood had, and let us meet lots of great people who make me feel good inside.* But I knew enough about God by now to know that he was going to do whatever the heck he felt like doing, and it didn't really matter how hard I prayed for something.

Our new house was way high up in Mountain Top, and as we drove up there, my ears popped. The house was in a housing development that was so high above the river that we could make *damn sure* that we would never ever lose the things that meant so much to us like First Holy Communion dresses and the new photographs that Linda had taken.

When we walked into our house for the first time, it didn't smell like it was *from the flood*. It was so brand new in fact that there weren't any rugs in the living room or the dining room, and there was only plywood flooring with numbers and letters and loops and arrows that the workers had written on there because they were sure that the whole thing would be covered up by some soft shaggy carpet, so why not?

This was where we had been waiting for two whole years to finally arrive because it was new and it was big and this was what real living was because we all had our own bedrooms and each room had brand-new shag carpet instead of linoleum on the floors like we had in the trailer. Every room had an intercom in it so that you didn't even have to walk up or down the stairs to talk to somebody. The house was much bigger than the trailer, so you couldn't open the windows and let the wind blow from one end to the other and call it clean. It was the most modern and fancy house we had ever owned, even more fancy than the house on Birch Street before it filled up with water.

The housing development was called Walden Park, but Walden Park wasn't a park like Kirby Park with tennis courts in the summer and ice-skating rinks in the winter, and it wasn't a park like Dorney Park, which was a local amusement park that was fun but not as much fun as the Jersey Shore boardwalk. It wasn't a park at all really, except for the name.

The roads were big, wide, and curvy, with smooth black tarmac and white curbs that had perfect square corners. The lawns in front of every home were large and well thought out and designed with shrubs and plants and covered in mulch and fertilizer that smelled bad. We were sure that there were fun places to explore and fun kids to play with, but everything in Mountain Top was far apart, so it was going to take a long time to find those things, so we begged Mom to invite Jamie and Christopher over to play because she had promised we would *make plans*, and we didn't want to leave Jamie and Christopher out of the fun of exploring our new neighborhood.

After we moved to Mountain Top, we didn't see Charlene as much because she now had to split her time between our house and Christopher's house and Jamie's house. One Saturday night, Char came to babysit us kids so that Mom and Dad could go see a movie, which they still did every single Saturday night. But this Saturday night, she came with a boy who she told us was her boyfriend, and she said we should call him Joe.

Joe was quiet and had a big red Afro on top of his head. He was skinny and had skin as white as cotton, and he spent most of the night sitting on the couch, watching TV with Char. We weren't too crazy about Joe because when Joe was with Charlene, she just didn't have the same kind of magic that she had when she was all by herself with us kids.

That fall, Mom started spending more time at school and doing something called *clinicals*. We didn't know what that meant, only that it meant that she had to be gone more. One thing we knew for sure was that those two years in the trailer neighborhood were a time of discovery for Mom too, except she wasn't discovering gems of magic doors or perfect branches to bounce on for hours in the woods.

Mom was discovering *herself*. We knew that because one night when we were supposed to be in bed asleep, we could hear Mom and Dad downstairs having a conversation that sounded more like an argument except no one was yelling.

Pam quietly opened the door of my bedroom and peaked her head in.

"Suzie, are you awake?" she whispered, but loud enough so that if I *were* asleep, her loud whisper would wake me up.

"What do you want?" I asked, sounding irritated but feeling very happy that Pam came into my room with what felt like something very important to report.

"Do you hear Mom and Dad?" she asked. She opened the door a bit more so that their muffled voices would travel up the stairs and into my room. I listened carefully and paused.

"Yeah," I said.

"Come spy with me," Pam said. I leapt out of my bed because doing something as cool as spying was exciting enough, but doing it with Pam was *extra* special.

Once I was on my feet, I looked at Pam and put my index finger in front of my lips, miming a *shhhhhh* sound. I was thinking, *We're in this together, Pam,* which meant that she definitely couldn't tattle on me like she sometimes did because this was *her* idea, so if she did tattle, I would definitely be pointing this fact out.

We got down on our bellies and army crawled along the hallway to the top of the staircase. We heard Dad say, "Jesus Christ, Peggy, you haven't even finished nursing school!"

It was quiet for a few seconds. Then Mom started talking in a very soft voice, so I slid down the stairs as far as I could without being seen by Mom and Dad, using the spindles of the banister to keep me from cascading all the way down the stairs on my stomach.

"I'm just looking for some *intellectual stimulation*," Mom said. "I have the right to it just as much as any *man* does."

Mom referred to Linda as an *intellectual,* but I wasn't sure what that meant other than she knew how to take black-and-white photographs and that Mom called her a doctor even though she wasn't the kind of doctor that I knew of.

"Well, can't you just read some damn books? I mean, it's hard enough right now with the *Charlene situation*."

I looked at Pam to fill me in on exactly what the *Charlene situation* was. Pam shrugged her shoulders, letting me know that just like me, she didn't know what Dad was talking about.

"Oh, believe me, I *am* reading books," Mom told Dad. "That's exactly why I want to take this course."

"Does it have to be *now*?" Dad asked.

"I'll figure it out," Mom said.

"How?" Dad asked.

"It's just one night in class. Women's studies," said Mom, ignoring his question.

I didn't understand why Mom needed to study how to be a woman. She already *was* one.

"It's not just one class. It's on top of everything else," Dad said, sounding frustrated.

"How is you staying at the club every night any different?" Mom was delivering a low blow.

"Jesus, Peggy, after the last two years, I think I deserve a little break!" Dad protested. "And it's *hardly* every night," he added.

Mom was quiet for a while, so I imagined her giving Dad her *Oh, you wanna go there with me?* kind of look. Finally, she said, "You *know* what I mean."

Dad paused. He took a deep breath. "I just don't think it's a great time."

"There's *never* a great time. I'll figure it out," she repeated.

It was silent for what seemed like a long time.

"Well," Dad finally said, "don't come crying to me when you need someone to pick up any extra slack."

"What else is new?" Mom quipped.

Dad walked out the front door, got in his new brown Mercedes that he had bought right before we moved out of the trailer, and drove away.

*Where the heck was he going?*

Mom didn't say anything. She walked toward the stairs, and Pam and I had to scurry backward up the stairs on our bellies using the spindles to hoist ourselves in the opposite direction. We scurried into our separate rooms.

I waited for about five minutes, then got up and walked over to the intercom on my wall. I set the dial to Pam's bedroom, pushed the talk button, and whispered, "Pam!"

There was no answer.

Again, I whispered, "Pam! You there?"

A moment later, I heard the crackle of the intercom, and an irritated voice came through the speaker.

"What?"

"Are you scared?" I asked, mostly because I was scared and I wanted her to know that. Ever since she had volunteered to sit with me outside of the haunted house that ill-fated summer night, I felt protected by Pam even though the kids never went back in because they were sure they would have been killed.

"Kinda."

"Do you think they are gonna get a divorce?"

On the rare occasion that Mom and Dad had an argument, I was convinced that this was it. They were getting a divorce; I was sure of it. We would all be orphaned.

"I don't know," she said. Then she was quiet, which told me that she was just as scared as I was.

I couldn't sleep that night. I just lay awake in my bed, imagining my future life as an orphan, like Oliver Twist. In my mind I wore oil-stained and tattered clothes and crept around the streets of town at night, raiding garbage pails for scraps of pork chop or fish bones and discarded potato peels. Alone, cold, and starving.

After a while, I couldn't take it anymore. I got out of bed and grabbed my sleeping bag, tiptoed quietly down the stairs, and walked out of the front door. The night was warm, but even if it turned cold, I was going to sleep on that porch until Dad came home. I crawled into my sleeping bag and drifted off to a half sleep.

A bit later, I heard the diesel engine of the Mercedes pulling into the driveway. I pretended to be asleep. Dad walked up the stairs of the porch, picked me up still in my sleeping bag, and carried me up the stairs and put me into my bed.

When he walked out of my bedroom and softly closed the door, a wave of relief washed over me. Mom and Dad wouldn't be getting a divorce. I was not going to have to live on the streets and scavenge for food. But as scared as I was about becoming an orphan that night, it also felt so good to be picked up and carried like a baby to my bed, like Dad used to do on Birch Street. And if Mom and Dad fighting and me sleeping on the front porch was the only time that would happen, then I would take it.

A few weeks later, Mom and Rosalie took me and Pam to the shopping outlets near Philadelphia to buy some new clothes for school. Pam and I sat in the back seat while Mom drove, chatting with Rosalie as if they hadn't seen each other in a few years instead of just a few weeks.

Mom and Rosalie didn't stop talking as they shared stories about nursing school and anatomy class and clinicals and their new homes and what it felt like to have such a big house with so much space. Rosalie told Mom that clinicals were really exciting because you got hospital experience and you could see what it was really like to be a nurse. I found the whole thing boring and drifted off to sleep.

A little while later, I woke up, but I kept my eyes closed, and I didn't sit up. I heard Mom say, "It sounds like she wants to keep it."

Rosalie replied with, "Catholic school, you know? I guess abortion is just not an option."

What was *abortion*? I wondered. I had never heard the word.

Rosalie said, "I thought being married at three months along was tough. But having a baby in high school . . ." She didn't finish her sentence and instead took in a deep, deep breath like she did when she smoked, then let it out.

Mom said, "Well, let's just be there for her. To support her. Emotionally."

Rosalie said, "Of course." Then she added, "There goes our babysitter."

There was a long pause before Mom finally said, "I think she'll be a good mother, you know?"

Rosalie gave a small grimace as if to say *I sure hope so*. Then they both were very quiet.

*Charlene? Our Charlene* was having a baby? It didn't make sense.

Charlene was not a grown-up. Charlene was more kid than grown-up, and only grown-ups had babies that came out of special spots. Did Charlene even *have* a special spot? I thought frantically.

So *this* was the Charlene situation?

I continued to pretend to be asleep, not wanting to miss a word and wondering what I had missed while I was napping. I looked over at Pam, and her eyes were still closed. I tried to tell if she was awake but just pretending so she could listen to everything, just like I was doing.

Us kids had definitely noticed that Char was losing some of her magic ever since red-Afro-Joe started coming around, because she spent more time on the couch with Joe, giggling and snuggling with him, and less time playing games of imagination with us, but I thought it was because there weren't as many fun and magical places to explore in Mountain Top and there definitely wasn't a golf course.

Still, I didn't know what I was going to do if Charlene, who was by now almost seventeen years old, couldn't be our babysitter anymore. One thing was for sure: I most definitely and without a doubt would not accept any substitutes, so Mom was just going to have to quit school and stop discovering herself with her intellectual curiosity and women's studies and all that other stuff, and Mom and Dad were just gonna have to stop going to the movies on Saturday nights. And that was all there was to it.

Us kids blamed that boy Joe for taking away some of Charlene's magic, and she didn't babysit as much but instead came to the house to get advice from Mom on having a baby, and since Mom had four babies and Rosalie and Marty each only had one, Mom was more of the expert on that type of stuff.

Mom had promised Dad that she would figure things out, and I guess that meant asking Pop-Pop-with-the-Chi-Chi to come watch us kids, because we started seeing him a whole lot more.

Pop-Pop-with-the-Chi-Chi wasn't Dad's real father, but he was the only grandfather on Dad's side that we had ever known. Dad's real father was killed when he and Grandma Gertrude were driving to New York City for the day and had a head-on collision with a Greyhound bus. Dad was only three years old.

Grandma Gertrude wasn't killed in the accident, but her legs were crushed like smashed-up twigs, and she had to stay in the hospital for one whole year, so Dad went to live with Nana and her husband, Daniel, and when Grandma Gertrude finally got out of the hospital and asked for Dad to come back to live with her, Nana refused to give him back. So for years after the accident that killed Dad's real father, whose name was Steven, Grandma Gertrude felt sad about not being able to have Dad back with her, and she stayed that way until she married Pop-Pop-with-the-Chi-Chi and they had some kids of their own, including Uncle Mark, who Dad had to fire and who was the reason that Dad and Grandma Gertrude didn't talk to each other for two years before she died.

We called Pop-Pop-with-the-Chi-Chi by that name because if we just called him Pop-Pop, we would get confused about which Pop-Pop we were talking about because we had another Pop-Pop. So Pop-Pop-with-the-Screwdriver was our Pop-Pop who made things out of things, and Pop-Pop-with-the-Chi-Chi lived with Grandma Gert, and they had a Chihuahua named Chi-Chi, which was the same Chi-Chi that Uncle Mark threatened to hold upside down by her tail.

Having Pop-Pop-with-the-Chi-Chi as our babysitter wasn't the same as Charlene because he didn't make up games of imagination and act like a kid like Charlene did, but he was funny and made us laugh because he called us goofy names. Sometimes he would say, *Oh, look at Lady Godiva!* or *Here comes the Queen of Sheba!* when one of us walked into the room. *Well, whaddaya know, it's the Dolly Sisters,* he sometimes said when Pam and I came down for breakfast, and most of the time, he called Paul *Gunga Din.* We didn't know who any of these people were, but the way that Pop-Pop-with-the-Chi-Chi said it made us laugh and feel a little special.

Pop-Pop-with-the-Chi-Chi had gray hair that wasn't long but wasn't short, and it stuck straight out from the sides of his head like Pippi Longstocking, except he didn't have his hair in pigtails. He had a scraggly gray mustache to match his hair, and sometimes he had stubble on his chin, but he never had a full beard.

Mom told us Pop-Pop-with-the-Chi-Chi was a hairdresser before he retired, and I guess he missed it a little bit because he always said things like, "Come sit down and let Pop-Pop put your hair in cornrows," to me and Pam, but we never let him do that. Most of the time he wore a sleeveless ribbed T-shirt around the house, and he had a big belly that looked like Mom's belly right before Baby Jessica came out of her *special spot*. He spent a lot of time sitting in the kitchen, smoking cigarettes, or drinking coffee that he made in our new Mr. Coffee coffee maker that kept coffee hot for hours and hours.

On hot days, Pop-Pop-with-the-Chi-Chi sat at the table without his sleeveless T-shirt, exposing a big white scar with dots running down either side that ran right down the middle of his round belly, which Pop-Pop said was because the doctors had to go in and fix his heart. He didn't seem to mind his scar, and he didn't seem to mind that he had to give himself a shot in the arm every day because he had what he called *the sugar*. Mom told us that the shot was something called insulin, and we could tell that she was learning a lot in that school of hers because she knew that. Pop-Pop-with-the-Chi-Chi sometimes let us stick that needle in his arm, which I told myself was good practice for becoming a nurse, which was something that I decided I would like to do, but I only wanted to be a nurse in the afternoon because in the morning, I wanted to be a teacher, and I wanted to be an actress at night.

Even if Pop-Pop-with-the-Chi-Chi sat smoking in the kitchen without his white sleeveless T-shirt, he wore a gold chain with a cross, and Jesus hung on that cross like the ones we saw in church. He wasn't like Aunt Sadie because he didn't pray the rosary or talk a whole lot about how much God loved us and would protect us, but I knew that when someone wore a cross like that, they believed in God, and I wondered why God would give someone who wore a gold chain of Jesus around his neck a bad heart and *the sugar*. I made a note to start praying a lot more to God, just in case.

All the grown-ups loved Pop-Pop-with-the-Chi-Chi too because he made them laugh when he said things like *Honey, she wouldn't know a diamond if it came out of her ass!* And we laughed right along with them even though he said a curse word. No one seemed to mind that.

Pop-Pop-with-the-Chi-Chi reminded me of Rip Taylor and Charles Nelson Reilly from my favorite game show, *Match Game*, and I thought that everyone should have a Pop-Pop who was as funny as Pop-Pop-with-the-Chi-Chi.

Even though Pop-Pop-with-the-Chi-Chi wasn't magic like Char, he did take care of us kids, and I don't mean just because he fed us and made sure that we did our homework and went to bed and were nice to each other, but because just like the time that Charlene protected me from getting a spanking when I tried to do loop-the-loops on the shower-curtain rod, pretending to be Olga Korbut, Pop-Pop *also* promised not to tell Dad when we did something bad, so we didn't get as many spankings as we would have if he weren't around.

But Pop-Pop-with-the-Chi-Chi was mostly there to take care of Jessie, who was still very little and couldn't take care of herself. When Jessie was not napping, Pop-Pop-with-the-Chi-Chi sat her in her high chair and fed her baby food while talking to her just like he talked to us kids. He didn't have to use a funny voice because his voice was already a little funny, and he talked to her as if she were talking right back to him, which she was not.

"You've gotta eat those peas, my precious little gumdrop!" Pop-Pop would say as he spooned some green mush into Jessie's mouth and scraped off the stuff that oozed out as she hesitantly gummed that nasty-looking stuff.

"Mmmmmm!" Pop-Pop would say. "Isn't that so *good*? I slaved all day over a hot stove to make that for you!"

Jessie only responded with baby sounds like *munnamunna* as she gummed more baby food.

"Well, thank you, my doll! I'm so glad you like Pop-Pop's food," he would continue, and it would go on like that whether he was changing her diaper or giving her a bath in the kitchen sink.

After her bath, Pop-Pop-with-the-Chi-Chi brushed Jessie's thin-as-silk hair, which she didn't have very much of, with a hairbrush that had bristles so soft, I really didn't see the point.

Only when he put Jessie in her swing and cranked the handle so that the swing would go forward and back did Pop-Pop-with-the-Chi-Chi light up a cigarette, pour himself another cup of coffee, and sigh as if the whole thing wore him right out.

The room with the bare floors with the arrows and words written on them was at the front of the house, so Mom put long, dark curtains on the windows so that people couldn't see inside and watch what we were doing, even though we never spent time in that room because there was no furniture in it.

One day, Paul and I decided to wrap our bodies up in those curtains and lean all our weight into them like we were lying in a hammock. Paul took one curtain, and I took the other curtain; both were on the same rod at the top of the window.

After we wrapped ourselves all up like mummies, Paul said, "Go!" and we both leaned forward and let the curtains hold all of our weight, but we bashed into each other before the curtain rod went *snap*, and we both tumbled to the floor.

I looked over at Paul, who had terror on this face. We both knew that this was a punishable offense, and we knew the punishment would be a spanking.

Paul was nearly hyperventilating as he repeated, "Are we gonna get a spanking? Are we gonna get a spanking?"

"Don't worry," I said. "I have an idea."

I went into the kitchen, grabbed a chair, and dragged it into the front room. The kitchen chairs were brand new. They had frames made from chrome and wood with curved lines, like the desk in Uncle Ray's office at the shop. The seat of the chair and the back of the chair were made of something Mom called *caning*, which was squishy when you sat on it and had lots of little holes all over it.

I dragged the chair over to the curtain rod, which was now snapped in the middle but still attached to the top of the window on either side. My strategy was to get rid of the evidence. Problem solved.

Just then, Pam walked into the room.

"What happened?" she asked, furrowing her brow.

"We broke the curtain," Paul said as he grimaced and started clacking his teeth together.

"You're in so much trouble!" Pam said. She seemed almost happy about that.

"I have an idea," I said as I stepped onto the chair and strained to reach for where the curtain rod was secured.

I managed to get one side unhooked, when my foot went clean through the caning of the kitchen chair!

"Oh no! Oh no!" Paul moaned. "We're *dead*!"

"Yeah, you're dead," repeated Pam.

They were right. If Mom and Dad saw that we had broken something in our brand-new house up on the mountain that wasn't *from the flood*, we were definitely dead.

Paul started moaning, "I don't want to get a spanking; I don't want to get a spanking." He curled his knees up to his chest, wrapped his arms around them, and started rocking back and forth and repeating *I don't want to get a spanking* over and over.

"We won't," I promised. "Here, help me."

Paul got up and took one end of the curtain rod from me. I pulled my foot out of the hole I had made in the chair, stepped out of the chair, and dragged it to the other side of the window.

I climbed back on the chair, only putting my feet on the edges that were solid wood, and removed the other end of the curtain rod.

"What are you doing *now*?" Pam wanted to know. I wished she would shut up.

"We're hiding these in the garage," I said. "Help me."

"No way," she stated. She told us to leave her out of it, so Paul and I dragged the broken curtain rod, the curtains, and the broken chair into the garage and hid them behind a pile of boxes that Mom and Dad hadn't unpacked since our move to Mountain Top.

I was pretty proud of myself and fully convinced that Mom and Dad would be none the wiser and wouldn't even notice that our window suddenly didn't have a curtain rod and the kitchen table was missing a chair.

A few minutes after Mom came into the house from taking Jessie for a walk in the stroller, she called out to us.

"Pamela! Paul! Suzanne!" She used our full names, which was not a good sign. "Come here now!"

We found Mom in the now-curtainless front room, waiting for us with her arms folded across her chest. Jessie was swinging back and forth in her mechanical swing. As she moved back and forth, the swing gave off a *click click clicking* sound until the sound slowed down and we had to crank the handle, which always woke Jessie up because it was twice as loud as the clicking sound.

"You wanna tell me what happened here?" Mom asked. *Click click click* went the swing.

Paul and I looked at each other. At five years old, Paul didn't have the best poker face. He had a wild look in his eyes, as if he were about to be eaten by wolves.

I shrugged my shoulders, as if to say, *Beats me!*

Mom looked at Pam, who she knew would give her the straight story. "Pamela?" she said.

"It was Suzie's idea!" Pam blurted out.

In that instant, I felt that familiar red-hot feeling suddenly course through my veins. *Traitor! Backstabber! Goody-goody!* I thought to myself, vowing never to trust Pam again as long as I lived.

I didn't understand how Pam could be such a fun kid one day, and the next day act like a grown-up. It made me feel confused and betrayed.

"Was *not!*" I lied, making a note to tell about this lie in confession.

"I don't care whose idea it was. Tell me what happened to the curtains and who was involved," said Mom.

Paul offered, "We thought it would be fun," and he gave me a pleading look.

"Thought *what* would be fun? Where are the curtains?" Mom asked again.

"They broke," I finally admitted. "We're sorry! We're sorry!" I began to cry, hoping that Mom would feel sorry for me and let the whole thing just fade away.

There was a pause, and Mom took a deep breath and exhaled in a huff while I continued crying and begging for forgiveness. Paul started crying too, which made Baby Jessica cry.

"Ugggghhh," Pam said with a hint of disgust in her voice. "They broke the kitchen chair too." It was a low blow. Mom hadn't even noticed the chair yet.

Mom lifted Jessica out of her swing and gently bounced her up and down in her arms. She looked at me and Paul and simply stated, "We'll deal with this when your father gets home."

And that only meant one thing. We were done for. Dad was going to spank us, and we had Pam to thank.

I refused to talk to Pam for the rest of the day. Every minute seemed an eternity as Paul and I waited for Dad to get home so he could deliver our spanking.

Dad hadn't given us a spanking since before the flood. Charlene had gotten me out of a spanking the day I broke the shower-curtain rod, and maybe Mom and Dad didn't care as much about things breaking in the trailer because it wasn't our forever home. But Mountain Top was, and we knew it took a lot of time and money to build, so Paul and I were as sure as anything we would get a spanking. But instead of sitting around, quaking with fear, and waiting for our spankings, I had an idea.

I ran into Paul's room and found him quietly playing with some Hot Wheels, driving them across the top of his dresser and making them fall off the edge, as if the car were plummeting into a ravine and dissolving into a ball of flames.

"Paul!" I said, closing his bedroom door behind me so tattletale Pam wouldn't hear.

Paul looked terrified. "Is Dad here?" he asked with a bit of panic in his voice.

"Not yet," I said. "But I have a plan for when he gets here!" I said excitedly.

"What?"

"Let's put on as many pairs of underwear as we can under our pants. That way, when Dad spanks us, it won't hurt as much." I felt especially brilliant at the moment.

"Yeah!" Paul shouted triumphantly. He jumped up from the floor, threw open his underwear drawer, and began ejecting multiple pairs of Fruit of the Loom Underoos. The Incredible Hulk, Spiderman, and Captain America sailed across the room as he flung each one out of his drawer. He counted out loud as he flung each pair—"One! Two! Three! Four! Five!"—until he emptied his drawer. There were nine pairs of underwear now strewn about his room.

"Wear your biggest pants. See how many you can fit under them," I instructed before heading into my own bedroom to do the same.

When I went back to Paul's room, he said, "I'm wearing nine." His butt looked like he was wearing a diaper, but I still thought it was worth a try. Maybe Dad wouldn't notice.

I managed to get eleven pairs of underwear beneath my jeans. My underwear was thin and silky, and I hoped that it would provide as much protection as Paul's thicker boy's underwear. *It's better than nothing*, I thought.

Paul and I tried to make ourselves scarce while we waited for Dad to come home. We didn't want Pam or Mom to be clued in to the fact that we were outwitting Dad, so we stayed in our rooms until we heard the diesel engine of the Mercedes in the driveway.

We could hear Dad and Mom mumbling down in the kitchen but couldn't make out what they were saying. Then Dad started walking up the stairs, and we knew that this was it. There was a knock on my door.

"Suzanne," Dad said sternly.

Dad opened my door, pointed directly at me with his index finger, then curled it toward himself in a *come here* motion.

I slunk from my bed, keeping my back turned away from him so he couldn't see my padded bottom, and followed Dad to Paul's bedroom, where he did the same. We followed Dad into his bedroom. Dad grabbed a yardstick from the corner of the room and sat on the bed.

"Come here and bend over," Dad said.

Paul went first, but when he bent over and when Dad saw his bottom, Dad smiled a little, which wasn't something I was used to. In the past, when Dad spanked us, he was serious, and we just did what he said and tried to get it over with. If Dad noticed that Paul had padded his bum, he didn't say anything or tell him to take off all that underwear. He didn't say anything at all. He just smiled.

Dad drew back his arm, his hand holding tight to the yardstick, then motioned as if to give Paul a giant whack, but he slowed down at the last minute and just gave Paul a light *bop* on all of those layers of underwear.

"OK, now your sister," Dad said.

"I'm done?" Paul asked, a little confused.

"What, you want more?" Dad asked, the corners of his mouth still slightly upturned.

"No!" Paul quickly assured him.

"Go wash your hands for dinner," Dad told Paul.

I walked over to Dad, preparing to bend over so he could spank me.

"I changed my mind, Suzanne," Dad said. "I'm not going to spank you."

I hadn't been praying my rosary at all lately but promised myself to do it more because God was certainly taking care of me!

"You're not?" I asked.

"You're getting a little old for spankings," he said, then added, "But you're also old enough to think before you decide to do something. All decisions have consequences, and the older you get, those consequences can be much worse than a little whack on the butt."

I didn't know what the heck he was talking about, but I was thankful that Dad was having this new outlook on life.

"Don't tell your mother you didn't get a spanking, OK?" Dad said. "I'll tell her later."

"OK," I said.

"Tell your brother too," Dad said.

"OK," I said.

Later that night, at dinner, Paul and I really wanted to make sure that Mom thought Dad gave us a spanking. We limped into the kitchen, holding our bums as if they were in great pain. We both supported ourselves on the edge of the table to help us sit down, which we made sure everyone knew was excruciating. We were quiet and pretended to brood, but when we looked over at Dad, he winked at us, and we couldn't help but smile a little.

*Take that,* I thought as I looked at Pam. But I just kept it inside.

## 29

# October 1974

Our brand-new house had a big front yard and a big backyard that was edged with wild blueberry bushes and then turned into a wild patch of woods. Pam and Paul and I tried to find a tree like the one in the woods by the dirt patch, but there wasn't anything like that in the woods behind our house in Mountain Top.

We missed playing with Jamie and Christopher, and even though Mom had promised that we would make plans, we weren't sure she remembered because we hadn't made plans yet, and we decided to start pestering her about it because we knew that we would have fun with Jamie and Christopher even though it wasn't the same as at the trailers.

Finally, just before Halloween, Mom told us that Jamie and Christopher were coming to spend the weekend, and I couldn't concentrate on anything much because I was so happy we would all be together again.

Rosalie and Marty arrived with Christopher and Jamie on Friday night, and we all had dinner around the kitchen table, except Mom had to bring out folding chairs because we didn't have enough to begin with, and now we had one fewer because Paul and I had broken the one.

After dinner, us kids moved down into the family room, and we talked about what our new schools were like and we laughed all together like old times until Jamie said *Let's play house!* which we did, and it felt almost as great as it had when we lived all together on the dirt patch.

Mom, Rosalie, and Marty stayed sitting at the kitchen table, with Jessie in the swing next to them, which was *click click clicking* her right to sleep.

I overheard Marty say, "It's such a great neighborhood, close to everything. Jamie can walk to school and come home at lunchtime every day."

"I miss that," Mom said.

"Me too," said Rosalie.

There was a pause.

Mom finally asked, "Are you nervous at all?"

"Not really," Marty said. "Lots of people moved back."

"It sounds nice," Rosalie said. Then she took a cigarette out of a red-and-white pack, lit it, and took a long drag.

I stopped paying attention and went back to having fun with the kids.

That weekend, we played all day outside in our Mountain Top neighborhood with Christopher and Jamie. We ran around our big backyard, playing freeze tag and crawling on the giant boulder that sat right in the middle of it. We explored deep into the woods at the back of our house, turning over rocks and finding bright orange- or purple-spotted salamanders that we wanted to bring home as pets. We walked along the curvy, broad, newly tarmacked roads until we discovered another wooded area that we decided to explore. Deep in the woods, there was a pond, and Jamie started chanting, "When the *moooooon* is full, and the *skkyyyyy* is black." We all joined in. "Ishkabibble prepares to attack!" But that made us a little sad because we missed Charlene and her magic, and we saw her less and less and Pop-Pop-with-the-Chi-Chi more and more.

After that weekend, we saw Jamie and Christopher more, sometimes at our house in Mountain Top, sometimes at Christopher's house, and sometimes at Jamie's apartment, which was in Kingston and had been in the flood but was all clean now.

We started playing new games like *The Six Million Dollar Man*, which was Paul's favorite television show. The game was just like tag, but everything happened in slow motion with sound effects. Every leap that Paul pretended to take had a soundtrack of *da na na na na na fa na na na na na*, which we didn't mind because sometimes Paul and Chris pretended to fight in slow motion with bionic sounds and Jamie pretended to be the bionic woman, whose name was also Jamie. It felt like a new game that we made up, and that made us happy.

The grass in our Mountain Top yard was starting to turn brown as the weather got colder, so we began collecting a bunch of small and perfectly smooth, round rocks that sat at the base of the shrubs that Mom and Dad had planted in front of the house. We weren't as excited about the rocks as we had been about our fossils and geodes because we didn't think regular rocks, no matter how smooth they were, would make us rich. But we saved them anyway because it seemed like a good idea.

One rainy weekend, Jamie and Christopher came to our house. Jamie suggested that we paint the rocks that we had collected with beautiful designs, or with faces, making them look like little people.

"That way we can sell them!" he suggested.

"Yeah!" said Paul, who was always up for anything.

Pop-Pop-with-the-Chi-Chi was babysitting, so we asked him if he could help us set up an art area on the kitchen table with paints and brushes and water for rinsing. We piled all of our collected rocks on the table while Pop-Pop-with-the-Chi-Chi plunked Jessie in her high chair and scattered some Cheerios on the tray for her to eat. With great concentration, Jessie grasped a Cheerio between the knuckle of her index finger and the pad of her thumb and popped it into her mouth. She began to gum the Cheerio with her back gums. A little drool spilled out of the corner of her mouth.

"Let me wipe that face of yours, Angel," Pop-Pop-with-the-Chi-Chi said as he drew a dishcloth across her mouth to wipe off the drool. She shook her head in protest but smiled when he was finished, exposing the only four teeth she had in her mouth, two top teeth in the middle and two on the bottom in the middle. She grabbed another Cheerio with her knuckle and thumb and popped it into her mouth.

"Pop-Pop is making potato pancakes for dinner tonight," he told us. "So I want this mess cleaned up, you hear? Or I'll put you out with the garbage, and the trash man can deal with you all!"

We knew that Pop-Pop-with-the-Chi-Chi was kidding because he gave a little smile every time he said something to us that sounded a little bit mean.

When our rocks were all painted, we lined them all up in a row and stood back to admire them. We were very impressed with ourselves.

"Let's set up a store on the front porch!" Jamie suggested.

"*Yeeeaaaahhh!*" we all squealed because it sounded like a fantastic idea.

The rain had stopped, and so we worked very hard to set up our little rock shop, lining all the rocks up for display. We scribbled a sign that read *Rocks for Sale*, then waited for all of our customers to come. We felt sure that we would sell so many rocks that we would get rich.

But Walden Park was very quiet, and the only people in Walden Park were the people who lived there, and most of them drove from their homes to get anywhere and back, so no one was really walking by. We waited and waited, but no one came.

Pam brought the tape recorder outside and suggested that we record *Jane the On-the-Spot Reporter*, so that's what we did while we waited for a customer.

The house across the street belonged to an Italian family that owned a small chain of pizza places called Dino's Pizza. Dad called them the *real deal* because once a year they set up a dozen gigantic black cauldrons in their backyard and filled them to the top with tomatoes and garlic and spices. They boiled those tomatoes down for days, making all the pizza sauce they would need for the year and filling the whole neighborhood with the smell of that delicious sauce.

We called the man *Dino*, even though we didn't know if that was his real name or not, and we really didn't see him very much, because Dad said a pizza place was a *tough business* and that was why he and Uncle Ray opened a printing business and not a pizza business, which was something they had considered.

We often saw his wife, who had long black curly hair that she pinned up on top of her head and always wore red lipstick, just like Miss Vasile. But she didn't speak any English, so she couldn't read books like *Jonathan Livingston Seagull*, which was just as well because it was a very boring book.

Dino's wife crossed the street in the middle of *Jane the On-the-Spot Reporter* interviewing disaster victims. When she approached our porch, we stopped our recording, and Jamie said, "Can I help you?"

Dino's wife lifted her hand, which held a one-dollar bill, indicating that she was interested in purchasing one of our amazing painted rocks. She looked over each one, picking one up and examining it before placing it back down and moving on to the next.

Jamie moved closer to where she was and leaned closer to her.

"Let me know if you need help with anything," he said, sounding just like the sales lady that we heard when Mom took us to the Boston Store, which was called Boscov's now that it had been all cleaned up after the flood and reopened with all brand-new clean and not *from the flood* clothes and jewelry and everything else.

Dino's wife looked at Jamie blankly and said, *"Non parlo inglese,"* then slightly shrugged her shoulders and gave a little grimace as if to say, *Sorry?* in the form of a question.

Jamie switched gears and took on the role of translator, even though he did not speak any Italian at all.

Jamie began gesturing all about with his hands and said, "You want to buy a rock?" Then he repeated *"Rock?"* as he pointed to one of the rocks.

"Rock!" she said, and she nodded her head.

"This one?" Jamie said, and he pointed to the rock again. Dino's wife shook her head.

"This one? This one?" Jamie pointed to different rocks.

Finally, Dino's wife picked up one of the rocks, smiled, and said, "This one."

"I taught her English!" Jamie squealed.

Dino's wife smiled and nodded her head and said, "Yes! English! Rock! This one!"

We all cheered and clapped. She handed us the dollar and took her rock back across the street to her house.

We were just about to resume our *Jane the On-the-Spot Reporter* tape recordings, when two kids came riding by on bikes. The boy looked to be a year or two younger than me, and the girl was young enough that she still needed training wheels on her bike. They stopped in front of our house, dismounted their bikes, and kicked down their kickstands, then walked up our sidewalk to our porch.

"Is this your house?" asked the boy.

"It's ours," Pam answered, pointing to Paul and me. "They're just visiting," she continued, pointing to Christopher and Jamie.

"We live right there," said the boy, pointing to a house down the street.

"What's your name?" Jamie asked.

"I'm Tony," said the boy. "This is Angie. She's my sister."

Angie looked to be about Paul's age, which was five years old. She was smaller than him, which made her very little because Paul was small for a boy, and he became really grumpy whenever anyone mentioned his small size. Angie had a mop of black hair that looked like she had just rolled out of bed after a really bad night's sleep. She had a lot of freckles on her face, which looked a little bit like Peppermint Patty's face from the Peanuts comics. Her face was smudged with dirt, and there were patches of dirt and grass stains on both knees of her jeans.

Tony wasn't as dirty as Angie, and his hair was not mussed up like hers. He had short brown hair that was neatly brushed, and a wide mouth that made him look like he was always smiling even though he wasn't.

"Are you *from the flood*?" Christopher asked. We were all surprised that he talked to a stranger because he usually didn't talk much at all to anyone.

"We're from Ohio," Tony answered.

"So your house wasn't in the flood?" Pam asked.

"What flood?" Tony asked.

"We had a treehouse in our backyard!" offered Angie with pride. "But we moved out of that house, and now we don't have a treehouse."

*Too bad,* I thought. A treehouse sounded fun.

Even so, I wasn't sure how I felt about kids who weren't in the flood. After trying to play with Bobby Skipalas, I didn't make friends with kids who weren't *from the flood*. But there weren't very many kids to make friends with in Mountain Top because it wasn't the kind of neighborhood where we always had kids around to play with and we shared Charlene as a babysitter and we walked in and out of each other's trailers whether anyone was home or not.

"Do you have bikes?" Tony asked.

"A few," Pam said.

Paul said, "I have a big wheel!"

"Wanna ride bikes with us?" Angie asked.

I said, "They can't," pointing to Christopher and Jamie. "They don't have bikes here."

"We can play taxi!" shouted Angie jubilantly.

Tony said, "Yeah! Let's play taxi. Then we can all play."

These kids seemed nice enough. I decided it might be OK to be friends with them, even if they played games like taxi instead of games about floods and tornadoes.

"How do you play taxi?" Jamie asked with a bit of suspicion in his voice.

"We give each other rides up and down the street like taxi cabs. One kid pedals the bike, and the other kid rides on the back." He paused to assess our reactions. "It's fun!" he added.

Paul, Pam, Jamie, Christopher, and I all looked at each other, trying to gauge how each of us felt about playing taxi with Tony and Angie.

"Yeah! It's fun!" Angie echoed.

"OK," we all said in unison.

And from that day forward, Tony and Angie became the first kids not *from the flood* that we had fun playing with and the only friends we had in Walden Park.

For the rest of the fall, Pam, Paul, and I rode our bikes and our big wheels all around and up and down those big, wide streets with Tony and Angie. We played taxi, which was one of our new favorite games, riding back and forth and back and forth as we dropped off and picked up from our house to Tony and Angie Patchik's house, which seemed like a really far way away compared to what we were used to, which was poking our heads out of our trailer and seeing everyone else's trailer so we could tell which kids were outside playing in the dirt or the stand of trees or the ditches.

When we *made plans* with Christopher and Jamie, we played taxi with Tony and Angie, and we taught them how to play the *Six Million Dollar Man* and the *Bionic Woman*, which had changed from being a game of tag to a make-pretend game. Pam was Oscar Goldman, who was the boss of Steve Austin and Jaime Sommers, and Christopher and I always played the bad guys, so Tony and Angie were bad guys too when they played with us.

We pretend fought in slow motion, adding the same *da na na na na na na* sound effects, but when Paul pretend punched one of the bad guys, he added *Doshe! Boshe! Oof!* As he pretend made contact with his fist on another kid's stomach or face.

By the time Thanksgiving came, we were getting a little more used to having to make plans to play with Jamie and Chris and to our new friends and our new games that were not *from the flood* and to Pop-Pop-with-the-Chi-Chi as our new babysitter.

# 30

# *December 1974*

When Christmas vacation came around, I had been in the fourth grade at Mountain Top Elementary School long enough to know that I did not like it one bit. I hadn't made any friends at school, with the exception of one girl named Lauren, who I didn't like much and who I liked even *less* after she told me she spied on her older brother and his girlfriend.

Lauren told me that her brother and his girlfriend went to a nearby meadow to have a picnic and that she hid behind a tree to spy on them. What she told me next was something that I wished I had *never* heard because it made me so upset. Lauren said that she watched her brother and his girlfriend lying on their picnic blanket and kissing, when suddenly he lifted up her shirt, pulled up her bra, and started suckling on her breast like Baby Jessica did with Mom.

"You should definitely call the *police*!" I advised Lauren. I had never heard of anything so lewd in all my life. Her brother needed to be behind bars, and that was all there was to it.

"You think I should?" Lauren asked.

"Definitely!" I affirmed.

I didn't like knowing there were people out there that did things like that, and it gave me a very bad feeling inside, and no matter how I tried, I just couldn't make it go away. It was like when Old Yeller got shot dead in that movie, and I wished I had never ever seen it because I couldn't make it leave my mind. It just stuck there, like the flies that I saw sticking to the yellow sticky flypaper at Nana's house. And that's why I never ever wanted to go into the haunted house with the other kids, because my brain didn't want to forget about things that I would really rather forget, like monsters and sad things about dogs and now Lauren's pervert brother and his girlfriend on the picnic.

Lauren was not a kid that was *from the flood*, and after she told me about her pervert brother, I decided that the only kids that weren't *from the flood* that I liked were Tony and Angie Patchik. I didn't talk to her as much after that, and because she was my only friend at school that meant that I didn't talk to anyone else either.

I was relieved when Christmas vacation finally came so I didn't have to go to school and feel lonely, and I could play with Pam and Paul and Christopher and Jamie when they came over to our house or when we went to theirs.

I was beginning to think that Santa wasn't real, even though Pam insisted that she saw his boot that one time. She had also told me that she saw the Easter Bunny's foot, which made me think that maybe she was lying to me because Santa and the Easter Bunny were supposed to be very, very sneaky, and no kids were ever supposed to see them.

So Pam was either making the whole thing up, because what kid would be lucky enough to see both Santa and the Easter Bunny's feet? As special as Pam was, could she be that special? I wondered. And if she told me she saw God's foot, I would know for sure she was lying because as far as I knew, no one ever saw him.

Jessie was still a baby that Christmas, so I decided to continue believing in Santa Claus because it felt as magical as Charlene and the imaginary games she taught us, and Jessie was feeling more and more precious to me every day, so I wanted her to feel what magic felt like.

"Do you still believe in Santa Claus?" I asked Pam one day.

"Do *you*?" she asked.

"I asked you first," I hesitated, not wanting to admit to believing in something if it wasn't true and run the risk of being called stupid.

"I don't believe the Santa at the mall is real, but I believe the Santa that brings our presents is real. I saw his boot," she reminded me.

This made good sense to me. The Santa at the mall with the fake white beard and the black-rimmed eyeglasses didn't look like an old man, which was a dead giveaway. Everyone knew that Santa was old, like both of our Pop-Pops. Besides, Pam was my older sister, and she always knew things before I did, like the fact that Miss Vasile was going to read *Jonathan Livingston Seagull* to us in the third grade.

"Yeah, me too," I said. Then I added, "Let's leave him a note and some milk and cookies this year."

"Good idea," Pam said, which made me feel really very good inside. I liked when Pam thought I had good ideas because a lot of the time, Pam thought I had bad ideas that would *get us in trouble*, like wrapping ourselves up in curtains and using them like hammocks. It turned out that really was a bad idea.

Mom was also on Christmas vacation from her school, so we asked her to help us make cookies for Santa Claus. On Christmas Eve, Pam and I wrote a note to Santa, and we let Paul sign his name, which he barely knew how to do. Then we told Jessie to scribble on it "Because," we said, "all the kids have to put something on the note, or Santa won't come."

We left a plate of the cookies we had made and a glass of milk out for Santa, and Pam and I decided to sleep together in Pam's room. But I couldn't sleep because I was too excited.

"Pam. Are you awake?" I asked.

"Yes," she answered.

"Are you gonna stay up?" I asked, wondering if she was going to try and get another glimpse of Santa's boot.

"I'm gonna try," Pam said.

"If you hear Santa, are you gonna sneak downstairs?" I asked.

"I'm gonna try."

I waited a few moments to see if she would invite me to come with her. She didn't.

"Can I come with you?" I asked.

"You probably shouldn't," said Pam.

This seemed extremely unfair to me. Why did Pam get to see Santa's foot and I didn't? Why couldn't I sneak downstairs with Pam if she heard Santa? Why did I have to stay hidden upstairs in the bedroom?

"That's not fair!" I protested. "Why not?"

"Because you have to be very, very quiet to see Santa, and you're a loudmouth," Pam said matter-of-factly.

I was so mad, but I also knew that she was partly right. Mom and Dad were always shushing me because when I got excited or upset, I got real loud without really realizing it.

"It's still not fair," I said, but what I really wanted to say was *I hate you*, but I knew if I said that, Pam would say *I hate you* back, and that would really hurt my feelings.

The next morning, we woke before the sun came up.

"Pam!" I whispered loudly. "You awake?"

"Yes!" she responded, sounding excited.

"Did you see him?" I asked.

"I heard him," she said. "I decided not to try to sneak down. I didn't want him to see me and get scared off."

That made sense.

"Let's go wake Paul," I suggested.

When we crept down the stairs, we could see piles of presents under our tree. I looked over to the table where we had left cookies and milk, and to my astonishment, all that was left were cookie crumbs and an empty glass!

"Pam!" I whispered, barely able to contain my excitement. "Look! Look!"

Pam hurried over to the empty plate and glass, looked down at the table, then up at me and opened her eyes really wide. Her mouth gaped open, and she said, "I *told* you he was real!" I made a note to listen to Pam and to believe what she told me from then on.

Later we learned that at Christopher's house, Santa Claus forgot to put any presents under their tree that Christmas, so when Christopher woke up and crept downstairs to look under the tree, he didn't find anything. Christopher's crying woke Rosalie and Ted up, and Rosalie tried calming Christopher's tears by telling him that sometimes Santa Claus hides presents in various places around the house and that they should look around. Sure enough, they found a whole closet stuffed full of wrapped presents, and while it wasn't *quite* as magical as finding them under the tree, he told us it was still kind of fun to find presents in a closet on Christmas morning.

After that, I guessed that some feelings of magic you could just decide to believe in, like the magic of Christmas, even if it wasn't always the kind of magic you planned for. And as long as I wanted to believe in that magic, I could because Christmas came every year, and so its magic wouldn't ever just *end*, like the magic of the trailer park or the magic of Charlene's imagination games.

# 31

# *April 1975*

That spring, Baby Jessica turned one year old. Pop-Pop-with-the-Chi-Chi made a birthday cake for her and put one candle right in the middle of it. We had a little party with just the family and sang happy birthday to Jessie and tried to get her to blow out her candle. Instead, she grabbed the dish towel from Pop-Pop and put it over her head like a bonnet. We all laughed because Jessie wasn't a boring sleeping-and-eating baby anymore; she was getting very funny and cute and starting to talk in ways that only *we* could understand.

Later, when Pop-Pop had gone home, Mom took Jessie up to bed. She rocked back and forth in a rocking chair as she held Jessie in her arms and sang the same songs night after night. "I've Been Working on the Railroad," "Bingo," and "The Teddy Bears' Picnic."

I learned those songs by heart just by listening to Mom sing them every night, which made me happy because now I could sing them to Jessie whenever I wanted and that made her smile. Her favorite was "The Teddy Bears' Picnic."

The Saturday after Jessie's first birthday party, Mom put her in her playpen so that she could study. Mom was getting very busy with night school and her clinicals and her women's studies class, so we saw her a lot less and Pop-Pop-with-the-Chi-Chi a lot more.

When Mom was home, she needed to study all the time so that she could finally become a nurse, and because Jessie was still very little, Mom needed to put her in a playpen so that she would be safe while Mom read from her books out loud into the tape recorder that Pam, Paul, Jamie, Christopher, and I made our pretend news broadcasts with.

Mom's school made her learn all about skin diseases and mouth diseases and other gross things that had long, hard names, which was why she needed to talk into the tape recorder so that she could listen to those recordings over and over until she knew everything by heart.

One day, we stole one of Mom's big schoolbooks and flipped through the pages, looking at the pictures of rashes and scabs that had nasty puss on them and mouths that were all misshapen and deformed with the big long complicated names, and we screamed *eeeeeeeww-wwwwwww!* and wondered why she wanted to learn about things that were so disgusting that we had to close the book and go back to running around, pretending we were bionic.

The day we knew that Mom's school was much, much different than ours was the day she came home from school crying, which was something I hadn't seen her do since Teddy/Licorice went back home with his owners. Mom didn't stop crying, and us kids started to wonder why you would go to a school that would make you cry so hard.

Later, we heard Mom telling Dad that she was crying because for school that day, she had to go to a hospital for *special* children, and some of the children had heads that were so big they couldn't lift them off the pillow, and the rest of the children had all sorts of other things that were hard to look at and made them stay in the hospital. I didn't understand why anyone would want to go to a school that made them go places and see things that made them cry. I was sure that Mom would have trouble getting that stuff out of her head when she was in bed trying to sleep, and I thought about telling her that if she just stopped going to that school, she wouldn't see any more stuff that she didn't want to see and everything would feel better from then on.

Even though I didn't like Mountain Top Elementary School one bit, I felt glad that my school wasn't like Mom's school because even though I hated it, I only had to do things like math and English and music and science and history. I didn't have to look at gross mouth and skin diseases or visit sick children who stuck in my mind and made me come home crying.

So on this day, Mom was sitting in the family room, reading from her disgusting book into the tape recorder; Jessie was babbling away in her playpen; Pam was making a pot holder on a weaving loom she had gotten for Christmas that year; and Paul was outside, playing with Tony and Angie. Or so we thought.

Just then, Paul walked in from outside and found us all in the family room. He was wearing a red-and-white baseball-style trucker hat with the slogan *Up your nose with a rubber hose* printed on the front. We had never seen it before.

Paul said he got the hat from his new friend, and by the way, we should all refer to him as *Starfish* from now on. When we asked him what on earth for, he told us in hushed tones that he met a kid who was the leader of a secret club. The kid's name was *Catfish*, and Paul wasn't just asked to join the club; he was asked to be Catfish's right-hand man. Catfish bestowed the name Starfish on Paul and told him that he had to go by that name from now on.

Who was this kid? We wanted to know. Where did he come from? How come we never saw or heard about him before? It was obvious he wasn't *from the flood*.

I looked at Pam, who looked just as concerned as I felt. As much as Paul bugged us, he was our brother, and we felt protective of him.

Since we moved into our big and perfect brand-new house with the intercoms and the nice yard and the plywood floors with the letters and the arrows, life felt very different, and not just because we couldn't find fossils or play on the golf course or take baths with a tub full of kids. It wasn't just because when we ran around calling out *Waterfence!* no one came, or that Char couldn't take us up to Ishkabibble's Pond at hole #4 or the Land of Magic Doors at hole #6 or that Jamie wasn't there to save us from the dungeon with his magic sparkly wand or to be our mother who cared so much for her babies, Paul and Chris, and made sure that we all had enough food and enough blankets and that every detail had been taken care of because *Lord knows your father can't think of these things what with the horrible mess from the flood he's trying to clean up!*

It was because we were now living in a place where we were out-numbered. Kids who weren't *from the flood* were all over the place, and we didn't like playing with those kids if we could help it. Now this *Catfish* character was dressing our brother, Paul, and changing his name?

It felt like a dangerous new world full of kids that we couldn't trust, and I just didn't know what to do about it.

When I didn't know what to do about something, I prayed about that thing to God. So that night, I asked God to help us find more kids to play with that were *from the flood.*

Then I thought up the club name of *Stingray*, just in case Catfish let me into his club.

# 32

# June 1975

My fourth-grade year at Mountain Top Elementary School was finally over, and we all started talking about our trip to the Jersey Shore that summer, where we could spend time with Chris and Rosalie and Ted and Mom and Dad and all us kids for a whole week without having to *make plans*. I dreaded starting fifth grade in Mountain Top, but I told myself not to think about it, just like I told myself not to think about other things that didn't feel great or that I was scared of.

One weekend, Mom and Dad told all of us kids that they had something to tell us, so they gathered us together in the family room. The last time they did that was when Mom had a baby in her belly, so I was expecting to hear that another brother or sister was on the way.

But they didn't tell us that we were going to have another brother or sister. They told us that the reason they never carpeted the plywood floors with the letters and the lines and the arrows was because pretty soon after we had moved in to the big brand-new house in Walden Park, up on the side of the mountain where it would never be filled with floodwater, they had decided that they didn't like it there and that we would be moving again.

"We just wanted to let you kids finish the school year before we moved again," Mom said.

*I wish you hadn't,* I thought. But I kept it to myself.

"Where are we gonna live *now*?" Pam asked, a touch of anxiety in her voice.

"Dad and I found a house in Kingston that we love. We have already started to fix it up. We think you kids are going to love it!"

*Kingston?* Kingston was where Dad's shop had been. It was just over the river from where our Birch Street house was, and it was a town that was also filled up with water and stunk with flood mud.

Pam beat me to the question. "What if there's another flood?"

Dad said, "There's nothing to worry about, Pamela. They have built the levees up much higher than they were before the flood. And besides, we know better than to leave everything behind if it should *ever* happen again." He saw the concern on all of our faces. "Which it won't," he added.

"Jamie lives just a block or two away from our new house, and guess what?" Mom said excitedly. "Christopher will be living just a couple of blocks away too!"

They explained how, around the time that Mom and Dad decided to move from Mountain Top to Kingston, Ted and Rosalie had also decided to move from their house up in the mountain to Kingston.

Paul began to jump up and down; then he began doing a weird stop-and-start sort of dance, as if his excitement were too much to stay contained in his six-year-old body.

"Oh yeah, oh yeah, we're gon-na live in King-ston! Oh yeah, oh yeah, it's gon-na be so great!" he chanted, in sync with his start-and-stop motion.

*Here we go again,* I thought. As much as I hated Mountain Top Elementary School and dreaded going to the fifth grade there, the thought of making *all new friends* and getting used to a *brand-new neighborhood* worried me. I hoped, at least, that there would be more kids who were *from the flood* down in Kingston because I was really tired of playing with kids who weren't.

For the last three years, we had been living in places that I loved, like Aunt Sadie's and the trailer neighborhood, and places that I didn't love so much, like Pop-Pop-with-the-Screwdriver's and Walden Park. We made friends who felt like our family, like Chris and Jamie and grown-ups who felt like family too, like Ted and Rosalie and Charlene. But I also made friends who didn't feel great, like Bobby Skipalas and Lauren with her pervert brother. So I guessed that it was the same with Mom and Dad and that maybe, this was like the time when Mom took us to get a dog that looked like Licorice-Teddy, but she realized it really wasn't the dog she wanted.

And maybe sometimes the things you *think* you want and that you *think* will make you happy and keep you safe, like a brand-new house on the mountain with a fancy new kitchen and a fancy black refrigerator and intercoms through the house and bedrooms for everyone and a big green yard with shrubs and boulders and the plywood floors with arrows and lines, don't make you feel those ways at all.

I closed my eyes and folded my hands in a prayer and quietly, in my mind, told God to take the Barbie Dream House off my Christmas list.

# PART IV

## Gibson Avenue

# 33

# *Autumn 1975*

In the fall of 1975, we finally were ready to move into our new house on Gibson Avenue in Kingston. The Gibson Avenue house was *from the flood*, but when Mom and Dad decided that they didn't like the house in Walden Park and bought the house on Gibson Avenue, they also decided that they didn't want an old house that smelled like it was *from the flood*, so they ripped out all of the old and smelly insides and built the insides brand new.

That way they got all of the smell of flood mud and mold out of the house, and they covered everything up with fancy, modern yellow plaid or blue-and-white flowered wallpaper and thick, thick gray-green shag carpet downstairs and red or blue shag carpet upstairs in our bedrooms.

Mom was so excited to leave Mountain Top that she loaded all us kids into the car with all of our sleeping bags and told us we were going to camp out at the new house because it didn't have any furniture yet. Dad stayed in the Mountain Top house with all of the furniture so that he could meet the moving truck the next day.

The new house was not like our Birch Street house or our trailer or the Mountain Top house. It was in a neighborhood sort of like Birch

Street. Houses sat one next to the other, lining a straight tree-lined street. But our new house on Gibson Avenue had two floors *plus* an attic *and* a basement, which Mom and Dad had made into a place just for us kids to play.

The house wasn't brick, like Birch Street, or metal, like the trailer, or brick and stone, like the house in Walden Park. It was made of wood, with wood siding and a wood fence, and the only thing that was brick or stone was the steps leading up to the front door. It was painted the same gray-green as the shag carpet and had a room on the front of the house that was covered with windows on all sides. That room looked like it had been slapped on the front of a normal house. That was the room that Mom had us set our sleeping bags up in, and she told us it was called the sunroom.

Before we settled into our campout spot in the sunroom, Mom took us upstairs to brush our teeth. We had never seen anything like the royal blue sink basin, and we *oohed* and *aahed* at the faucet of that sink because it looked like a big round crystal and reminded us of the gems we found in the trailer park. Our new house might have been *from the flood*, and it might not have been built brand new, with inter-coms in every room, but Mom and Dad had fixed it up very fancy, and I already thought it was *just great*.

After we finished brushing our teeth, we all crawled into our sleep-ing bags and looked up at all the windows surrounding us. There were no curtains on the windows, and we could see the night sky.

"Look, you can see the moon," Mom said, and she pointed to the moon through the wall of windows. "It's full."

"Mom?" I asked.

"Mmmmm?"

"Does the moon follow us?" This question had been burning in my mind for as long as I could remember.

"It seems that way, doesn't it?" Mom said.

"Does it? Actually *move*?" I wanted a straight answer.

"No, it doesn't move," she said.

I was confused. How could something look like it was moving, look like it was following me everywhere I went, and not be moving?

"Then why does it look like it's following me wherever I go?" I pressed.

"Suzie, shut up! I'm trying to go to sleep," griped Pam.

Mom lowered her voice to a whisper. She leaned her head closer to me, which felt good. "It's just that the moon is so far away that we can see it from wherever we are. It looks like it is moving, but *we* are actually the ones that are moving."

I paused, thinking this over. Then I said, "So the moon never moves?"

*"Shhhhhh!"* whispered Pam loudly.

"Well, it does move," said Mom.

Paul was suddenly alert. "I wanna see!" He hopped out of his sleeping bag and went right to one of those windows, flattened both palms and the tip of his nose onto the glass panes, and peered out to look out at the moon.

"Oh, you can't see it move right now. It moves very slowly, so you would have to stay in one spot for a long, long time to see it moving," Mom said.

Stay in one place for a long time. That sounded pretty appealing to me at this point.

"Mom?" I said, after a pause.

"What is it?" She sounded a little bit impatient.

"Are we gonna stay *here* for a long time?"

"Would you like to?" Mom asked.

Pam, Paul, and I answered in unison, "Yes."

"We'll see," said Mom. My stomach filled with dread, before she added, "But I think we've finally found our forever home." I felt a wash of relief. Then Mom added, "Now, go to sleep."

# 34

# *September 1975*

I began fifth grade at our new school, Rutter Avenue Elementary School, which everyone called *Rutter Ave*. In the Mountain Top house, we had our own bedrooms and our own beds. In the new house in Kingston, there weren't enough bedrooms to go around, and Paul got his own room because he was the only boy. Jessie got her own room because she was a baby. So Pam and I went back to sharing a room and sleeping in the same bed. I pretended to be annoyed, but secretly I was happy that I got to talk and play and giggle with Pam at night again.

The night before the first day of school, Pam and I lay in bed.

"Pam?" I said.

"What?" she answered.

"Are you awake?"

"What do *you* think?" Pam quipped.

I took a deep breath in and out. "Are you scared to start school?" I asked her.

"I don't know," she said.

"I hated going to school in Mountain Top," I told her. "Did you?"

"Not really," she answered. "Some of the kids in my class up there moved here over the summer too. They'll be in my class here." Then she added, "They're my friends."

I was glad that none of the kids in my Mountain Top class were going to be at Rutter Ave. But I was nervous anyway because it was a new school and I didn't know anyone and I would have to try to make friends all over again.

"Do you think Paul is scared?" I asked.

"How should *I* know?" She sounded irritated.

We stayed silent for a few minutes.

"Pam?"

*"What?"* she said, still sounding irritated.

"Do you think we'll move again next year?"

"I hope not," Pam said.

"Me too," I agreed. "Can we make a promise?" I suggested.

"What?" Her tone softened slightly.

"Can we promise to always live together for as long as we live? That way even if we move more times, we'll always be together."

Pam paused, thinking about my suggestion. "What if I get married?" she asked.

"That doesn't matter. We can still live together even if you get *married*. Your husband can live with us too!" It seemed perfectly sensible to me.

"What if I want a lot of kids?" she continued.

"We can get a bigger house!" I offered.

"What about Mom and Dad?"

"They can live with us too. We can have a gigantic house with everyone living in it together. Even Chris and Jamie!" I was starting to get excited about this idea and made a note to bring it up to Mom because I was *sure* she would love it.

"OK," she finally said. "I promise."

The next morning, Mom helped us get ready for our first day of school. Our new school was the first school I didn't have to ride a bus to since before the flood at Lafayette Elementary School.

"Walk all the way down to the corner. Turn left, and walk all the way until you see the school. You'll have to cross one street, but there will be a crossing guard to help you," Mom told us.

Pam, Paul, and I did what Mom said. We walked on the white sidewalk lining Gibson Avenue all the way to the corner of Dorrance Street, then turned left. We walked down that sidewalk, and with the help of the crossing guard, who was a kid, we crossed Westmorland Avenue and walked to the corner of Rutter Avenue and Dorrance Street.

Rutter Avenue Elementary School was a large brick building that almost took up the entire block. It had giant metal double doors on the front, but no one used those doors to go in and out of the building. Instead, we saw kids going in and out of smaller metal doors on either side of the building.

When we entered those doors, we could see stairwells that led to the first and second floors. The stairwells led to more doors that opened into hallways lined with wooden doors that each had a window with a number painted on gold smack in the middle.

The stairwells were filled with kids moving up and down as they made their way to their classrooms. The shouts and laughter from all those kids bounced around from wall to wall, up and down the stairwells, and all around, like the little white ball in the game of pong that we discovered that summer in the arcade at the Jersey Shore.

Christopher, who had moved into his new home just a couple of blocks away from our Gibson Avenue house, was in the first grade at Rutter Ave. with Paul. Jamie, who already lived a couple of blocks away with Marty, had gone to Rutter Ave. last year for first grade while I was at Mountain Top Elementary with kids like pervert-brother-Lauren. Now he was starting second grade.

As soon as I walked through the side door into the cavernous stairwell, I was intercepted and greeted with a warm *hello* and a stiff handshake by a girl with straight shoulder-length dirty-blond hair wearing a pair of corduroys and a bright orange crossing patrol sash across her torso. It had an impressive silver badge that said *Patrol Captain*.

"Hi! My name is Susan. You're new, aren't you?" Susan asked as she held out her hand.

"My name is Sue too, but it's *Suzanne*, not Susan," I said, feeling clumsy and awkward.

"Did you just move here?" Susan asked.

"Yes. From Mountain Top," I said, then added, "We moved there after the flood."

"Our house was in the flood too! But we only got water on the first floor, so we cleaned it up and moved back in," Susan informed me. I instantly liked her.

"Where did you move? What street? I'm on Butler."

"Gibson Avenue," I said.

"We're neighbors!" Susan said excitedly.

The truth was that every kid at Rutter Ave. Elementary School was my neighbor. It wasn't like Hoyt Elementary or Mountain Top Elementary. Those schools were full of kids who took the bus every morning and came from all different places that you had to drive to if you wanted, and mostly you didn't.

Rutter Ave. was different. Every kid at Rutter Ave. lived within a few blocks of our new house on Gibson Ave. Every kid's house had been in the flood, like ours on Gibson Ave. and Susan's house had. It was a whole school of kids that were *from the flood!*

"We put an in-ground pool in after the flood too! You should come over to swim sometime," Susan said.

I made a mental note of this. A girl with an in-ground pool was someone I definitely wanted to be friends with. It didn't hurt that Susan was so friendly and outgoing.

"Cool!" I said.

Susan made me feel immediately welcome, and I was feeling less and less nervous about starting a new school. Susan showed me around the stairwell, the hallways, and the classrooms. She escorted me to the top floor of the school, where all the fifth- and sixth-grade classrooms were.

Susan was like the mayor of Rutter Ave. She knew every single student's name and introduced me to each one that we passed.

"This is Sue. *Suzanne*, not Susan. She moved to Gibson Ave. from Mountain Top. She's new here."

We'd exchange fifth-grade pleasantries and continue walking down the hall until we met the next student, and the next.

Susan walked me right up to the fifth-grade teachers as if she were a teacher herself!

"This is Sue. She's a new student here," she said, introducing me to the English teacher, Mrs. Gallagher, the math teacher, Mrs. Stevens, and the science teacher, Miss Hahn.

"Come on," she said. "Let's go say hi to Mr. Sarochek," and she led me straight to the Rutter Ave. principal's office and walked right through the door without even knocking!

She turned and whispered in my ear, "He's also the mayor of Kingston!" then raised her eyebrows as if to say, *He's one impressive guy.* I had never even spoken to any of my school principals, let alone stepped foot in their offices.

Mr. Sarochek sat behind a huge desk, reading a newspaper when he heard us walk in and looked up. He was the biggest person I had ever seen, even bigger than Aunt Sadie's brother, Uncle Pete, who was so big he had a heart attack and died.

He smiled and said, "Hey, chief!" to Susan, who responded with, "This is Sue. She just moved to Gibson Ave. She's new."

Mr. Sarochek had an enormous round belly, but not like Pop-Pop-with-the-Chi-Chi, whose belly looked like it might have a baby in it, except he was an old man and Mom said it was just beer. Mr. Sarochek was big and fat from head to toe, and he had a big round head that looked like a giant pumpkin. He didn't have much hair, but the hair that he did have was long enough for him to comb over the bald top of his head so that maybe it looked like he had hair there when he really didn't.

Mr. Sarochek huffed and puffed as he hoisted himself up from the chair behind his large oak desk to come shake my hand. He smiled wide, and his cheeks got round like two Ping-Pong balls.

"Well, welcome to Rutter Avenue Elementary School!" said Mr. Sarochek, still with his Ping-Pong cheeks. Then he swallowed my hand with his large mitt of a hand and shook it so vigorously that my whole arm shook and I thought my shoulder might pop right out of its socket.

"Stick close to Susan here; she's the right person to show you around," he said.

I looked over at his oak desk and spotted a large wooden paddle, the kind that would be used to whack a kid's bottom. Etched into the wood were the words *The Board of Education.* Mr. Sarochek caught me looking at the paddle and said, "Oh, don't worry about that. You look like a good kid, so you have nothing to worry about."

Susan saw that I looked worried and said, "Come on," then grabbed my arm and pulled me out of the office.

"Does he ever use that?" I asked.

Susan chuckled. "No. Bunky is the greatest."

*Bunky?*

"Bunky?" I asked.

"That's what the kids call him. Bunky," she explained.

"To his *face*?" What kind of school *was* this?

"Of course to his face!" Susan confirmed. "He loves it!"

I was starting to like my new school already.

Rutter Ave. felt very good because we also got to see Christopher and Jamie every day, and at lunchtime all of the kids went to their own homes to eat lunch, but we all walked to Jamie's apartment every day for lunch just so we could be together.

We all ate peanut butter and jelly or tuna fish sandwiches, except for Christopher, who only ate toast with butter and carrot sticks because he was a picky eater. We watched reruns of *Batman and Robin*, which was one of our favorite shows. But when Batman and Robin were trapped on a giant table saw or dangling over shark-infested waters at the end of the episode, we always had to return to school and miss the episode where they escaped and beat the bad guys.

So we played Batman and Robin in our yard after school because our yard was the biggest. Paul always had to be Batman, and Chris was, of course, Robin. Pam was Batgirl, of course, and we acted out the capture of Catwoman, played by Jamie, or the Riddler or Joker, played by me because the one thing I was getting very good at was being funny and making people laugh.

Jamie and Christopher came over almost every weekend, and we didn't even have to *make plans* because just like at the trailer, Rosalie or Marty and now Linda, Mom's women's lib friend, just showed up whenever they wanted. The weekends were still warm enough for us kids to run around the neighborhood, over lawns, and through backyards playing freeze tag or Batman and Robin or Dolley Madison, which was our new game where Dolley Madison was a terrible monster that chased and imprisoned me and Pam. The only way for us to escape was if Jamie, who was a magic fairy, unlocked our cage with his magic wand. We had made up that game because Jamie always wanted to pretend to be a fairy and Paul and Chris always wanted to be bad guys or monsters, so Pam and I didn't mind being the prisoners who Paul and Chris could capture and Jamie could free. We all felt happy.

We stayed outside until it was too dark to see much or we heard our mothers calling our names from the front porch, letting us know it was time to come home. We went barefoot for as long as we could because the lawns were so soft and the sidewalks so even and smooth, and our feet were so thickly callused and tough that we didn't need shoes to walk over pebbles or rocks or hot tarmac.

One Saturday, Pam, Paul, Christopher, Jamie, and I decided to explore. Christopher and Jamie lived near us on our side of Dorrance Street, and we knew that area pretty well because of walking to Rutter Ave. during the week, to Jamie's for lunch, and to Christopher's when we wanted to play on the weekends.

"Let's cross over Dorrance Ave.!" Jamie suggested.

Pam said, "I don't know." She had a hint of worry in her voice.

"Why not?" Paul protested.

"It's a busy street," said Pam. "And there is no crossing guard."

"Mom lets *me* cross busy streets," Christopher offered.

It was true. Since Christopher moved to our Kingston neighborhood, he did a lot of things that we still weren't allowed to do, like crossing busy streets and staying home by himself for little bits of time.

"Come on, Pam!" I said. "Don't be such a fraidy-cat!"

"Fine," she said, giving in. "But we all hold hands crossing."

"Fine," we all said, then skipped down the sidewalk of Gibson Avenue toward Dorrance Street.

Gibson Avenue continued on the other side of Dorrance Street, so once we crossed over, we walked all the way down until the street ended. It was just one block, but it felt like unexplored territory to us, which felt like an exciting adventure, almost, but not quite like the adventures we had in the trailer.

We decided to turn right and continue walking down a street called Hamilton. For one second, I got a little worried that we would get lost, but before I could get so worried that I wanted to go home, we spotted Cam's Little Red House, a penny-candy store on the ground floor of an old woman's house.

"Let's go in!" shouted Jamie, and we all walked through the door into Cam's, and instantly we were in candy heaven. There was a long counter along one side of the room, and behind the counter were wooden shelves stacked with big glass jars with glass lids. Each jar was filled with a different penny candy! There were Swedish Fish and jaw-breakers, candy cigarettes and Bazooka bubble gum, wax soda bottles with brown sugary liquid inside and Pixy Stix, and every other kind of penny candy that you could want, and some that you didn't even *know* you wanted!

"Who has money?" I asked. My mouth was already watering at the thought of a bag of Swedish Fish.

"Not me," the group said in unison.

"Darn!" yelled Paul, and he plunked himself on the creaky wooden floor of Cam's, crossed his legs, and crossed his arms in front of his chest in an *I'm not budging* manner.

Just then, an old woman as small as Mum walked into the store from a door in the back. She had gray hair that was pulled back tight in a bun. She walked over to where Paul was sitting, still wearing a grumpy look on his face. She looked down at him, silently. Paul peered up at her.

"We don't have any money," he said.

She still didn't say anything but turned around and walked behind the counter. She got out a piece of scrap paper and a pencil that didn't have any eraser left because it had been all used up. She had gnarled, arthritic hands just like Mum, which made it hard for her to use the pencil, but she managed to scribble something on the paper, then held it up for us to see.

Pam, Jamie, Chris, and I all carefully shuffled closer to the counter to see what Mum had written. Paul stayed where he was, making us walk around him.

The paper said *IOU*.

"That means we can owe her the money," Jamie said. "Right?" He looked at Cam, who nodded her head.

"We can bring the money later?" I asked. Just wanting to be sure. Cam nodded her head again.

Pam, Chris, Jamie, and I all looked at each other, then smiled as wide as we could and yelled, "Yeah!" in unison. Chris went over to

Paul, crouched down, and said, "We can get some candy!"

Paul shot up, came over to the counter, pushed his way in front of all of us, and said, "I want a pack of Bubble Yum! Grape!"

"Me too!" said Chris.

Bubble Yum was a new type of bubble gum that didn't stick to your mouth when a bubble that you blew had popped. If Paul and Christopher got their hands on a pack of Bubble Yum, they stuffed the whole pack into their mouths and had a bubble-blowing contest, seeing who could blow the biggest bubble.

Cam turned to face the wall of glass jars and pulled a large jar full of Bubble Yum packs off the shelf, grabbed two with her gnarled-up hands, and put them on the counter. Then she looked at me.

"Can I have some Swedish Fish?" Again, Cam pulled a big jar full of Swedish Fish off the shelf, set it on the counter, removed the lid, and scooped a handful of Swedish Fish out, laying them on the counter. She used her knuckles to count out twenty Swedish Fish, then put them all in the brown paper bag the size of a deck of cards and handed it to me. It was the smallest paper bag I had ever seen.

Pam got a Charleston Chew, which I thought was the most disgusting candy that ever there was, and Jamie bought candy cigarettes. Cam wrote the total of the candy, which was fifty cents, on the IOU and handed it to us. We took it from her and walked out the door.

Standing on the sidewalk in a huddle, we began to eat our candy. Paul and Christopher unwrapped every square of gum in the pack and shoved them all in their mouths. They had so much gum in their mouths, they could barely fit their teeth around the gigantic purple gob. Purple drool began oozing out of their mouths.

Jamie pretended to inhale from one of his candy cigarettes and exhaled the powdery fake smoke, saying, "That's disgusting." He then waved his hand as if to whoosh the smoke away from his face.

"That's gross," confirmed Pam.

Watching them navigate their jaws around the giant gob of gum in their mouths made *me* drool. I stayed silent.

Just as we were about to leave, a kid from my fifth-grade class at Rutter Ave. rode up on his bike. His name was John. Paul, who was still trying to navigate his teeth and tongue around the giant sugary purple glob of gum in his mouth said, "Hey, kid."

John looked a bit startled but answered with a small wave and a quiet and bashful, "Hi."

"I think you're in my grade," I said to John.

"You're the new girl," John confirmed.

"I'm Sue," I reminded him. Then I gestured toward the others. "This is Pam, my sister. She's in sixth grade."

"We're in first grade!" Paul chimed in, speaking for himself and Christopher, who was still shy and also trying to get control of the giant purple glob in his mouth.

"And he's in second grade," Paul said, pointing to Jamie.

Jamie extended his arm, let his hand dangle a bit off his wrist as if to offer it for John to lift up and kiss, and said, "How do you do?"

John briefly looked perplexed, then said, "Have you been to Hamilton Park?"

We told him *no, we hadn't.*

"Wait for me," John said. "I'll show you."

After John bought his candy, he walked his bike along with us and led us a few blocks down Hamilton Street to Hamilton Park. Hamilton Park had a playground, a baseball field, and a basketball court. Next to Hamilton Park was the Kingston public pool, which was closed until next summer. *Now I have two pools I could swim in,* I thought. Susan's pool and the Kingston public pool. I was starting to feel very happy with our new house and our neighborhood.

We sat on the swings and the merry-go-round, talking with John, who told us that he had been at Rutter Ave. Elementary School since the second grade. He told us which teachers were the best ones and which ones to stay away from. He told us that he had five brothers and sisters and that he was the oldest.

We liked our new friend John. He told us that his father was a pastor, and I felt a little bit jealous because pastors are really close to God, so God probably listened to John's prayers a little more than mine.

John told us about the Little League team that he was on and the games they played on the Hamilton Park baseball field, and when Paul and Christopher showed a bit of excitement, John told them they should join the peewee team.

"My dad's the coach!" John told them excitedly, and I wondered why pastors also had second jobs, like the dad of my friend Christy

from Hoyt Elementary, who was a pastor but also owned a movie theater. I made a note to ask John this question later because I couldn't
ask Christy since she wasn't my friend anymore since she moved to
Ohio.

After we finished eating our candy and were learning more about
our school and neighborhood from John, we told him we needed to go
home.

"Where do you live?" John asked.

"We live on Gibson Ave.," said Pam.

"I live on James Street!" said John, excitedly.

James Street ran perpendicular to Gibson Avenue, and was very
close to our house, since our house was on the corner of Gibson
Avenue and James Street. James Street was a long street, like Dorrance
Street and Rutter Avenue. But we knew that even if John's house was
all the way at the end of James Street, he still wouldn't be that far away
from us.

Once again, John walked his bike alongside the rest of us as we
made our way back up Hamilton Street, down the other part of Gibson
Avenue, across Dorrance Street, and down our block to the end of the
street where our house sat.

John was such a nice kid that I didn't think I even had to ask him if
he was *from the flood*. He just felt like he was.

But when I did ask, he said that no, he wasn't in the flood, but his
mom and dad bought the house on James Street that was *from the flood*
because his dad had gotten a job at Saint Stephen's Episcopal Church.
He told us that the house on James Street was really cheap on account
of it being in the flood and smelling like flood mud and gross mold, so
they moved into the second floor and cleaned and rebuilt the house
while they all lived there.

"It was gross," John said. "But it's nice now."

I was worried that I couldn't tell that John was not *from the flood*.
He was the nicest kid who wasn't *from the flood* that I had ever met,
but I wondered if he was just pretending to be nice. I wondered who
else in my class wasn't *from the flood* and was just pretending to be
nice.

"We moved to Mountain Top!" Paul shared.

"Only for a year," Pam added.

"Why'd you move back here?" John asked.

"We didn't like it there," I said.

"It was too far away," Pam said.

I wanted to say, *Because we didn't like kids that weren't* from the flood, *like Catfish and Lauren with the pervert brother,* but I didn't want to hurt John's feelings in case he was actually a nice kid even though he wasn't *from the flood* either. I was kind of starting to like him.

"Oh," John said simply.

When we arrived at our house on Gibson Avenue, John said, "Hey! My house is right around the corner!"

"Where?" Jamie wanted to know.

"Over here," John said as he pulled us around the corner to James Street and pointed to a house that was three doors down.

"We can play after school!" I said, remembering my ill-fated play-date with Bobby Skipalas but already feeling like things would be different with John.

"Sure!" John said. "See ya later!"

I was excited to have a new friend as nice as John who lived so close to our house. The corner of our backyard almost touched the corner of John's backyard, like the diagonal squares on a checkerboard. The corners were separated only by a six-foot section of John's next-door neighbor's property, which was behind their garage anyway, so we only had to hop the fence of our yard, sneak behind John's neighbor's garage, and we were in John's backyard.

It was fantastic! Except for one thing. John's neighbor's name was Mrs. Egan, and she was the meanest lady I had ever met. Mrs. Egan didn't seem to have anything better to do with her time than stare out the window and wait for us to cut behind her garage, because every time we did it, she seemed to know what we were up to and came out screaming for us to stay out of her yard.

John told us that Mrs. Egan confiscated any basketballs, baseballs, or soccer balls that accidently got thrown, kicked, or bounced into her yard, and she wouldn't give them back.

But Mrs. Egan couldn't stop us from cutting behind her garage to get to John's house because with all of those kids who lived there, we could always find someone to play with, and I felt like we were in the trailer neighborhood, which was a feeling I hadn't had since we moved to Mountain Top.

Soon enough, we were playing with those kids almost every day, whether we cut behind the garage to get to them or they cut behind the garage to get to us. Just like when we lived in the trailer, we didn't have to make plans, we only had to listen for kids playing and follow that sound.

# 35

# *November 1975*

By November, Mom had made friends with our next-door neighbor, Diane, and the woman who lived next to Diane, whose name was Maureen. Diane and Maureen both had children the same age as Jessie. Diane's son was Erik, and Maureen's daughter was Johnna. Mom, Diane, and Maureen took turns watching all three kids. That way they didn't have to pay for childcare or a babysitter and could still get things done like shopping, running errands, and other things like going to nursing school for Mom.

The two women could not have been more different. Diane was a prim and stiff woman who would have reminded me of Jackie O if it weren't for her two crooked teeth in the front. She was quiet and demure, with mousy brown hair cut and shaped into a sensible bob. The house she shared with her husband, her son Erik, and her baby, Matthew was stately and regal. It was a large brick structure with white trim and two white columns that bordered the front door.

Diane's house was flanked by our house on the left and Maureen's house on the right, all perfectly lovely houses, but Diane's house dressed them both down in a subtle yet noticeable fashion.

Maureen was a platinum blonde. She wore bright blue eyeshadow and pink lipstick every day. She had a baby-doll sort of voice, like the one Marilyn Monroe used in the movies. She liked to drink, and sometimes she seemed less in charge of her faculties and would clumsily move her arms about, knocking things over or spilling items out of her handbag as she searched for something in particular.

Maureen lived with her daughter, Johnna, her son, Todd, and her small mustached bulldog of a husband. Maureen's husband was short and had permed hair. He never said hi to us; we never saw him smile, and he wasn't very nice to Maureen. Diane's doctor husband wasn't friendly either, but Mom said his job was very important and he needed to rest when he was at home, which was why he didn't waste time talking to the neighbors.

Maureen's husband was grumpy and rude, and us kids tried to avoid him, which wasn't very hard because other than work and mowing the front lawn, he didn't leave the house. Mom called Maureen's husband *a real jerk.*

We overheard Mom tell Dad she didn't like the way Maureen's husband spoke to her, and by the way, she didn't think it should be only her job to clean up after dinner just because she was a woman, so from now on, it was going to be a family activity. Everyone had to participate, but Paul always found a way out of it by claiming he had to go number two and spending the entire time in the bathroom.

Mom also spent more and more time with Linda, who gave her books on feminist theory to read, like *A Century of Struggle, A Doll's House,* and *Feminism: Old Wave and New Wave.* We heard them having conversations about all sorts of things that made them mad, like the fact that women couldn't get a checking account in their name or a loan from the bank and that women were considered the possessions of men and were financially dependent on their husbands.

One morning after Sunday school, Pam informed Mom that everyone was born with something called original sin, and that it was Eve's fault because she made Adam take a bite of the apple. As soon as Mom heard that, she grabbed her purse and sped off in the car to give Monsignor Clark a *talking to.* We never went to church again after that, except for on Christmas Eve because you had to at least go to church one time each year to confess all your sins and receive Holy

Communion so that you had a chance of getting what you wanted for Christmas. Not going to church was just fine by me, but I felt worried that God would be mad and make something bad happen, but I guessed I would just have to wait and find out.

Mom had heard about an all-men's club called the Westmoreland Club that would not let any women go there, not even to have dinner with their husbands. It was the kind of club where men got together to drink whiskey and smoke cigars and *feel superior* as Mom said, so together, Mom and Linda started an all-out crusade against that club and their *male chauvinist* rules, which was causing a lot of trouble and getting their names in the paper.

If Dad objected to the division of labor or Mom making a stink about her getting her own credit card or scolding the monsignor or causing a ruckus about the Westmoreland Club, he didn't act like it. The only thing he told Mom was that he didn't think Paul should have to do all the chores that the rest of us did, but Mom said that because one day Paul had said, "I wanna be like my dad," Dad had to participate in the housekeeping because she wasn't about to raise a male chauvinist son.

Dad went along with the changes that Mom was making as long as she promised him that she wouldn't complain about how much time he was spending at the golf club.

In fact, we complained more than Dad, because now we had to help with the cleaning up after dinner, which we never had to do before, and Mom said she was going to teach us how to wash and dry and fold clothes so we could all do a load of laundry once a week.

Mom was also getting very touchy when we told jokes. One day at the dinner table, I decided to repeat a joke I had heard at school that day.

"How many Polacks does it take to screw in a lightbulb?"

"Suzanne, that's not funny," Mom immediately shot back.

"But you didn't even hear the punchline," I retorted.

"I don't need to," Mom said. "That joke is racist, and 'Polack' is derogatory, and it's not funny."

I didn't know what *derogatory* meant, but I shut up all the same. I looked over at Pam, who rolled her eyes as much as she could without

Mom seeing. I gave Pam a subtle grimace and felt wonderful that Pam and I bonded over what we saw as Mom's waning sense of humor. If I had to choose between Mom being funny and Pam being on my side with something, I would pick Pam every time.

# 36

# December 1975

The first Christmas in our new Gibson Avenue house was fantastic. Mom had gone all out with Christmas decorations, covering almost every surface in every room. Real pine boughs wrapped around our banisters, hung across our fireplace mantelpiece, and framed every doorway. Thick red and white candles inside tall glass hurricane lamps and slender candles stuffed into brass candlestick holders were set atop every available surface. Statuettes of male and female carolers wearing red felt jackets, holding sheet music, and singing with their mouths wide open stood in little groups on top of end tables. Mr. and Mrs. Claus figurines filled in any available spaces, and white twinkle lights were wrapped and strung all over the house.

Each window of the house had an electric candle set in the middle of it so that when you looked at the house from the outside, there was a glowing candle in every window. The eight-track stereo started playing the *Andy Williams Christmas Album* or Percy Faith's Christmas album the moment we finished our Thanksgiving dinner and stayed on repeat every hour of every day all the way up to and including Christmas Day. But the best thing about our first Christmas in our Gibson Ave. house was the Christmas party.

Mom and Dad hosted our first ever Christmas party, and they invited all their friends from the trailer park, their new friends from Gibson Ave., and Dad's friends from the club. I was in charge of watching Jessie, which was fine by me because I adored dressing her up and curling her hair and showing her off to anyone who was around. Pam was in charge of passing the *hors d'oeuvres* and making sure the trash didn't get too full of paper plates, napkins, and plastic cups.

Mom put a white tablecloth on the dining room table and set out trays of shrimp cocktail, chafing dishes with homemade meatballs, a big ham that was all sliced up, and soft little buns so people could make sandwiches. There were bowls of Mom's homemade potato salad and delicious ambrosia, which was made with mini marshmallows and fruit cocktail and mandarin oranges and all mixed up with Cool Whip and sour cream and was just about the most delicious thing I had ever tasted. For dessert, Mom made a rum cake, which would have been delicious if it didn't have rum in it. After Mom added the rum, it tasted like wet shoe leather.

The Christmas party was the first grown-up party that I had ever been to, and it was loud, chaotic, and kind of exciting because it was the first time I had seen adults act silly and laugh at each other and not talk about the flood for once.

Pop-Pop-with-the-Chi-Chi was there with his friend named Joe, who had started coming around the house more and more when Pop-Pop-with-the-Chi-Chi came to babysit. Joe lived with Pop-Pop, and they were best, best friends, which I knew because they shared a bedroom and slept in the same bed just like me and Pam. Joe wasn't bald like Pop-Pop, and he wasn't funny and didn't make us laugh like Pop-Pop did. He had a full head of salt-and-pepper hair and wore heavy black-framed glasses that slid down his nose, pinching it and making his mopey voice sound nasal.

When Joe came to the house with Pop-Pop, it felt like Joe was dragging a dark cloud in behind him. He was always complaining about one thing or another. When Mom asked him *How've you been?* or *How's it going?* Joe just sighed and moaned and said through his nasal voice something like *I've been better* or he'd list off a string of physical ailments that we didn't understand like *my pressure is up*, and he didn't stop complaining until Mom got out her blood pressure cuff to take his blood pressure.

Maureen from two doors down loved Pop-Pop and Joe, and when they came to the house, she almost always came over to drink beers and smoke and laugh with them, which was the only time we saw Joe smile.

After all the grown-ups ate and it started getting late, Mom told me to put Jessie to bed. I felt happy that I got to rock Jessie in the rocking chair and sing her "Bingo" and "The Teddy Bears' Picnic" and "I've Been Working on the Railroad." I rocked her in my arms and looked down at her as I sang. My long hair hung down, the tips of it brushing her body. She lifted her chubby little toddler arm up and played with my hair the same way I ran my fingers over cool sheets when I sucked my thumb. I had a very strong feeling that I had never had before. It filled my chest with a warm ache. I wondered if it was the feeling of God living inside of me, the feeling Aunt Sadie said I would feel. Now that I was finally feeling him, I hoped that God wouldn't leave me since we stopped going to church on Sundays and I stopped taking Communion and confessing my sins.

I decided that I wanted to live with little Jessie for as long as I lived and sing to her and let her play with my hair and protect her so that nothing could ever, ever happen to her. If it wasn't God I was feeling, maybe it was the feeling of being a big sister. I wondered if this was how Pam felt about being a big sister to me.

When I went back downstairs, there was a small group of adults left at the party. They ended up in our play area in the basement so they wouldn't wake little Jessie up. Several of them sat on the stairs, holding their drinks and laughing loudly as Pop-Pop and Joe told funny stories. Maureen was laughing the loudest. Her *real jerk* of a husband wasn't there.

"Tell them about the shirts!" Maureen encouraged, wiping tears of laughter from the corner of her eye and gesturing with her glass with such animation that the liquid sloshed over the side and onto the floor. "Whoops!" she said and laughed some more.

"Oh yes, honey. These are our lucky shirts!" Pop-Pop said as he presented the black shirt he was wearing and the gold chain hanging heavy with a big crucifix. Joe was wearing an identical outfit.

"Well, you know, Joe and I like to *socialize* from time to time," he began with a wink. "So we put on our outfits that you see here and headed to Lucky's Tavern."

"A real night out!" Ted said sarcastically. He was making a joke, because most of the bars in Pop-Pop's Lee Park neighborhood were just converted first floors in residential homes and had names like Lucky's Tavern or Frank's Pub or Vinnie's Place, and that's how you knew who owned the house.

"Oh yes, honey, only the best for us queens," Pop-Pop said, and everyone erupted with laughter. I didn't really know what they were laughing at.

"So we were there for a couple of hours and had had a few drinks before we decided to pay our tab and head to another bar," continued Pop-Pop. "And you know, we didn't think anything of wearing our black shirts here because we're good church-going Christians," he said and glanced over at Joe, who made the sign of the cross on himself and said, "Praise Jesus."

"So when we stood up to pay the bar tab"—Pop-Pop started laughing—"the bartender took one look at our outfits and said—" Pop-Pop and Joe began laughing, which made Maureen laugh, and even though they were the only ones who knew the story, all the other adults, who had now formed a tight circle around Pop-Pop-with-the-Chi-Chi and Joe and were holding their clear and amber drinks, started laughing too.

"Spit it out!" someone yelled.

"The bartender took one look at us and said—" Pop-Pop was laughing so much, he had to wipe a tear from his eye. "He said, 'It's OK, Father, we don't charge for clergy'!"

The whole room seemed to erupt with laughter, like the end of a fireworks show when everything gets real chaotic.

Then Pop-Pop sputtered through his tears of laughter, "So we said, 'Bless you, my son,' and went to the next bar!" He held his arm out and made the sign of the cross in the air, which made the room erupt in laughter again.

Finally, Pop-Pop said, "We got free drinks for the rest of the night, and we've never gone out without our lucky black shirts and crosses since."

A final eruption of laughter petered out as the grown-ups wiped tears from their eyes and quietly said things like *Oh, that's funny* or *Oh Lord* and *What a couple of characters.*

Pam and I got to stay up way past our bedtime, which felt very special. The last people at the party were Mom and Dad, Rosalie and Ted, Maureen, Pop-Pop-with-the-Chi-Chi, and Joe.

Ted was telling a funny story about being a boy in Catholic school. "Those nuns scared the shit out of me," he said. "Especially Sister Mary Eloise. If you crossed her, she'd whack you with a paddle. Even if you so much as *looked* at her wrong!"

Someone said, "That's how it was in those days." I thought of the Board of Education paddle I had seen on Mr. Sarochek's desk and wondered if he ever used it.

"She was our music teacher, and I was so scared of her that I practiced all the words to 'I Am Jesus's Little Lamb' until I could sing that hymn in my sleep! I still remember every word," continued Ted.

Maureen, whose mascara was smeared down her cheeks by now because of all the laughing she was doing, grabbed a ukulele from a pile of our instruments and thrust it toward Ted.

"Sing it! Sing it!" she demanded.

Ted grabbed the ukulele, and the crowd got quiet. He began to strum the instrument, producing a sound that made it clear that he didn't know how to actually play the ukulele, and started singing.

> I am Jesus's little lamb,
> Ever glad at heart I am.

The crowd began laughing. Ted continued.

> For my Shepherd gently guides me,
> Knows my need, and well provides me.
> Loves me every day the same,
> Even calls me by my name.

The room erupted in laughter again, and everyone started chanting, "Ted! Ted! Ted! Ted!" and laughing some more.

I was so tired, I could barely keep my eyes open, but I didn't want to go to bed because this night felt very special. It was the first time that we got to have fun with the grown-ups instead of being made to sit at the kids' table or being told to *go to bed* or *go play outside.*

It felt like being let into a secret world, and I wanted to hang on tight to the feeling. For just one night, the grown-ups didn't speak in hushed tones and weren't careful about what they said in front of us. For this one night, everyone was just happy and free. It was how us kids felt in the trailer neighborhood after the flood. But the flood wasn't over for all these grown-ups when we were in the trailers. Maybe, I hoped, all the Christmas decorations and the Christmas party with the delicious food and everyone laughing so much they were crying meant that the flood was finally over for everyone, including Mom and Dad.

I soaked in every minute of that night.

# 37

# January 1976

After we moved to the Gibson Avenue house and stopped going to church on Sundays, we saw a lot more of Momo. Momo spent her weeks working at the Planters Peanuts factory or all alone in her one-bedroom apartment with painted cinder block walls and ugly carpets that weren't shag like ours, but low pile and formed into squiggly shapes that looked like intestines. The smoke from the packs and packs of Salem menthol cigarettes that Momo smoked stained the walls, giving them a yellow tone, and there were a few burn marks in the carpet from lit cigarettes that had dropped there and hadn't been picked up fast enough. But from the time she was a baby, Pam spent every Saturday at Momo's for a sleepover.

Once or twice Momo agreed to let me sleep over too, but I had to sleep on a foldout cot that squeaked and groaned when I rolled over in my sleep instead of in the bed with Momo, which was where Pam slept. I mostly didn't mind because on those few Saturday nights, I felt a little special too. Momo served us dinner on foldout TV trays, and we sat down on the couch or the recliner to watch *Hee-Haw*, *Mary Tyler Moore*, and *The Bob Newhart Show*. After dinner, Momo poured

Cheez Doodles and Wise potato chips and malted milk balls into little serving bowls, and we settled down for my favorite program, *The Carol Burnett Show*. I thought Carol Burnett was the funniest woman to ever have lived, and she was the reason I decided that I wanted to be funny too and make people laugh like she made me laugh.

On Sundays, after we stopped going to church once Mom gave the monsignor a *talking to*, we started going to Momo's for Sunday dinner instead. Dad didn't come to Momo's, just like he didn't go to church, because golf was still *his church* and he didn't see any reason to stop going.

Paul and Jessie, who almost never had sleepovers at Momo's, came to Sunday dinner with me and Mom unless it was a special weekend where I got to stay at Momo's with Pam. Dinner was usually a roast chicken with gravy and vegetables out of a can.

After we finished eating dinner, we'd all sit on the couches and chairs in front of the television and watch the Sunday noon matinee, which was always an Abbott and Costello movie.

I thought Lou Costello was the funniest man to ever have lived, but I especially liked him because like me, he was scared of monsters and was always meeting one monster or another in those movies. Lou Costello met Frankenstein one week, Dracula the next, the Mummy the next, and the Wolf Man the next. Watching those movies helped me feel less afraid of monsters because whenever a scary monster came into my mind at night, I could immediately picture Lou Costello trying to scream but not being able to or finding out that the shoulder he was grasping was the Mummy's and not, as he thought, Bud Abbott's, and that made me laugh instead of feel scared.

I decided that I really wanted to meet Lou Costello someday, so I could tell him how much he helped me feel less afraid of the monsters that always came to my head at night. So one day, after we arrived back at Gibson Avenue and after Mom put Jessica in her room for a nap, I found her sitting on the living room love seat, reading one of her disgusting books.

"Mom?" I said as I sat down next to her.

"Mmmmm?" she said without looking up from her book.

"I want to meet Lou Costello. Do you think I can?" I asked.

"He died a long time ago, Suzanne," Mom said, looking up. Then she went back to reading her book.

I was crushed. It didn't seem fair to me that someone who was so funny and seemed so alive in the movies that I loved to watch was not alive. I didn't understand how someone that I watched being so alive and funny every week on television was gone forever. Mom didn't seem sad or confused at all.

I started getting so sad that some tears dripped out of my eyes, and I sniffled. Mom looked up at me.

"Suzanne, what's the matter?"

"I'm sad that Lou Costello is dead," I told her.

"Dying isn't so bad," she informed me.

"How do *you* know?" I asked her.

"Because I died for a little bit when I was fourteen years old," Mom said matter-of-factly.

This confused me even more.

"But you're still here!" I said. "Why isn't Lou Costello here?" I was feeling confused *and* angry now.

"Because I didn't *die* die. I died for just a while," Mom explained.

"What does *that* mean?" I needed her to explain more.

"Well, one Saturday when I was fourteen, me and my friend Suzie, who you were named after, decided to walk downtown to go to Woolworths," she began. "We walked along the sidewalk. I was on the outside, closest to the street," she continued. "All of a sudden, a drunk driver came speeding up over the curb and hit me."

"What happened? Were you hurt?" I asked.

"Oh yes! I flew way up into the air like a rag doll and landed with a thud in the middle of a busy intersection." She seemed to be thinking back, reliving the moment. "That's when things got very peaceful. I floated above everything and was just looking down at everything. I was watching what was going on," she told me.

"Like a ghost?" I asked.

"Not quite," she said, pausing. She seemed to drift off in a memory; then she said, "I just felt very peaceful. But down below me, it was a lot of chaos. I could see myself lying there in the middle of the street. I was totally still. The man who hit me was crying into his hands. An ambulance arrived, and then Momo arrived. She ran to me and collapsed onto her knees next to me; she was screaming and crying. I had never heard a noise like that come from anyone!"

"Then want happened?" I was riveted.

"I just kept saying, 'I'm OK! I'm right here! Don't cry; I'm OK,' but no one could hear me."

"Then you came alive again?" I asked.

"No. I watched as Momo continued to scream and cry over me in the ambulance until we got to the hospital. Then they had to take me to the operating room, and Momo was still screaming and screaming. I kept trying to tell her that I was OK, but she didn't hear me."

"Then what?"

"Then I was above everything again in the operating room, and I could see them cutting my favorite sweater off me with a pair of scissors. I kept trying to yell for them to stop; I was so mad they were ruining that sweater!" It seemed like she was still angry about them cutting her sweater.

"The next thing I knew, I woke up in my hospital bed, and that was it." She paused for a moment, lost in the memory again. "I never told anyone about that except your dad. And now you." She looked exhausted.

"So you think you *actually* died?" I asked.

"Oh, I know I did," she said. "That's why I'm not afraid of dying. It felt very pleasant, actually."

We sat in silence for a good long time.

"Mom?" I finally asked.

"Yes?"

"Do you think Lou Costello is watching us and feeling peaceful?" I would have felt a lot better about Lou Costello being dead if I could think of him like that.

"Yes, he probably is," she assured me.

After this conversation with Mom, I had some questions for God. Why did Mom come back after being dead but Lou Costello didn't? Do you just float around after you die and watch what's going on down below? Or do you go someplace else after a while? Why does *anyone* have to die? I hated that God never answered my questions, especially really important questions like these.

Then I started to think about Mom and Dad dying, and I got a feeling inside my body that I didn't like at all, so I decided to think about
rocking Jessie in the rocking chair and singing bedtime songs to her so
I could have the good feeling instead, and that worked.

# 38

# *February 1976*

The year 1976 was called the *Bicentennial*, which meant that America was two hundred years old. This was obviously a very big deal because no one could stop talking about it and it was all over the television all the time.

Jimmy Carter had been nominated as the next presidential candidate to run against Gerald Ford, who was president only because Richard Nixon resigned. Dad called Richard Nixon a crook, and he said Gerald Ford couldn't *find his way out of a paper bag*. I guess Jimmy Carter was the best guy for the job even though everyone talked about him being a peanut farmer. I wondered if he had ever heard of Planters Peanuts.

*Happy Days* and *Laverne and Shirley* were our favorite television shows, and Richie, Potsie, Ralph, and the Fonz gave me and Pam a glimpse of what lay ahead of us—adolescence.

I was intimidated by teenagers and steered clear of the middle school girls that I saw each morning walking to school. The bus stop to the middle school was on the corner of Rutter Avenue and Dorrance Street, which was where Rutter Ave. Elementary School was too. Each morning, teenage girls gathered in small groups. They wore makeup and short skirts with bare legs in the warm weather and tights covering their legs in the cold weather. They wore tight sweaters that showed off their small breasts and whispered and giggled with one another in a way that made me feel like along with their developing bodies came a secret that only *they* would understand.

I tried not to look at these girls, and they thankfully had no interest in me. But I was also intrigued because this strange new place was just ahead of me, and I wasn't sure I wanted to go there. What was it like to not feel like a kid anymore? Would I still like playing with Pam and Chris and Jamie and Paul and now our new friend John from around the corner? I wished I could know without going there myself.

There were things I did like about getting a little older. I liked feeling grown-up enough to choose a prime-time television show to watch, and it felt even more special when Mom and Dad watched and laughed along with us. Dad and Paul loved when the Fonz put his thumbs up and said *aaaaeeeeeeyyyy*, and they began using that as a way of saying hello to one another.

But there were also tales of the perils of being a teenager that permeated these last years of pure childhood. On the news, we heard about girls like Patty Hearst getting herself brainwashed and being forced to do things that were against the law. We heard about Karen Ann Quinlan, who drank too much alcohol and took too many pills at a party one night and was now a vegetable and probably would be allowed to die any day because her parents wanted to *pull the plug.*

I wasn't sure how you could wash someone's brain without taking it out of their head, which was impossible, or how a human being could turn into a vegetable or what *pulling the plug* meant, but the stories of these girls made me very frightened of becoming a teenager.

As frightening as the stories of Patty Hearst and Karen Ann Quinlan were, they couldn't even touch the terror I felt when I found Mom and Dad's copy of the book *Helter Skelter.* I didn't read the book; I just flipped to the middle where there were several pages of black-and-white photographs of crime scenes and groups of crazy-looking teenage girls with long hair.

These teenagers killed some famous people and wrote on the walls in blood and shaved their heads and carved things in their foreheads, and now that Lou Costello had helped me feel a little less afraid of monsters, I had new things to be terrified of, including teenagers and Mom's health.

One day after school, I was in the sunroom practicing *the bridge* shuffle with a deck of cards. I had been secretly practicing ever since the day on Aunt Sadie's porch, and now I was *very* good at it! After about a dozen shuffles, I looked up, and Pam was standing between the two open French doors. I hadn't heard her walk in.

"Hey," I said, then casually showed her how great I was at the bridge without looking away from her. I kept my eyes locked on Pam so I could see the jealousy in her eyes.

My excellent bridge shuffle made Pam turn white because she was as pale as a ghost. I felt a little bit bad.

"I can teach you!" I offered.

She somberly said, "Come with me. I need to show you something." She remained white.

"What's the matter?" I asked her.

"Just follow me," she repeated.

"Where?"

"Upstairs," she said.

There was obviously a very serious secret that Pam wanted me to know, which made me feel special and important. "OK," I said, leaving my cards on the table and following her.

She led me up to the bathroom, pulled me in, closed the door, and locked it. The royal blue basin of the sink was streaked with toothpaste dribble that had dried to the sides.

"You better sit down," she said, pointing to the squishy toilet seat that was also royal blue. Mom had replaced the hard toilet seats with squishy foam seats that were covered in shiny latex and made a *pfffffft* sound when you sat on them.

I closed the lid of the toilet and sat down. *Pfffffft.*

"What?" I was impatient for her to get to the secret.

"Look what I found in the wastebasket," she said, pulling out a big wad of toilet paper that was obviously wrapped around something to hide it.

"What is it?" I asked impatiently.

"Just wait a minute!" she said with irritation. "I'm going to show you!"

Pam slowly unrolled the toilet paper and revealed something rolled up like a *Yodel*, which was a chocolate sponge cake, spread with cream and rolled up like a pinwheel. It was one of my favorite special treats.

But this was not a treat. When Pam unrolled the thick pad, we saw blood. Lots of blood.

I gasped.

"What *is* that?" I wanted to know.

"I think it's from Mom," Pam said. I thought she was going to cry.

"Is she dying?"

"I think she might be!" Pam said.

We both sat in the bathroom, me on the squishy toilet seat, Pam on the floor. Both of us had tears in our eyes.

"What are we gonna do?" I wanted to know. "Should we tell Dad?" I suggested.

"I don't know," Pam said. This was the first time Pam seemed as scared as me about something. Usually she wasn't scared, and I could count on her to know what to do.

Mom didn't look or act sick. Maybe she just had a cut somewhere and it healed up. I decided to make a suggestion to Pam and see what she thought.

"Maybe she just cut herself," I suggested.

"Maybe," Pam said. "It's a lot of blood." Then she paused and looked at the unrolled pad with the blood on it. "And it smells terrible!" she added.

"Yeah," I said. "I'm worried."

"Me too," Pam said. "I don't want Mom to die." She was crying now.

"Me neither," I said. I knew that Mom already died once. I didn't think God would give her another chance to come back if she died again. But I didn't tell Pam that. Instead, I said, "Let's wait and see how she seems."

Pam said, "All right," and we made a pact to keep a close eye on Mom.

The next day in school, I couldn't stop thinking about Mom and the bloody thing we found and if I had to start preparing to be an orphan again, at least a half orphan. I didn't much feel like doing anything at recess, and when we went to Jamie's house for lunch and to watch

*Batman and Robin*, I could tell that Pam's mind was occupied too because she was more quiet than usual, and she didn't act irritated with me once.

When the school day ended and all the kids went into the coatroom to put on their coats, hats, gloves, and scarves so they would be warm enough on the walk home, Kim Manganella called my name from across the coatroom.

*Me?* I thought. Kim Manganella was the one girl in the class who wore a bra. Kim Manganella was more like the teenagers that I saw waiting for the middle school bus than a fifth-grade kid like the rest of us. She didn't run around playing games at recess but instead snuck around the corner of the building with Jim McAvoy, who was the handsomest boy in the class. All the kids called Jim McAvoy *Leonard*, for no particular reason that I could tell.

Kim and Jim were the only boyfriend-girlfriend couple in the fifth grade, and the rest of us observed them with curiosity, the way that Jacques Cousteau observed underwater sea life in the specials we saw on TV. We were interested but didn't want to get too close.

So when Kim Manganella called to me in the coatroom that day, I couldn't for the life of me think of what she would want. She hadn't said a word to me since I'd started at Rutter Ave. that fall. I didn't even think she knew my name.

I pointed to myself and mouthed, *Me?*

"I need to talk to you," she said. Her tone was serious.

What on earth could Kim Manganella possibly have to talk to me about? She was an untouchable fifth grader. Our worlds did not coincide. She was more teenager; I was more kid. My heart started to beat fast.

"OK," I said.

I must have looked like a trapped wild animal because as Kim walked toward me, she said, "Calm down. I'm not going to hurt you or anything." She reminded me of Pinky Tuscadero from *Happy Days*. She seemed way older than a fifth grader. Kim *knew* things that the rest of us did not.

All the kids had grabbed their winter gear and gone by now. Kim got real close to me. My palms started sweating.

Kim brought her mouth so close to my ear that I could feel her breath send warm air directly into it. Her voice was several decibels lower than those of the rest of the kids.

"What I'm about to tell you is for your own good," Kim began.

*Oh God!* I thought. *What? WHAT?* But I was frozen, and no words came out of my mouth.

"When you get home from school today, tell your mom to take you shopping for a training bra," instructed Kim.

*A training bra?* I thought. *What on earth for?*

"Why?" I managed to spit out.

"Because you're *developing*, and people can see through your shirt. It's *inappropriate*," said Kim. I detected some disgust in her answer.

I was so horrified. I felt ashamed. How many kids had seen my *development* through my shirt?

"OK," I said. "Thank you." And I kind of meant it. If what Kim said was true, then she was the only kid with enough guts to tell me.

"Don't mention it, kid," she said. Then she winked and walked out of the coatroom, where Jim/Leonard McAvoy was waiting to walk her home.

When I got home from school that day, I ran up to my bedroom. Pam was sitting on the bed, propped up with a stack of pillows at her back, and reading a book called *Are You There God? It's Me, Margaret.* It was written by someone named Judy Blume.

I stood in the doorway, trying to think of a way to tell her what Kim Manganella had told me in the coatroom that day. Finally, Pam put the book on her lap and looked up.

"What?" she said.

"Pam?" I said, wearing a look on my face that told her I had something serious to talk about.

"Suzie, what's wrong?" she asked, sounding concerned. I had thought about telling Mom what Kim Manganella said, but the idea felt mortifying. And scary. I decided I would go to Pam. She would know what to do.

"Do you think I need a training bra?" I asked.

"Why?"

"Just, do you?" I wanted to hear it from Pam.

"I don't know," Pam quipped. "Why are you asking *me*?"

"Because Kim Manganella told me I needed to buy a training bra," I admitted.

"*Okaaaayyy? Soooooo?*" Pam was waiting for me to say more.

"So, I don't want to tell Mom, and I don't know anything about training bras," I said. I made my way to the bed and plopped down on the mattress by Pam's feet.

"It's no big deal," she said. "It's OK." Then she shifted one of her feet to make contact with my hip. I felt better instantly.

"Do *you* have one?" I asked.

"Yes," she said. "But I don't wear it much. I don't really need to," she added.

"Do you think *I* need one?" I asked.

"If you *want* one. But you don't have to wear it all the time," she told me.

"Did Mom buy it for you?" I wanted to know.

"No," Pam said. "Marcy Williams and I went shopping for them at the Kiddie Shoppe."

I sat quietly for a while. Pam sat up and scooched next to me.

"Do you want me to take you there and help you buy one?" she offered. "It's not that bad."

"Would you?" I asked.

"Sure," she said. "It's really not that bad."

We sat for a while in silence. I was feeling glad that Pam was the first person I told about what Kim said to me in the coatroom.

Pam lifted the book off her lap and showed me the cover. "I've never ever read a book like this in my life," she informed me.

"What do you mean by that?" I asked.

"It's hard to explain," she said. "You just have to read it."

She began telling me more about the book and about the girl named Margaret, who was the main character in the book and was exactly Pam's age and in the same grade. She told me that Margaret was waiting for something called a *period* and that all girls get a period eventually. She explained what a period was, and the whole thing sounded dreadful to me. I thought a training bra was bad, but this sounded a thousand times worse!

Pam looked at me with a goofy grin. I looked back at her, confused.

She raised her eyebrows and said, "Get it?" I didn't.

"What are you *talking* about?" I said. She was acting crazy.

"Suzie!" she said, with exasperation. "Mom isn't dying *after all!*"

I hadn't the faintest idea what she was talking about until she said, "Those things we found in the wastebasket? They were Mom's period!"

I had to admit, I was glad to hear the news that Mom wasn't dying, but now I didn't know what to think! *Dying* blood was scary, but *period* blood seemed much worse. Just in a different way.

"That's not happening to *me*, is it?" This day was getting worse and worse.

"Of course it is. You're a *girl*, aren't you?"

My shoulders slumped. I hung my head low. I took in as deep a breath as I could and blew it out. I resisted the urge to slip my thumb into my mouth. Mom said I was getting a little old for that and that the gap in my two front teeth couldn't be fixed until I stopped the habit. We still had the liquid that made my thumb taste like earwax, so I silently vowed to paint it on my thumbnail that night.

Lately, I had been keeping my thumb-sucking mostly a secret. So I decided I had to also keep my quitting-my-thumb-sucking a secret. I considered sitting my family down for a family meeting to tell them that I still sucked my thumb, just so I could tell them that I quit all by myself. But when I showed Pam how great I was at the bridge, she didn't seem to care at all, so I decided I'd rather keep it to myself, which felt better than feeling really proud about something and finding out that no one really cared.

"Don't worry," Pam said. "I'll probably get my period before you do."

That made me feel a little bit better. When we were little, having an older sister who did things first like receive First Holy Communion and have a birthday every year a week before mine felt unfair. But now that we were getting a little older, having an older sister who did things first like buy a training bra and get a period felt very good. I knew that Pam would tell me all about it and how it felt and if it was scary or not.

I looked at Pam and smiled. "OK," I said.

"OK," she said, and she gave one nod of her head as if to say, *And that's all we'll say on the matter.*

I went downstairs, feeling relieved that if Mom was down there,

I wouldn't have to bring up the subject of training bras or periods or anything else like that. I had a big sister, and that was all I needed.

The next day Maureen brought her daughter Johnna over to play. Johnna had become Jessie's best friend, and they played together now almost every day. I could hear the two girls playing in the basement and decided to go see them.

As I rounded the corner, I found Mom sitting in the kitchen at the table with Maureen. Maureen was holding an ice pack to her eye with one hand and smoking a cigarette with the other. Her lip looked split.

"What happened to *you*?" I asked her.

"Oh, I walked into a wall!" she told me. "I'm such a klutz." She laughed.

Mom looked very serious, which was a look she had when she was working on changing something she didn't think was fair, like complaining about the Westmoreland Club not letting women in.

"Go check on the girls," Mom told me. "And don't make a big deal about the socks," she added.

"I won't!" I barked.

The week before, when Maureen brought Johnna over to play with Jessie, Johnna's once long blond hair was chopped into a short Dorothy Hamill bob.

In my opinion, the only reason to watch the Winter Olympics that year was Dorothy Hamill, and every girl wanted a haircut like hers. So when Johnna asked her mom to get her long blond hair cut into a Dorothy Hamill–style bob that was what she did. Except it didn't really look like Dorothy Hamill's hair; instead, it just looked like a boy's haircut.

After Johnna got her hair cut, Jessie begged and begged Mom to take her to get the same style, and so she finally did. But hours after Jessie's hair had been cut short, she started screaming and crying that she wanted her hair long again, and no matter how much Mom tried to explain that you could cut your hair short but you couldn't cut your hair long, Jessie just didn't want to hear it.

So, to get Jessie to stop screaming and crying, Mom attached one sock to each side of Jessie's head with a barrette, which satisfied Jessie. But Paul laughed at her one day and made her cry again, so Mom was always reminding us to just act like those socks on the side of Jessie's head were the most normal thing in the world.

*Stop reminding me!* I thought when Mom told me not to make a big deal of the socks. Then I shot Mom a grumpy look and went down to see the girls.

When I landed on the bottom step of the basement, Jessie spotted me and ran into my arms for a hug.

"Play airplane?" she asked. *Airplane* was a game we had come up with where I lay on my back and lifted her up by the stomach on the soles of my feet. Jessie would hold her arms out like an airplane and squeal with delight. We had gotten so good at airplane that she could now stand upright on the soles of my feet as I lifted my legs vertically into the air.

I took turns playing airplane with Jessie and Johnna, who was a lot wobblier than Jessie. We gathered all the couch cushions from the other room around us so that if Johnna fell, which she did, she would land on the soft cushions and wouldn't hurt herself.

Finally, Maureen called for Johnna to go home with her, and Jessie and I continued the game by ourselves.

For once, I was glad I was the middle sister because it felt very good to have an older sister like Pam and it felt wonderful to have a younger baby sister like Jessica. I silently thanked God for putting me in the middle of two sisters, just in case he was still listening.

# 39

# June 1976

By June of 1976, life was just about back to normal. People still talked about the flood, but they didn't have the same sad and tired sound to their voices. It was the same way people talked about where they were when they heard that President John F. Kennedy was shot. Like it was a time in their lives that they would never ever forget, and they only had to start talking about it for all of the memories to come flooding back and they could almost relive it, but this time they knew how everything ended.

The world was gearing up for the Summer Olympics, and America's July the Fourth Bicentennial celebration was all anyone seemed to be talking about. Jamie's mom, Marty, had a new rich boyfriend, and she was moving Jamie to his big house in a place called Bear Creek, which was far away and meant that we had to go back to *making plans*.

But for one more month, Jamie was still in Kingston, and Pam and I still liked to play outside with Paul and Christopher and Jamie and our neighbor John, who was just about the nicest kid I knew and lived so close to us, we never had to *make plans*.

One day, we were all playing in our backyard when John cut through the back of Mrs. Egan's garage and hopped the fence into our yard.

"Hey!" John called to us.

"How come you're alone?" Pam asked. John always had a sibling or two in tow with him when he hopped over the fence to see who was around.

"I'm sick of them," he said. "They're just a bunch of babies. I'm tired of always having to watch them."

"Oh, I *know* what you *mean*," said Jamie. "Kids are *exhausting*!"

Paul furrowed his brow and said, "*You're* a kid!"

"Yeah!" said Christopher. "And you're an only child like me!"

Just then, the tall pine tree in our yard caught John's eye.

"Hey! We should climb that tree!" he said with excitement.

"We can't," I said. "The branches are too high to reach."

It was true. The first six feet or so on the trunk of that tree had no branches whatsoever. You would have to be ten feet tall to reach the lowest branch and hoist yourself up.

John surveyed the tree for several minutes. "Hmmmmmmmm," he said.

Pam, Paul, Christopher, Jamie, and I were just as happy playing in the shade *under* that tree. We still played the occasional game of house, collecting pine cones as food to stockpile for the coming hurricane, or we used the trunk of the tree for home base in games of freeze tag. We thought the tree would be fun to climb, but we resigned ourselves to the fact that it just wasn't possible and found other ways to have fun.

John seemed determined to figure out a way to climb the tree.

"I have an idea," he said. "Wait here." Then he disappeared back behind Mrs. Egan's garage.

About twenty minutes later, John returned with a few two-by-fours, a hammer, and some long nails.

"What's *that* for?" asked Jamie, seeming part excited and part apprehensive.

John explained that we should nail the two-by-fours into the trunk of the tree to make a ladder. He said we could climb up the two-by-fours until we reached the branches and could climb the rest of the way up the tree.

I thought John was the smartest kid I knew. We got right to work. We took turns holding the pieces of wood against the tree trunk while

John nailed in several long nails. Once the first couple of boards were nailed in, we needed a volunteer to climb on the boards that were already nailed and nail in the higher boards.

"I'll do it," I said.

Pam was immediately opposed. "Suzie, don't," she said. "You could get hurt."

Normally, I would have felt very irritated with Pam's insistence on safety. But after our conversation about training bras and periods, I decided I would listen to her a little more so that she would still talk to me about the things I would need to know about getting older and not think that I would just ignore her.

"I promise I won't get hurt," I tried to reassure her.

"You could fall and break your arm. Then we'll *never* be allowed to climb the tree!" Pam insisted.

She did have a point. If I fell and hurt myself, we'd have to tell Mom, or worse, Dad. Dad would rip the boards off the tree, and we'd never be allowed to climb it again. Now that John had a plan, I was *dying* to climb that tree.

"So, who's gonna do it?" I conceded.

"I'll do it," said John.

"Yeah, *you* do it!" shouted Paul. "Let's go; we wanna climb that tree!" He jiggled with excited anticipation.

It was a group effort. John climbed on top of the first board. Pam passed the board to John, and I handed him one nail at a time. Paul, Christopher, and Jamie shouted encouragement as John nailed in one board after the other until he reached the first set of branches.

"I'm going up!" he yelled.

"Me too!" shouted Paul.

"Paul, wait!" warned Pam, but John, then Paul, then me, then Chris, and Jamie all hurried up those boards one after the other and hoisted ourselves onto the first branches. We made our way up, up, up that gigantic tree, all the way to the top where the branches were thin and the tree swayed this way and that in the breeze. Sap stuck to our hands and adhered to our clothes.

"*Woooooooooow!*" exclaimed Paul.

"Pam! Come up here!" shouted Jamie.

John said, "Look; you can see the courthouse and the Market Street Bridge. It feels like you can see the whole world from up here!"

And it did.

We all got quiet and looked out at the expanse before us. We could see the whole valley.

And at the base of the mountains was the Susquehanna River, winding its way right down the middle of the valley, through neighborhoods and under bridges. It looked small and thin, like a piece of yarn that had fallen on the floor.

I looked at the dikes, trying to imagine a river so wide it went all the way up and over the top of them. It seemed impossible. I looked at the houses and the churches and the hospitals and the new indoor shopping mall, and I couldn't tell which parts of town were *from the flood* and which weren't. It all had been cleaned and rebuilt, and everyone had moved back.

I looked at John. His eyes were wide with wonder, even though he wasn't *from the flood* and probably wasn't thinking the same things that I was thinking, so I decided not to say anything to him about the river and the flood and all the homes and churches and libraries and businesses that it had destroyed.

Maybe John really *was* a nice kid, and maybe there were a lot of other nice kids around who weren't *from the flood* too. I just needed to stop caring so much about that so I could find them.

When I walked in through the back sliding door, I heard the kitchen phone ring. I lurched to pick it up. Before I could say *hello*, I heard Mom say *hello* from the phone that she had answered from her bedroom.

"It's Marty," I heard Jamie's mom say.

"It happened again," Mom said.

"Oh fuck," said Marty.

I couldn't believe my ears. I knew Marty had a dirty mouth, but I had never in my life heard someone use *that* word, let alone one of Mom's friends! I was shocked beyond shocked. I felt dumbstruck. My opinion of Marty was instantly changed. She felt crude and gruff. Tough and certainly not ladylike. I wondered what Mom thought about this.

"Yeah. When she dropped Johnna off this morning, she wouldn't take off her sunglasses. I could see the bruising anyway, and she had a split lip," Mom told Marty.

"So, are you doing it?" Marty asked.

"Definitely," Mom said. "That asshole has thrown his last damn punch."

*Doing what?* I wondered. *What asshole?*

# 40

# *July 1976*

The next month, Jamie had moved into the big mansion of dirty-mouth Marty's boyfriend in the country. We got to see him for the Fourth of July Bicentennial celebration in Kirby Park, but after that I wouldn't see him until our trip to the Jersey Shore in August. We all couldn't wait for the shore because it was a time when we were all together again and it felt good, the way it felt in the trailer park.

Rosalie and Ted, Linda the feminist and her friend Jenny, our neighbors John and Christopher, and Pop-Pop-with-the-Chi-Chi, even Uncle Ray and, on very special occasions, Aunt Sadie popped in and out of our Gibson Avenue house. Even if Mom or Dad wasn't home, everyone walked right in without knocking, made themselves a snack or poured a glass of ice tea or diet soda, which was becoming very popular, and stayed a bit to chat with whoever was around. Even Char came once to visit with her baby, who was just a little younger than Jessie, and even though Char didn't have the same magic that she had when she was our babysitter, it still felt like when we lived in the trailer, and it made me happy that our Gibson Ave. neighborhood was more like the trailer neighborhood than the Walden Park neighborhood.

Lately, Maureen was coming to visit more and more because

Jessica loved to play with Johnna more than anyone else. Sometimes Maureen even came by herself when Mom wasn't home and sat at the kitchen table, smoking one cigarette after another. On those days, she was real quiet and didn't much want to talk.

One Wednesday morning, I woke up to Pam nudging my shoulder to wake me.

"Suzie, get up!" she said urgently.

"What's wrong?" I asked groggily.

"Come look," Pam said. She went over to the bedroom window, which faced the street. I slowly slid out of bed and joined her.

We could see down the street a bit to the front of Maureen's house. There was a big U-Haul truck in front of the house on the street. The back of the truck was wide open, and we could see that a few pieces of furniture had been placed in there.

"Let's go spy!" Pam suggested.

I loved when Pam had an idea that was sneaky and she wanted me to join.

"Yeah!" I said enthusiastically.

We went downstairs and outside, still wearing our nightgowns. We crouched down behind the front steps of our house and peeked out just enough to see and hear what was going on.

Mom and Maureen came out of the house together, carrying a large armchair. It looked like Dad's special La-Z-Boy recliner.

I heard Mom say, "How much time do we have left?"

Maureen said, "He'll be home for lunch in about an hour and a half."

"Let's pack up as much as we can in the next hour. You don't want to have to come back here once he sees that you and the kids are gone," Mom said.

Maureen looked at Mom. She had tears coming down her cheeks. "I couldn't do this without you, Peggy," she said. "Thank you." Then she hugged Mom.

Mom pulled out of the hug and grabbed Maureen by both shoulders, looking straight into her face. "Enough is enough. He's not laying another finger on you *or* your kids," she said.

Maureen nodded.

"Let's get moving. We still need to fit the beds. There'll be time for tears later." And she walked back into the house.

Pam said, "Come on," and she started back into the house.

When we got into the entryway, I asked Pam why Mom was helping Maureen move everything out of the house.

"Because her husband is mean," Pam said.

I thought about this for a moment. Sometimes Dad was mean when he lost his temper and scolded us. Did that mean that Mom was going to move us out of our house too? The thought upset me very much. Worrying about being an orphan that night on the porch in Mountain Top was terrible, and I didn't want to have to worry about that again.

"Where will they live?" I asked.

Pam said, "Mom helped Maureen find an apartment a couple of blocks away. On Rutter Avenue."

"How do you know all this?" I asked. I didn't know a thing about any of it.

"Momo told me," Pam said.

Of course. Mom told Momo, and Momo told Pam. But no one told me.

# August 1976

Everyone was excited for our trip to the Jersey Shore, which always happened right in the middle of August. Mom and Rosalie had invited Linda and Jenny and another mom named JuleAnne, who had four kids, along with dirty-mouth Marty and Jamie. Dad and Ted weren't even going to come this year, not even for one or two days. We always had so much fun with all those kids together that we didn't really mind if Dad and Ted didn't want to be there. We always drove to the shore on a Saturday and drove back home the next Saturday.

The day before we planned to leave was a Friday. Us kids had been at John's house playing freeze tag that morning. Mom could call us home just by standing on our back porch, which was what she did.

"Pam! Suzie! Paul! Come have some lunch!" We heard her.

For lunch Mom gave us peanut butter and jelly sandwiches with Wise potato chips. We started talking excitedly about what we were going to do at the shore.

"Can I swim out deep?" Paul asked.

"Can we go to the boardwalk?" Pam asked.

"Can we get saltwater taffy?" I asked.

Mom's answer was always, "We'll see."

There was a lull in the chatter.

"Where's Jessie?" I asked.

"She's napping," said Mom. Then she said, "It's been quite a long time. Can one of you go up and peek in at her?"

"I will!" I said excitedly. I loved Jessie, and I especially loved when I peeked into her room in the morning and saw her sitting up and smiling in her little bed, which by now was not quite a crib but not quite a big-kid's bed. I loved Jessie's smile because her dimples were so cute and her smile made my heart feel like it was smiling, which I guessed was what Dad felt because he did a lot more smiling after Baby Jessica was born.

When I got to the top of the stairs and just outside her room, I put an ear to her door to see if she was awake and babbling in her bed. It was quiet.

I very gently turned the doorknob so I wouldn't wake her if she was still asleep. The door made a low creaking sound as I slowly opened it enough to poke my head in.

I peered in and looked into Jessie's bed. It was empty.

"Mooooooooooooooom!" I screamed. "Come up here! Jessie is *gone!*"

I didn't even hear Mom's footsteps before she was in the room and screaming her head off. I had never seen Mom so hysterical.

"Oh my God! Oh my God!" Mom screamed. "Find her!"

Pam came upstairs with a confused look on her face. "What's happening?" she said, sounding scared.

"We can't find Jessica," I informed her.

"What do you mean you can't find her?" Pam asked.

"She's just *gone!*" I urgently said. "When I came up here, she wasn't in her room or her bed."

"We need to find her!" Pam said frantically. "You check the attic; I'll go downstairs with Mom!"

*Of course,* I thought. *Send me up to the scary attic by myself while you search with Mom like you're one of the grown-ups.*

But I didn't have time to wallow in the unfairness of having an older sister who bossed me around.

Mom had already gone downstairs, and I heard her shouting frantically to Dad on the phone. She slammed down the receiver and shouted to no one in particular, "Your father is coming!"

Mom and Pam then started walking through the house, screaming, "Jessica! Jessica!"

I went into our bedroom to access the creepy attic. There was a door in our bedroom, next to the closet that we kept closed at all times because I was scared that the monsters from Abbott and Costello or a Sleestak, a creepy creature from my favorite morning show, *The Land of the Lost*, would bust through that door in the middle of the night and rip my body to pieces.

I said a quick prayer to God, hoping he was still watching me, flung the door open, and ran up the stairs to the attic. When I neared the top of the creaky wooden stairs, I felt a wall of heat hit my face. It felt like it was one hundred degrees.

I ignored the heat and any potential hidden monsters because little Jessie was missing and I *had* to find her. I just didn't know what I would do if Jessie was suddenly gone, like Lou Costello was gone. Even if Jessie was hovering over our screaming family like Mom had been hovering over a screaming Momo, I didn't care. I wanted her here, with me, cuddling in bed or playing airplane.

"Jessica!" I screamed. I considered that maybe she was hiding to be funny, and that made me feel mad at her. "*Jessica!* If this is a joke, it is *not* funny!" I shouted sternly.

Jessica still didn't emerge.

I went back downstairs, and Dad was there. Mom and Dad had gone out back, and now everyone, including Paul, was frantically running around and checking every corner of the house and yard for Jessica. We couldn't find her anywhere.

I went out back to join Mom and Dad.

"I didn't leave the house. *I barely left the kitchen!*" Mom was saying to Dad through tears. "Oh Jesus, Bobby. Where *is* she?" she added, her voice becoming high pitched and frantic sounding.

"OK, OK," Dad said. "Let's think." Dad paused, to think. "She could be hiding somewhere in the house. Or maybe she went to Maureen's old house?"

The house Mom helped Maureen move out of was two doors down, and it was now just Maureen's husband's house. He lived there alone.

Maybe Jessica went there to find Johnna, not knowing where Maureen and her kids were now living?

"I'll go check," said Mom.

"Can I come?" I asked.

From one corner of the yard, Pam yelled, "I'll go!"

"No!" I said firmly. "*I'll* go!"

Mom said, "Both of you go. If she's not there, I'm calling the police."

Pam and I ran from the backyard, through the side yard to the front of the house. We took a sharp left and ran past our front stairs, through the front yard, through Diane and her doctor husband's front yard, and through what used to be Maureen's yard but was now Maureen's *asshole husband's* yard to the front door.

We knocked on the door. There was no answer. We knocked and knocked again. No answer.

"Let's check the backyard," Pam suggested.

"OK!" I said. It felt like we were a real team.

We ran around back and didn't see anything but the backyard. Pam went to the back door and knocked again. I joined her, cupped my hands around my eyes, and peered through the glass. No one was there.

Pam said, "No one's here. Let's go back," and we both ran back through the yards to our house.

When we walked into the house, Mom was sitting at the kitchen table with her face in her hands.

"Oh my God, oh my God," she was softly saying to herself. I wondered if Mom prayed to God after she stopped going to church. I hoped that she had, even just a little. Even just on Christmas Eve.

She heard us enter the kitchen, and she looked up from her hands. "Is she there?" she asked, a hint of hope in her voice.

Pam and I silently shook our heads.

Mom suddenly sprang up from the chair, grabbed the headset of the black rotary phone with the extra-long cord that was mounted on the kitchen wall, and dialed 911. Dad, Paul, Pam, and I all gathered around so we could hear.

"911, what's your emergency?" we heard the woman on the other end of the line ask.

"My daughter is missing. She's just a toddler, and we can't find her," Mom said. Then she said, "She was napping in her room, and when we went to check on her, she just wasn't there!"

"OK, ma'am. What's your address?"

Mom answered all the woman's questions, and the woman told Mom to hold on a minute. Then we heard a man come on the phone, asking Mom a bunch of questions. How old was Jessica? What color hair did she have? What was she wearing?

"She was only wearing a diaper and a little T-shirt," Mom told him. She started crying but tried as hard as she could not to make a sound. Then she tried to collect herself.

"Ma'am? Was she riding a big wheel?"

"I don't think so. She's too little. She doesn't know how," Mom said.

The man paused for a moment. "Ma'am? Did your little girl have socks in her hair?"

That instant, we all knew that the girl the man was describing was *our* Jessica!

Mom turned to me and put her hand over the mouthpiece of the phone.

"Suzie!" she said. "Go and see if Paul's big wheel is out there!"

I sprinted to the side yard where Paul kept his big wheel. Nothing was there.

I sprinted back into the kitchen and breathlessly blurted, "It's gone!"

"That's her! That's her! That's *definitely* her!" Mom shouted into the phone. She was crying harder now. "Where is she?"

There was a pause.

"Ma'am, everything is OK. She's OK. Your daughter is enjoying a snack of milk and cookies around the block at a neighbor's. On Westmoreland Street."

Mom cried even harder. "Oh, thank God! Thank God!"

So, I did.

I peered up toward the sky and silently said, *Thank you.*

Mom wrapped her arms around Dad and kept crying into his shoulder, repeating, "They have her! They have her!" Dad was crying a little too, but I could tell he didn't want anyone to see.

"I'm going to get her now," Mom said. Pam and I insisted that we come. Dad stayed home with Paul.

When we got to Westmoreland Street, we saw a police cruiser outside of a house. There was a big wheel out front on the sidewalk.

"There it is," Mom said.

We walked through the front door, and there was Jessie, sitting on a kitchen stool with her feet dangling and her legs swinging to and fro, one sock attached to each side of her head. She munched on a chocolate chip cookie. A half-full glass of milk was sat in front of her.

Mom scooped Jessie into her arms and said, "I have been looking *all over* for you!"

Jessica looked at Mom and said, "I ride bike to Johnna's new house." She was clearly very proud of herself.

"My *goodness*!" Mom said, "But Johnna doesn't live here!"

Mom then looked at the neighbor lady, who had seen Jessie alone on the sidewalk and invited her in before calling the police.

Mom said, "Thank you. Oh my God, thank you."

The woman smiled and said, "Well, when I saw this little toddler with socks in her hair, scooting along on her big wheel in nothing but a diaper, I knew something wasn't right." Then she added, "I have kids too. I would hope anyone would do the same for me!"

There was a pause; then the woman said, "I lost everything in the flood. That really taught me that kindness toward others and helping others is more important than anything else. I guess I'm paying it forward."

Mom looked at the woman, who looked like she was thinking about the kindness of others, and said, "I know what you mean. Us too."

They didn't have to say anything more about the flood after that.

The policeman looked kindly at Jessica and said, "No more going out without your mom or dad, OK?"

Jessie said, "I like cookies," and Mom, Pam, and I all laughed.

The policeman laughed a little and said, "OK, but you're only gonna eat cookies at *your* house, OK? Unless you're with Mom or Dad, right?"

Jessie buried her face in Mom's neck. Mom looked at the police officer and mouthed, *Thank you.*

That night, Mom held Jessie in her arms while she rocked her in the rocking chair and sang her some bedtime songs. Pam and I lay at the top of the stairs, outside the door of Jessie's room, and listened.

We had heard Mom sing "The Teddy Bears' Picnic" to Jessica at least a hundred times, but this time when Mom came to the part about it being better not to go alone and safer to stay at home, we could hear Mom's voice catch.

Just then, I felt Pam take my hand. I turned my head to look at her, and she had tears in her eyes. My eyes started to fill up too.

"I'm glad you're my sister," she said.

"Me too," I said. I really, really meant it.

There was a pause.

Then Pam said, "Let's promise to always look after each other and to always look after Jessie, OK?"

"OK, I promise," I said.

I loved Jessica so much, and I felt I would die of sadness if we hadn't found her that day. And when I imagined something happening to Pam, I also felt I would die of sadness. That was the moment I decided that I didn't want to be anywhere else but in between sisters.

We listened to Mom finish the song, and after that everything was just quiet.

I squeezed Pam's hand. She didn't say anything for a moment or two.

Then I felt her squeeze my hand back.

# Epilogue

One day about ten years ago, Dad asked me and Pam and Paul what our favorite memories of childhood were. We immediately said in unison *the trailer years*. He stared at us in disbelief. Losing everything Dad had built after the flood of 1972 was the most devastating, dark, and difficult time of his life. He could barely wrap his mind around the worst time in his life being the best time in ours, and thus was planted the seed that grew into this book.

It's true that Hurricane Agnes wreaked devastation on our family and our valley. Hundreds of thousands of households were impacted in ways that radically changed their lives.

It wasn't just the furniture and the clothes and the toys and household items that were hard to lose to the flood and its all-destructible mud. Those could all be replaced. It was the things that couldn't be replaced that we all grieved the longest.

For my family, it was the sentimental items like love notes that were neatly folded and tucked into the back pages of books. It was high school senior photos inscribed with hopeful proclamations for the future on the back and lockets and bracelets given as gifts to mark the memory. It was the hundreds of photographs documenting Mom and Dad's journey from fourteen-year-old high school sweethearts to their wedding day, through their honeymoon and newlywed life, first house, and first pregnancies. It was baby books so lovingly and painstakingly filled with locks of hair and baby hospital bracelets and ink prints of newborn soles of feet as well as all the carefully documented moments like first steps and first food and first baths. Moments that had been captured on film and printed on paper and counted on being there as documentation of the lives that Mom and Dad were building.

Even so, the flood was not all loss for us. Through the flood, we received the gifts of friendship, of community, and of family. While we eventually lost touch with Marty and Jamie, Mom and Rosalie and Dad and Ted remained best friends. As couples, they vacationed together, spent every Thanksgiving and Christmas together, and we all continued annual trips to the Jersey Shore together. They feel as much like family as any family could.

Paul and Christopher have remained best friends to this day.

All of us have grown, married, some divorced, and had children. Through the good times and challenging times, my family and the extended family we gained in the trailers have been there. And in my darkest moments, both of my sisters were there by my side, loving and supporting me. I remain grateful to be the middle sister of three.

Through the flood, the people we met inspired Mom to change and grow in so many ways. She became a strong and fearless woman and has been a role model for all of us. She fought for what she felt was fair—for herself and for others. She went on to become a nurse who served the migrant population, walking through the tomato fields of Pennsylvania to administer medicine or change bandages within the Haitian migrant community. Her story of having a sit-down with the voodoo medicine man where she asked him to teach her about his medicine stays with me to this day. She taught me about caring for others, advocating for women, and about cultural sensitivity. In my opinion, my mom is as much the superhero of this story as my dad is.

But to us kids, the real superhero of the flood years was Charlene. Charlene went on to become a nurse, to get divorced and remarried, have more kids, and eventually become a grandmother. I don't know if Charlene knows how deeply she touched the lives of all us kids during the trailer park years. But we will never forget her. Charlene taught us about the magic that is always just within reach.

This book began as a story of what happens when a family's life is destroyed in one night. But the writing of it has shown me the unforeseeable gifts that we discovered in the process of picking up the pieces and putting our lives back together.

# Acknowledgments

This book would not have been possible without the help, encouragement, and guidance of so many people, beginning with my friend and colleague Nicole Burrill, who in 2011 told me to "write the flood." Her words of encouragement stayed with me for over a decade and gave me the confidence to finish writing this story ten years later. Thank you, Nicole. You planted the seed that became this book.

I could not have written it without the support of my incredible wife and best friend, Jude Ierardi. Jude, your support and encouragement has never, ever wavered. Even while in the throes of a stressful house renovation, you continued to assuage my fears and my self-doubts, and you consistently reminded me that this book needed to be published. I could not have done this without you. I love you.

This book would not be what it is without the support and guidance of my incredible mentor and editor, Gail Hudson. When I sent Gail the pages I had written in 2011, she saw an important story to tell, and from that moment on, Gail helped shape this book into what it eventually has become. Gail, your gentle and intuitive guidance has always been spot on. This book truly feels as much yours as it is mine.

I would like to express love and gratitude to my mother and father, who sat with me for hours, describing every detail of what was a terribly difficult time for them. Mom and Dad, thank you for helping me understand the practical and emotional details of your experiences. Thank you for your patience and your willingness to relive the flood in order to answer the many questions I had. I truly could not have written this story without you both.

To Michelle Bedwick, who helped me bring Aunt Sadie back to life in the pages of this book. Michelle, you helped me remember why Aunt Sadie and the whole Bedwick family were so special to me and how you all shaped the woman who I have become. Our conversation made me realize how important Aunt Sadie and your family are in my life and to this story. Thank you for helping me feel her presence as I wrote this book. It has been a true gift.

To my entire Girl Friday Productions team. The care you took in helping me get this from a Word document manuscript to a beautiful book is deeply appreciated. But more than that, the words of praise and encouragement from every individual on the team have helped me feel supported and confident through the vulnerable process of publishing a memoir. It has been a pleasure producing book number two with this wonderful company.

To John Feyrer. John thank you for helping me remember those wonderful Rutter Ave. years. Our conversations helped me write over one hundred pages, most of which got cut from the book. They will surely find their way to another story! But most of all, thank you for being one of my first friends when we finally found our forever home in Kingston and helping me learn that kids who weren't *from the flood* could be good friends too.

To my brother, Paul, my sister Pam, Christopher, and Jamie. You made the years after the flood the most magical time in my childhood. Without all of you and our experiences together, this book would have no heart. And to Charlene, the most magical fifteen-year-old that ever lived. Charlene, our time with you in the trailer was the driving force behind this story. You gave us kids the gift of play, imagination, and magic at a time when the adults around us were deeply struggling. I hope you find this book someday and, in these pages, read how deeply you touched all of our lives.

To my sister Jessica, whose arrival into the world taught me what deep and unconditional love is. Jessica, you came along and were the start of a new life for all of us. Your support through the writing of this book helped me to just keep writing. I love you as much now as I did when you wore socks in your hair.

To all the people, from Rosalie and Marty to Linda and Ted, to Pop-Pop-with-the-Chi-Chi, who helped change the course of my family's life and taught us what family and community really meant. You may never have known, but you gave us permission to just be kids and provided the feeling of security within which we could let our imaginations run wild. It wouldn't be until decades later that I would truly conceptualize the gravity of what all of you were going through.

And finally to my sister Pam. Pam, from the moment I began writing this book, I knew that this story would be a story of sisters. We have been through floods and friendships, fights with Barbies and tears over boys. I have never known a life without you. You were my best friend from the moment I was born, and you have been by my side through every triumph and tragedy of my life. The writing of this book gave me the gift of reliving our lives together and reminded me of how lucky I am to have you as my sister. This book is for you.

# About the Author

Suzanne Jones is an expert in the field of trauma recovery through somatic methods. She has presented workshops and led talks at Omega Institute for Holistic Studies, the Kripalu Center for Yoga and Health, mental and behavioral health facilities in the greater Boston area, and national conferences. She has been profiled on CNN and in *Yoga Journal*, the *New York Times*, *Shape*, and *Whole Living*. Since the start of the COVID-19 pandemic, Sue has supported hundreds of women through her online trauma-recovery program (TIMBo). Her first book, *There Is Nothing to Fix*, received international acclaim and won several awards. *From the Flood* is her second book and is a retelling of the events of Hurricane Agnes that she and her family lived through.

CPSIA information can be obtained
at www.ICGtesting.com
Printed in the USA
BVHW070326310522
638437BV00006B/224